Innovations in Indian Education System

Innovations in Indian Education System

Editors

Kalika Yadav
(Director, Deptt. of Continuing Education & Extension,
Barkatullah University, Bhopal)

H.K. Khandai
(HOD, B.Ed. Deptt. of Continuing Education & Extension,
Barkatullah University, Bhopal)

Anshu Mathur
(Assistant Professor, Bhopal School of Social Sciences, Bhopal)

SHIPRA

ISBN: 978-81-7541-574-4

First Published in India in 2011

Innovations in Indian Education System

Published by:
SHIPRA PUBLICATIONS
H.O.: LG 18-19, Pankaj Central Market, Patparganj,
I.P. Ext., Delhi-110092, Tel: 91-11-2223 5152, 2223 6152
Br.Off.: 4617/18, Ansari Road, Darya Ganj,
New Delhi-110002, Tel: 6594 6453, 9810522367
E-mail: info@shiprapublications.com
www.shiprapublications.com

Foreword

Innovations in Indian Education system has always been a major focus of policy makers and thinkers. We are going through a reform and experimental process of education system in which RTE bill, semester system, grading, use of ICT, scraping of board exams and new methods of teaching-learning are being introduced. Learning community as a new model for teaching-learning process is being practised and implemented as experimental basis. I am very convinced and optimistic for the same and there will be revolutionary changes in whole process in near future. Learning communities means Teacher, Students, Management, and Principal with Parents work together to achieve the aims of education. It is a co-operative movement in educational process to attain the goal of learning with shared vision.

Several papers in this publication will not only provide information about the topic but also lead present and future scholars to look up. I am also confident that this publication will prove to be a guideline for policy makers and those who are engaged in the area of reforms.

I congratulate Dr. Kalika Yadav, Dr. H.K. Khandai and Ms. Anshu Mathur for having such an admirable idea in front of all to get benefit. I especially appreciate all contributors who have shared their vision and knowledge with this publication.

Dr. B.K. Passi
Former VC, NCTE, New Delhi

Preface

In the era of Shining India as a "skill capital" for the world, we are facing new challenges in our path of progress. We have to change and we are in a process of reforms too. While India's future lies in the classrooms it is very necessary to understand and ensure that the talent being churned out from the Indian education system has the capability to match the best in the world. Keeping this viewpoint in mind the book attempts to provide an extensive as well as an in-depth analysis of the various innovations in education system by many scholars. In the present social system, globalization demands compulsive use of new methods and technology and we necessitate with passion a learning environment to match with global needs as learning and sharing the knowledge to widen it, as this is the only way to go forward. We need to stimulate learning culture by promoting innovations in our system because the advancement in system yields rich dividends in future.

This book is designed as a guide to road ahead for innovations and to indicate the barriers of the desired path. Thoughts are original and very innovative for the future of Indian education system in every aspect. We thank the scholars for their valuable contribution to this timely volume. However the views expressed in the papers are those of the individual contributors and not necessarily of any institute. We are grateful to Dr. B.K. Passi for his support and guidance for the same. We also extend our thanks for extending support in publishing this volume to Dr. Vashishtha, Dr. Nityananda Pradhan, Dr. Baiju. K. Nath, Dr. Poonam Singh Kharwar, Dr. Noushad Husain, Dr. S.S. Chaugule, Anjum Ahmed, Prof. Girijesh Kumar, Dr. Smriti Bhosle, Dr. D. R. Kapoor, Dr. Kajal Manhas, Dr. Gaurav Singh, Dr. S.K. Gupta, Dr. D.D. Pandey, Mrs. Rucha Gujar, Dr. Vadnere, Dr. (Mrs.) Vani N. Laturkar, Dr. C. Naseema, Mr. V.K. Jibin, Geetika Agarwal and Dr. Loknath Mishra. We firmly hope that the book will give larger vision and vitality to the readers.

Prof. Kalika Yadav
Dr. H.K. Khandai
Anshu Mathur

Contents

1

Shared Learning—A Vital Approach for Teachers Education in India

B.K. Passi, Hemant Kumar Khandai and *Anshu Mathur*

Today, India claims to be the biggest human resources supplier for the world. We supply bureaucrats to the government, software engineers to the IT companies around the world, managers to the multinationals, engineers and scientist to the foreign universities. For this, India needs a huge force of innovative teachers who could make the end product excellent and self-contained. Educator is the key for that, with his knowledge, attitude, abilities and qualities. As the hands of a clock are powered from the center that remains ever still, so the teachers as a society maker remain ever at the center of human life, no matter where the hands of time are pointing—past, present or future. Here when we are stepping towards the era of 'Shining India'. The challenge will be not only to develop new frameworks, and new educational environments to support the system, But also to support by overcoming the limitations of the individual human mind of educationist as a society maker. A good teacher with knowledge, attitudes and skills will turn out the potential of our school children. We still follow the old model of teacher's education in traditional classrooms where knowledge transmission from a teacher to students based on "instruction approach". Students are not required to be active learners and only be passive recipients. Teaching skills may develop through "Microteaching", but all other information or knowledge related to learning is automatically given through a teacher irrespective of the students' needs or problems. In such situations, learners are not motivated to learn. In this era of becoming superpower we are facing the challenges of profound change, there is no substitute for collaboration and group work. We need personal reflection and shared vision that is done collectively to create solutions, Individual accountability, Incentive for working effectively together as a team Supportive and shared environment, Collective creativity, and shared personal practice. As a course of action shared and collaborative learning must be supported because the individual Human mind is limited. This occurs several levels simultaneously: to provide enhanced learning opportunities for the individual members. Building shared vision, developing personal mastery, appreciating a diversity of mental models, embracing team learning and combining these four together through working at a commonplace with an active participation is the vision of this approach.

CONCEPT OF SHARED LEARNING

The formal definition of learning describes the process as "a relatively permanent change in behaviour based on an individual's interact experience with its environment." As such, learning is an important form of personal adaptation. But we cannot escape the fact that, in order to learn, we need other people. Both formal and informal learning requires human interaction–whether that can be the words of someone written down, media others have created or the acknowledgement from others of our grasp of concepts. So, personal learning also requires others. We need to transform our classrooms into workplaces in similarity, if learners solve their own problems for their own sake; they try to actively acquire required knowledge and skills. Therefore, active learning happens when learners are self-directed to learn for themselves.

Just as a drop of water is powerless, similarly a student alone can't do much without sharing knowledge. If the students energy, talents, vibrancy, passion can be organized with everybody of same field in an interactive way of learning, it will be more fruitful for individual development and upliftment of our Teachers education system. Use of classrooms as a workplace with sharing, collaborating, exchanging and understanding of knowledge by different ways with students, teachers, B. Ed. students of other colleges and Teachers of other B. Ed. colleges at a commonplace. We should begin to create a shared learning system. With an idea of development and channelized growth that will transform learning from an individual to complex with the involvement of persons at all levels of the teachers education system and goal of their actions is to enhance their effectiveness as professionals so that students benefit. Shared learning is the accumulation of individual learning. It's a structure that facilitate team learning with features such as boundary crossing and openness, therefore it is important that team members develop open communication, shared meaning and understanding.

Shared Learning can be defined as:

"Groups of people, engaged in intellectual interaction, for the purpose of learning."

In this concept for teacher's education, decentralization of organizational structure is necessary, which allow creation, acquisition, dissemination, and implementation of the knowledge, skills and attitude.

Design

1. *'Speak' 'Connect' and 'Reflect'*: These three behavioural forms are the foundation stones to build an environment for Shared Learning. *Speaking* as a tool to connect when combined with one-to-one dialoging to explore interpersonal sticking points, a powerful combination of learning comes out. This unites emotional growth with intellectual knowledge.

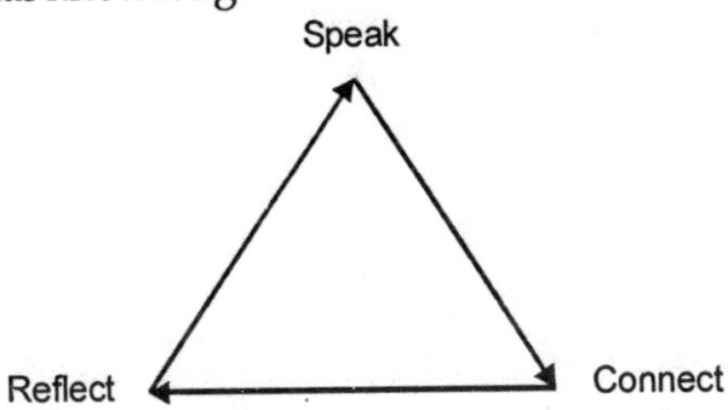

Connect is a process completed by listening others voice Listening relation generates dialogue, and dialogic communication constructs reflections.

Reflection as a learning device is not well respected and so learning risks either being lost or remaining at the level of data acquisition. Yet, both intra-personal and inter-personal learning suffer, when the learning cycle does not include reflection. Reflection helps us to realize a sense of meaning from complex issues, it takes us out of the present moment, and allows us to see a world through a self with the added dimensions. Only these three basics can help building the positive environment for Shared learning, for the intelligence and development of each member.

2. *Democratic Environment*: Colleges should be opened inside and outside to exchange different voices through dialogic communication. These voices may be of experienced schoolteachers, students/teachers from other B. Ed. colleges and classmates. Democratic environment provides a platform open for everyone

to participate as a protagonist with his or her own role and responsibility. Variety of thoughts and visions can discussed through interactive communication in a democratic environment.

Democracy in education is "A way of associated living" as per Dewey definition.

3. *Collective Approach*: The most effective method to transfer wisdom/practical knowledge is for the inexperienced to learn through practice under the supervision and guidance of the experienced teachers in a collective approach. Building relationships and collaborating with others in the discovery process is essential. Teachers share the teaching experiences, express their own practical knowledge related to practice, and create new practical knowledge through discussion, case studies, presentations and observations. The growth of every kind of teaching skill depends on shared practice and honest dialogue among the group of people who do it.

4. *Active Participation*: Learning as a quantitative increase in knowledge: Learning is acquiring information or 'knowing a lot'. Individual accountability what is called Readiness, active participation will give ample opportunities to learners for better educational practice and professional development. Pursuit of the best participation through utmost efforts brings deep humility and modesty to teachers and learners. "Active participation" is in which students and teachers work together to create a better classroom and they organize activities in which they share the responsibility for improvement of education.

5. *Integration of Working and Learning*: Learning as interpreting and understanding reality in a different way. Learning involves comprehending the world by reinterpreting knowledge. In a shared learning organization, each individual must excel at his or her discipline with Positive, productive, collaborative and relationship-building skills. It will allow progressively learning through multiple interactions and therefore progressively build in intelligence among cluster of educators.

Methodology of Shared Learning

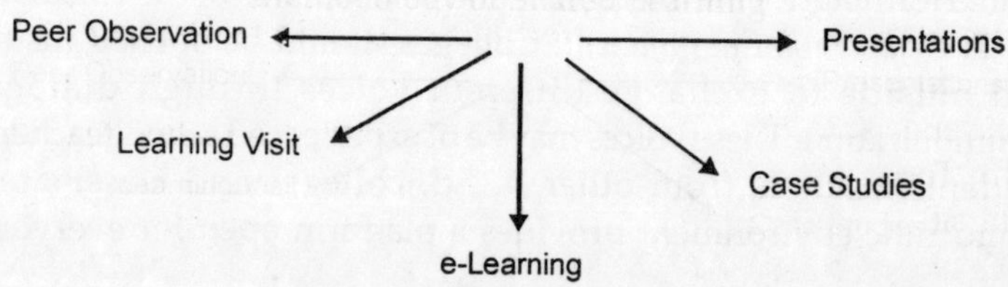

1. *Cluster of Educators*: B. Ed. Teachers + B. Ed. Students + Experienced Teachers of various schools + Students of other colleges of Education, with each other build a cluster of educators. It is a set of persons who embedded into the day-to-day processes of learning, such that team members continuously learn and develop their knowledge, skills and attitude together.

2. *Share Knowledge*: A shared vision is at the heart of all that is significant to the constituent of a learning environment with all teamwork. Jointly experienced the knowledge and develop togetherness for the interrelationship between content and context in Shared Learning. Shared vision for knowledge is based on effective and active Participation of everyone. In order to move into the area of shared knowledge, teachers and students need to develop trust and mutual respect in spite of diversity of styles or practice.

3. *Peer Observations*: Isolation and remoteness, is a part of most teaching, must be overcome and teachers made to feel the need for peer interaction and support. The interaction required encourages sharing and assisting one another to enhance respective instructional techniques as well as professional practice. In this way, individuals as well as the cluster of teachers benefit and move forward together. Observations and experiences at all level of teaching and learning process intend to give more emphasis on methods for capturing knowledge from experts or students.

4. *Learning Visit*: Learning visit is the process of putting either different kinds of information or people together by visits to internalize existing contents or come up with new patterns or ideas. Teachers and students not only experiment with their own beliefs about teaching but also learn new things from visits to different institutes of education and as well as schools also where they experience classroom teaching, behaviour and methods. That can nurture and develop teachers' professional growth. Learning by viewing will boost the level of pragmatic knowledge of learners and they will move towards expertise.

5. *E–Learning*: Electronic way of teaching and learning that includes, Learning from Internet, Video conferencing, Tele conferencing, thru emails, e-books or e-journals. Increased meaning and understanding of the content and provide more knowledge globally. Today's society is characterized by increased professional specialization changes in marketplaces (local and global are no

longer clearly distinguished); and new technologies for information sharing, communication, and collaboration, made possible by Internet technologies and specialized applications. The skills required for educators in these environments are more than the basic skills traditionally taught in our classrooms. They should be motivated towards e-learning in form of their projects and presentations.

6. *Case Studies*: Case study is an empirical inquiry that investigates a phenomenon within its real-life context. They provide a systematic way of looking at events, collecting data, analyzing information, and reporting the results. As a result the researcher may gain a sharpened understanding of why the instance happened as it did, and what might become important to look at more extensively in future research. Teachers can know about different cases through this procedure and can enhance their knowledge of behaviour in practical. Educators can get benefit of learning psychology and behavioural science thru this.

7. *Presentations*: Presentation is the practice of showing and explaining the content of a topic to an audience or learner. It's a better way of communicating ideas and information to a group. It improves understanding and attracts learners towards new knowledge. In teachers education this may helpful in various topics related to curriculum and to break the monotony of the class. Presentations increase attentive listening and communication skills of an individual, which is required in shared learning.

8. *Group Discussion:* Group discussion refers to the nature of communication that occurs in groups. Group discussions have a high apparent validity-since the idea is easy to understand, the results are believable. Also, they are low in cost, one can get results relatively quickly, and they can increase the sample size of a report by talking with several people at once. Face-to-face contact as a part of shared learning is supportive in building and sustaining knowledge.

In this system teachers' role undergoes massive change. Teacher is no more, the reservoir and sole dispenser of knowledge. He/she is a planner, Initiator, climate builder, facilitator and guide, mediator, knowledge organizer and evaluator. From another angle, teacher writes the script, sets the stage, directs and produces the drama (learning), leaving the actual acting to the learners with himself. Shared learning can be integrated in the regular subject teaching. Also, various extramural activities can form part of a well-designed experiential curriculum form. This model will accomplish the need, because the design is based on essential components of quality basic education that aims to build the Knowledge, skills, attitudes and values that will able to make an educator complete.

Learning cycle of Shared Learning

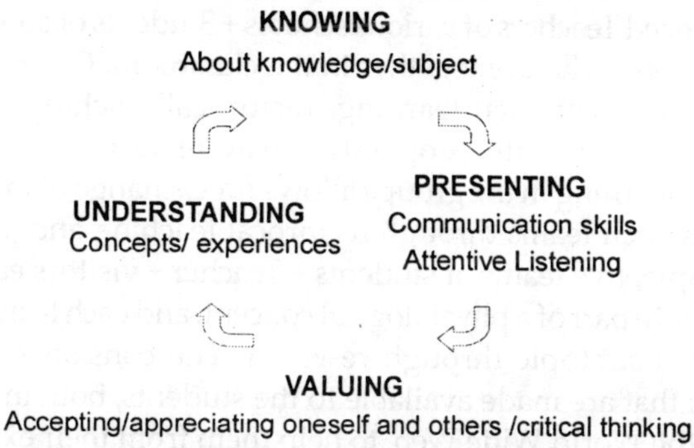

The process of shared learning goes in a cycle where *Knowing* about the subject as knowledge of each appears by *presenting* thru communication. It may include self-learning, cooperative learning to share knowledge, case studies, e-learning, peer observation, learning visits, discussions, presentations, problem solving by group work, etc. Learning with all discussed methods promotes attentive listening for reflection to others by appreciating and critical thinking of knowledge. The acceptances of knowledge generate *value* for whole range of instructional processes. At its next stage development process of teacher's knowledge, skills and attitude drives towards *understanding* the knowledge with various experiences. This cycle continuously gives opportunities to learners, to be active and engaged in constructing their own learning.

MECHANISM OF SHARED LEARNING

Indirect Teaching and Direct Learning in a Group

Indirect teaching and direct learning is the student centered instructional practice in the constructivist paradigm. This may include a whole range of Instructional processes and opportunities created by the teacher for the students to be actively engaged in constructing their own learning. Such Instructional processes may include self-learning, cooperative learning; case Studies, projects, problem solving, research etc. Collective lesson planning; peer observation and evaluation and critique; Observation of demonstration or model lesson plans, including the watching of videos of model lessons; and the production and consumption of research about teaching and learning, including by publishing articles are the jobs for Cluster of educators (B. Ed. Teachers + B. Ed. Students + Experienced Teachers of various schools + Students of other colleges of Education), who are together in the classroom. Group works as designers of their own learning, reciprocal teaching, in shared learning concept with cooperative way of learning. They may distribute learning in the groups allows for exchange of information across research teams through reciprocal teaching and jig-sawing. For example, five teams of students + Teacher + visitors each are set up to explore part of a physiological concept, and each team becomes expert in a subtopic through research. The consists of research materials that are made available to the students, both in print and through the World Wide Web, to help them from their expertise on the topic. The teacher acts as learner and facilitator in the process, rather than purely as the expert. When each group attains a level of expertise, the teacher then asks the groups to present their topics by different way of shared learning. Each member educates the others through answering questions, summarizing, clarifying, and predicting. Then jig-sawed groupings can takes place by one expert from each team comes together to form a new team until a complete mix of groups has occurred, to combine the expertise in the sub topical areas. This process can give expertise to each.

Techniques to attain the environment for shared learning are-

- Improve human relations among teacher-student, teacher-teacher and students themselves.
- Develop good attitudes in students and teachers as well, e.g.

Co-operation and Mutual Respect

- Healthy emotional development in students.
- Facilitate socialization through participation in interaction and cooperative Learning activities.
- Improve student's discipline and sharing behaviour.
- Develop creativity both in students and teachers.
- Improve standard of quality of teaching and learning by discussed methods.

Hurdles in Implementation of Programme

- Teachers are always the instructors, and there is almost no opportunity to learn mutually or interchange roles between teachers and students.
- We are taught to respect our teachers and are required to be listeners and followers. Students and instructors are never at the same level, how they will from become co-learners.
- By learning the skills of collaboration through opportunities to practice and observe others proficient in that skill already, teachers will not be so quick to resort to old habits.
- Organizational barriers may come, as A Shared Learning Organization needs to fully embrace the removal of traditional hierarchical structures.
- There is a big question. Do the teachers of other institutes will come up with same support.
- Lack of a pro-learning culture in some organizations can be a barrier to learning. These are the barriers in development of shared vision and the sharing of knowledge.

Advantages of the Concept

- Exploration of Different Learning Paradigms
- Re conceptualization of the Role of Teachers and Learners
- Educators to Become Lifelong Learners
- Support to New Interdisciplinary, and inter organization Collaborations
- Balance Economics and the Quality of Education
- Move beyond standard curriculum and simple notions of efficiency
- Support Collaborative Knowledge Construction

Disadvantages

- Dependency upon "Basic" Skills of presenter
- Students often express dissatisfaction with team-based learning
- Regular chances to reflect on everybody and at every topic will lead to indiscipline
- Evaluation must be difficult
- The gaps and overlaps on subject learning will take places
- Best Orator will steal the show.

Conclusion

The end product of this exercise will lead to an improved system of teacher's education in India. The impact of Shared Learning will be meaningful only if the contents ultimately transmit the information to the minds of the learners, with impact on their aptitude. In this ever-changing world, every aspect of life is based on a never-ending race for satisfaction. Teachers have to face new challenges in future with changing curriculums, patterns of teaching and learning environment for quality education in India. We need progress and a deeper understanding of new theories, innovative systems, practices, and assessment. We have to create new intellectual spaces, new organizational forms, and new Structures to make learning effective. We need individuals, contribution groups, and organizations to personally engage and experience these new forms. We need to ensure that the authorities "create, support, and sustain high-performing colleges. In fact, we need risk takers who use their creativity and imagination to explore this alternative way of learning.

REFERENCES

Hinman, C. (2007). Developing a substantive professional learning community. *National Forum of Educational Administration and Supervision Journal*, 24 (1), 29-35.

Huffman, J. B. (2000). One school's experiences as a professional learning community. *Planning and Changing*.

Manabu, Satu, (2008), Philosophy on the restoration of schools in Japan: The principles and activity system of the Learning Community, *Journal of All India Association for Educational Research*.

Murphy, C. (1997). Finding time for faculties to study together. *Journal of Staff Development*.

2

Changes and Challenges of Teacher Education

Issues Ahead for Quality

U.C. Vashistha and *Hemanta Kumar Khandai*

> *"Nothing is more important than securing a significant supply of high quality recruits to the teaching profession, providing them with the best possible professional preparations and creating satisfactory conditions for work in which they can be fully effective."*
>
> *Education Commission (1964-66)*

As we all know that education is an important instrument in bringing out potentialities of human being while effectiveness of a system of education is mainly depend upon its teachers. So, teacher education is considered to be most crucial among all the dimensions of education. Now we are in 21 century where knowledge, communication and information play very significant role, teacher education has to address to cope within this changing scenario. If NCTE frequently changes the norms and conditions of teacher education, then maintaining quality is a great threat and challenge before the education institutions, students and teachers.

By a resolution of government of India the non-statutory NCTE was set up in 1993 maintain standards and norms in teacher education. It evolved a documents called "Teacher education curriculum a frame work" with the involvement of U.G.C. panel on teacher education which was the first attempt to revamp teacher education pertaining to all states of education.

NCTE has taken number of steps for raising the quality of teacher education system. In 2000 the council also developed "curriculum frame work for quality teacher education" for up grading-the quality of teacher education programmes as per with international standards.

FACTORS THAT MAKE THE PRESENT TEACHER TRAINING PROGRAMME INEFFECTIVE

1. Recently the NCTE changed norm in teacher education by which dozens of questions arise before maintaining quality education. As we all know M. Ed/M.A. (Education) is eligible for teaching in B. Ed. or M. Ed. level at University or college but suddenly the NCTE changed the qualification of teachers that any master degree with B. Ed, will be eligible for lectureship in B. Ed. colleges and also not permitted the M.A. in Education equaling to M. Ed. or eligible for B. Ed./ M. Ed. lectureship.
2. Various committees and commissions constituted for time to time are in opinion that teacher education to day is far from reality.
3. Quality issues of the teacher education programmes can be examined by analyzing the quality of input, quality of process and quality of output. Any deficiency in the above said quality determinants will influence the effectiveness of the teacher education programme.
4. The Impact of privatization and globalization increase competition every where. In this era of competitions most of the teacher educational institutions face difficulty in surviving.
5. Present teacher education programmes does not have meaningful linkage with school, peer institutions, other institution of higher and the community.
6. Curriculum reforms and pedagogic reforms are not coping with teh rate of advancement of knowledge.
7. Mushroom growth of ill equipped, ill provided and ill planned teacher education colleges has led to the production of ineffective teachers in the name of teachers.
8. Administration of undeserving candidates based on caste, creed, religion etc. and political interference for admission of students and for the recognition of the institutions.
9. Delay in starting the courses due to conflict between the central/state governments and the teacher training institutions with regards to obtaining NOC, minority status, reservation norms, admission norms.
10. Poor quality of teacher training due to poor learning resources and with higher teacher educators-student teacher ratio.
11. Poor assessment, appraisal and monitoring systems.

12. Lack of preparation of the teacher trainers with regard to the contemporary global and national issues.
13. Lack of committed and dedicated teacher educators and appointment of unqualified or under qualified teacher educators.
14. Evaluation system is qualitatively poor and corrupt.
15. Evil practice of collecting fees from the students for admission.
16. Present duration of the B. Ed., and M. Ed., courses makes the courses more examination oriented and not oriented for professional preparation.
17. No intensive microteaching and macro teaching practices to understand and learn the teaching skills.
18. The teacher education institutions do not have link with their similar institutions and do not involve themselves in consultant jobs for the government or other private agencies.
19. Skill of "learning to learn" is lacking among teachers and teacher educators.
20. Lack of involvement of teacher trainees, school teachers, teacher educators, research scholars and principals/ administrators of teacher education instates in framing policies with regards to teacher education.
21. No research exposure to teacher trainees and no interaction with the community.

PRESENT SCENARIO OF QUALITY IN TEACHER EDUCATION

Teacher education is deteriorating day by day and there is sincere need for drastic changes in every sphere of teacher education so as to facilitate the teacher to face the challenges of the dynamic world of twenty-first century.

LOSS OF QUALITY IN SHORTAGE OF TEACHER

- Lack of innovation.
- In securing job.
- Use of teacher for 4-5 months in some institution.
- Salary is not up to the mark.
- Over burdened
- Not good rapport between management and teacher.

It is clear that the teacher at any stage is expected to bring the best in the child and the youth and help them to realize their maximum potential—intellectually and spiritually.

The teacher education system should ensure adequate supply of such professional trained teacher to teach and guide those who study in colleges and institutions of higher learning.

Quality has become the defining element of education in the 21st century in the context of new social relations. The information communication, revolution knowledge of economy and globalization are greatly influencing the "next society".

Our teachers are still uncomfortable with the use of technology in the classroom. They should be trained to use the technological innovations that are readily available. Effective use of information communication technology in teacher education institutions can improve the quality of teacher education.

School curriculum is becoming more and more complex. Many new areas of knowledge are getting in to the curriculum. Many new areas of knowledge are getting into the curriculum. In this situation, one time teacher training of a particular duration may not serve the purpose. These should be continuous in service programme organized both through face to face and distance made in order to make the teachers cope with latest development.

Each teacher is expected to involve in undertaking action research for qualitative improvement of class room teacher. These should be continuous monitoring of teacher education institutions by NCTE, particularly the privately managed self financing institution in order to maintain the standard of teacher education programme and its quality enhancement.

REFERENCE

1. Ministry of Education (1964-66), Education Commission, Government of India, Govt. of Indian Press, New Delhi.
2. Ministry of Eduation (1968), National Policy on Education, Govt. of India, New Delhi.
3. NCERT (2000), National Curriculum Frame work for School education, NCERT, New Delhi.
4. NCERT (2004), Curriculum frame work for Teacher Education, NCERT, New Delhi.
5. NCTE (1998), Curriculum, Frame work for Quality Teacher Education, NCTE, New Delhi.

3

Role of Continuing Education and Extension In Globalisation Era under University System of Higher Education

Kalika Yadav and *Hemant Kumar Khandai*

As we know education starts from womb and ends in tomb. So the concept of education is so broad that one can not keep it in water tight compartment. So far as Continuing Education is concerned that is to help in pursuing life long learning. Continuing Education provides an opportunity for all citizens to integrate learning, working and living. These three aspects is important for the development of the individual and society. In 1977 the UGC first incorporated extension into its policy statement for higher education when it started that "If the University system has to discharge adequately its responsibilities to the entire education system and to the society as a whole it must assume extension as the third important responsibility and give it the same status as teaching and research". It was way back in 1960 that the Kothari Commission first articulated the concept of extension and the trinity of Teaching, Research and Extension.

UGC stated that extension was essential for:

- Making education relevant to real life situations.
- For preventing the alienation of the educand from society.
- For developing in the educand a sense of responsibility towards society.
- For deepening the teacher's knowledge through a winder exposure to real life situation.

The main thought of University Grants Commission is to include extension as third dimension was to promoting a meaningful sustained rapport between the Universities and the community. The extension will act as a bridge between society and the University.

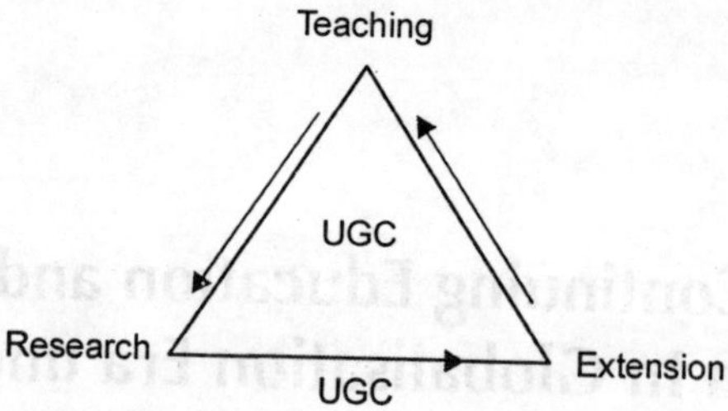

CONCEPT OF GLOBALISATION

Globalisation is a process of integrating the whole world into one village *i.e.* global village. The main aim of globalisation is "whole earth is one family" and "All people shall be prosperous".

According to IMF-Globalisation as the growing economic inter dependence of countries would wide through in creating volume and various of cross broder transaction in good and services.

According to chanles U.F. Hill-Globalisation as "The shift towards a more integrated and interdependent world economy.

Globalisation does not take place in a single instance. It takes place gradualy through an evolutionary approach. Globalisation means globalising the marketing, production, investment, technology and other activities.

The changed scenario is marked by the phenomenon of "Global Village" through efficient modes of communication, distance have reduced, world is now like a global village and continuous international interaction has become an essential component of human survival. There is a process of global and cultural unification. Revolutions in the scientific and technological fields and cybernetic and electronic information transmission are sweeping the world. We are challenged with changes that the taking place in the world at large. We are challenged with changes that are taking place in the world at large. Today it is increasingly realized that knowledge is universal and its creation and dissemination cannot be confined with national boundaries.

Now the experts, educationists, planners and members of various comission and committee has realized that the impact of globalisation has placed new changes, challenges and demands on education system in current situation in nationally and internationally. Transformation with rapid change is taking place every where. The student, youth, housewife and adult have to be prepared by the university to adopt change and learn new skills in accordance with new demands of the world of work. In other words the university system of education has to prepare the student to be a life long learner. Then only the student should be able to sustain his knowledge and skill at global level. Private universities are being setup and international universities are entering in the country also information and communication technology (ICT) is being more frequently used in the field of learning. Online learning and e-learning will soon become feature of university course. It is now realized the department of continuing education and extension should interact and collaborate with private sector. E-learning and on-line mode for the conduct of courses are be utilized for continuing education to cater to the needs, interests and problems of various section of society. So the department will therefore, have to play a more dynamic role and move from the periphery to the centre stage of the university system.

THRUST AREAS

The following thrust areas are adopted by the UGC keeping globalisation in to account. The major thrusts are-

1. The acceptance of the philosophy of Continuing Education as a part of total education programme of the institution.
2. Reaching out to the larger sections of adults through the university system and specially deprived groups for the purpose of equalization of educational opportunities.
3. Environment of the learning process of faculty and students through exposure to community needs, problems, issues and reaching out to socio-economic and cultural groups.
4. Introduction of courses offered on campus, on-line and through e-learning.
5. Development of courses linked specially to business and industry which world includes work ethics, work culture and preparation for the changing world of work.

ROLE AND FUNCTIONS OF THE DEPARTMENT

The department of Continuing Education and Extension would full fill the following role and functions for changing society *i.e.* the globalisation era.

1. Teaching, Training and Reserch

- Conducting needs based continuing education course,

including online courses on credit or non-credit basis.
- To assist in the development of a curriculum for multi-disciplinary programmes.
- Training for human resource or skill development for the different target groups.
- Under taking various need based action research.

2. Catalyst Role

- Acting as a focal agency in the University System for all extension and field out reach programmes with the involvement of University department and colleges.
- Serving as a technical resource centre for University's Community based activities.
- Assessing the needs of the University students and out of University learner for Continuing Education programme.

3. Collablorative and Net Working Role

The department shall under take collaborative programme and new work with.

- Business and Industry.
- University departments.
- International organization/Universities and agencies, such as UNESCO, UNICEF, UNDPA etc.

4. Documentation and Dissemination

Publication of News letter, Journal, Magazine, E-Journal, creation of an interactive website, dissemination of materials and information:

In this globalization era, it is necessary that our planners and educational administrations must expedite the process of reforms and encourage innovation. We have to wake up from the deep slumber and discard the old, rusted and out dated skills. We must replace the superstition, traditional thinking, and orthodox culture in the society and help them to adopt a new more dynamic approach for the improvement of self and society.

4

Right to Education Bill

An Awaited Drizzling

Hemant Kumar Khandai

We the largest democracy in world, land of more than a billion people, having great cultural heritages of various regions and religions, the history of over 5000 years, but the second half of the 20th century witnessed an educational miracle all over the country. Educational explosion in terms of numbers, students, teachers, schools and colleges and even public expenditure have been phenomenal, though the growth was not smooth, but the most notable among them is the wave of reforms. Education as a fundamental right cannot be denied in any democratic society. It is the duty of the Government to provide for and guarantee this fundamental right. It is the very foundation of good citizenship. More than six decades after Independence, the Indian government has cleared the Right to Education Bill that makes free and compulsory education a fundamental right for all children between the ages of 6 and 14.

The Right of Children to Free and Compulsory Education Bill seeks to provide education to children aged between 6 to 14 years. The Bill, one of the flagship programmes in the 100-day agenda of the UPA government, also earmarks 25 per cent seats to weaker sections in private schools. HRD minister Kapil Sibal describing it as "harbinger of a new era" for children to meet the challenges of the 21st century.

HISTORY OF THE BILL

December 2002: 86th Amendment Act (2002) via Article 21A (Part III) seeks to make free and compulsory education a Fundamental Right for all children in the age group 6-14 years.

October 2003: A first draft of the legislation envisaged in the above Article, viz., Free and Compulsory Education for Children Bill, 2003, was prepared and posted on this website in October, 2003, inviting comments and suggestions from the public at large.

2004: Subsequently, taking into account the suggestions received on this draft, a revised draft of the Bill entitled Free and Compulsory Education Bill, 2004, was prepared and posted on the *http://education.nic.in* website.

June 2005: The CABE (Central Advisory Board of Education) committee drafted the 'Right to Education' Bill and submitted to the Ministry of HRD. MHRD sent it to NAC where Mrs. Sonia Gandhi is the Chairperson. NAC sent the Bill to PM for his observation.

14th July 2006: The finance committee and planning commission rejected the Bill citing the lack of funds and a Model bill was sent to states for the making necessary arrangements. (Post-86th amendment, States had already cited lack of funds at State level).

19th July 2006: CACL, SAFE, NAFRE, CABE invited ILP and other organizations for a Planning meeting to discuss the impact of the Parliament action, initiate advocacy actions and set directions on what needs to be done at the district and village levels.

The Lok Sabha on Tuesday August 4, 2009, passed the right to education Bill to provide compulsory schooling for all children between 6 to 14 years. The Right To Education Bill, 2009, will operationalise the fundamental right mentioned in Article 21-A as part of the 86th amendment of the Constitution *i.e.*

The Right of Access to Education: Education must be available for, accessible to and inclusive of all children.

The Right to Quality Education: Education needs to be child-centered, relevant and embrace a broad curriculum, and be appropriately resourced and monitored.

The Right to Respect Within the Learning Environment: Education must be provided in a way that is consistent with human rights, equal respect for culture, religion and language and free from all forms of violence.

PRESENT SITUATION AND NEEDS

- Out of 200 million children in the age group of 6-14 years, 59 million children are not attending school. Of this 35 million are girls and 24 million boys.

- There are at least one-lakh habitations in the country without schooling facility within one kilometer.
- There are problems relating to dropout rate, low levels of learning and low participation of girls, tribal and other disadvantaged groups.
- Coupled with it are various systemic issues like inadequate school infrastructure, poorly functioning schools, high teacher absenteeism, large number of teacher vacancies, poor quality of education and inadequate funds.
- 70 per cent of all child laborers work in agriculture in rural areas where access to schools, availability of trained teachers and educational supplies is severely limited.
- Though, the education gap runs much deeper than a rural-urban divide. Even in urban areas, poor and marginalized children are unable to benefit from greater access to school facilities because of cost, caste and culture

RTE CONTAINS

- Every child in the 6-14 age groups will be eligible for free education
- Every school will have to earmark at least 25 per cent seats in class 1 for free and compulsory elementary education.
- Do away with the practice of school taking capitation fees before admission and subjecting the child or parents to any screening procedure.
- Ban private tuition by teachers and ensure that no child is subjected to physical punishment or mental harassment.
- It shall be the duty of every parent or guardian to admit the child to a neighborhoods school for elementary education
- No child should be denied admission for lack of age proof.
- No child shall be required to pass any Board examination till completion of elementary education.
- Calls for a fixed student-teacher ratio
- Schoolteachers will need adequate professional degree within five years or else will lose job;
- School infrastructure (where there is problem) to be improved in three years, else recognition cancelled;
- Financial burden will be shared between state (25%) and central (75%) government

Children from even the poorest families can hope to study in good schools with a provision that schools will have to keep aside 25 per cent seats in class 1 for such students.

There's some good news for children, especially those belonging to the weaker sections. They can now hope to realize their education dreams, courtesy a Bill, which promises radical changes in the primary education system of the country and seeks to make free and compulsory elementary education right of every child.

According to Right to Education Bill, schools will not be allowed to force a child to repeat a year or expel students until class VIII for any reason.

"People normally think kids won't take studies seriously if there is no failure and no exams. We're saying that kids don't necessarily have to learn out of fear. Instead, they'll learn if you provide them with a learning environment.

The RTE bill aimed for systemic reforms in the elementary education. It is aimed to provide quality education.

It promises to counter the growing lobby for the privatization of school education.

The legislation is a step towards the common school system, first proposed by the Kothari Commission

The biggest hurdle will come from the growing and influential private players in education sector and their votaries among the country's political leadership

Bill says the onus of students' learning and performance is on the school.

Schools will be banned from holding admission tests or seeking "donations" from guardians if a bill to be tabled this week is passed without change. The Bill also prohibits physical punishment, expulsion or detention of a child and deployment of teachers for non-educational purposes other than census or election duty and disaster relief. Running a school without recognition will attract penal action

The bill prohibits the teachers from taking private tuitions and schools from deploying them for non-educational purposes other than decennial population census, disaster relief and election duty.

The Bill also prohibits physical punishment, expulsion or detention of a child and deployment of teachers for non-educational purposes other than census or election duty and disaster relief.

Running a school without recognition will attract penal action Schools cannot deny admission to a child for lack of age proof and no child can be detained or expelled till the completion of elementary education. Physical punishment and mental harassment will attract disciplinary action under service rules.

WIDE OF THE MARK

Multi Layered System

The Bill perpetuates a discriminatory and non-inclusive system in which the quality of education is dependent on the social classes to which the school caters. For the mass of government schools, funding is extremely tight and thus, quality is largely missing. Here the expenditure on a child's education can be as little as Rs 900 annually although some NGOs are getting close to Rs 3,000 per child for running *Mobile Schools* which operate out of buses.

Exclusion of Children below Six Years

One of the serious drawbacks of the Bill is that it excludes children below six years of age from its provisions. This is a denial of the fundamental right of children already given to them by the Supreme Court through the Unnikrishnan Judgement of 1993. The judgement declared 'free and compulsory education' a fundamental Right of all children until they complete the age of 14. The bill will result in 170 million children below six years of age losing their fundamental right to balanced nutrition, health care and pre-primary education in what are undeniably the most formative years.

Dilemmas on Disability, Child Labour and Minority Schools

In this Bill, *'disability'* has the meaning assigned by the Persons with Disabilities Act, 1995, which does not include such other disabilities as defined by the National Trust Act, 1999. The Bill prohibits any person from preventing a child from participating in elementary education; it does not adequately address the issue of child labour. Minority schools are not exempted from provisions in this Bill. It is possible that this will conflict with Article 30 of the Constitution, which allows minorities to set up and administer educational institutions

Lack of Assurance and Accountability

The Bill provides for the right to schooling and physical infrastructure but does not guarantee that children learn. It exempts government schools from any consequences if they do not meet the specified norms. lack of focus on learning achievement instead of just inputs, treating schools for the poor (government schools) unequally with the schools of the rich (private schools) in terms of infrastructure requirements and recognition process, and not empowering the School Management Committee to manage school finances and functionaries, to cite just three. Both the state government and the local authority have the duty to provide free and compulsory elementary education. Sharing of this duty may lead to neither government being held accountable.

The Most Stunning aspect of the Bill

There is no acknowledgement of the role to be played by the owners, founders, trustees, and management of the school themselves.

Children will have to get their caste certificates ready at Kindergarten level.

Till date, schools at least in urban areas have largely been free of caste identity.

The school management committee, if workable will also have to meet caste quotas in addition to the 50 per cent women quota.

Gives power to the local politics. Has the ability to undo decades of hard work for the school boards.

CONCLUSION

The Right to Education Bill, which makes education a fundamental right of every child in the age group of 6 to 14 years, however, needs deep consideration. In its present *avatar* the Bill suffers from major anomalies which must be given due consideration, Laws and Bills don't make children go to school. Initially, there will be problems because while everyone must understand their social responsibility, what matters is whether the right children will have access to this programme. The quality of education for children below six years should not be overlooked because that is the foundation of education of children. Minority institutions also have some reservations about the bill.

As the purpose of this legislation is to set a certain benchmark for school education, the Bill details punitive action for running unrecognized schools and also provides for de-recognition of institutions which do not meet the standards. These standards in terms of the qualifications of teachers and their duties, and pupil-teacher ratio have been specified. How are they going to coop with the remaining population in the school that comes from a much richer background without feeling deprived, it is fact and may scar the poor kid for life? Going further, the schools does not charge any fees from these 25 per cent, but who is going to pay for the books, dresses and other things. Effort is excellent but it would be beneficiary if it will be in actuality not just as reality of "reality shows".

5

Innovation in Teacher Education

Poonam Singh Kharwar

Teacher Educators are responsible for producing quality teachers as per changing need of society. Skill based practices and change of attitude in teacher education programme mostly depends upon research and innovation in teacher education. In spite of many innovations in this area abroad, they are almost static in India. Any innovation in Teacher education should consider proximal, distal, and confluent properties of innovation. The success of innovation is to a great extent dependent upon the activities and abilities of individuals who enthusiastically support the new product or process. An innovative practice in teacher education would remain an innovation until at least half of the industry has adopted the innovation. Teachers as action researchers can discover innovative curricular, instructional, and management strategies that will effectively benefit their respective classes and may be transported to colleagues. Different qualities of newness (decency, originality, and similarity) of innovation should also be applied in teacher education. Multiple sources of influence impact the decisions about what and how teacher educators are expected to operate. Several factors facilitating the spread of innovation in teacher education in India are awareness and interest, incentive, service and support, leadership role, problem solving approach, prestige value of innovation, and intrinsic value of innovation and evaluation process.

The very fact that teaching is a profession entails that teaching is a specialized activity for which specialized knowledge and training is required through specialized institutions. Apart from the institutions, it is the teacher in the institutions who produce desired individuals. Teacher Educators are responsible for producing quality teachers.

NEED FOR QUALITY AND INNOVATION IN TEACHER EDUCATION

Teacher education programme is based predominantly on skill based practices, understanding of different school situation, inculcation of values, change of attitude etc. Among this, skill based practices and change of attitude mostly depends upon research and innovation in teacher education. One way to improve the situation is to absorb the innovation in the field of teacher education because modernization of education depends to an extent on modernization of teacher. Innovation turns ideas into useful practicable and commercial services.

There is a need to revamp today's teacher education system in tune with the changing need of society and particularly changing need of school education. So it is necessary to prepare practicable quality norms for our teacher education programmes and to implement these norms optimally in teacher education institutions. Nowadays the quality has become the key word due to liberalization, privatization and globalization; and there is no existence without quality. Since quality needs intensive capital investment, talent and hard work, therefore there is no short cut to quality. In general, the quality in education means pursuit of excellence, consistency and fairness, satisfaction of client needs and appropriate development of resources. Competent and honest teachers, need based curriculum, adequate infrastructure and ideal student teacher ratio are some of the parameters of quality education. (Singh, 2008)

The purpose of teacher education is to produce teachers who have competencies. As teacher education meant for preparing future teachers who will lead society and nation, the responsibility of teacher increases many folds. The role of the teachers is no longer confined to teaching imparting knowledge alone; they need to be thorough professionals, fully equipped with high academic standard, pedagogical and practical skills, ethical and more values. Teacher education has to play special role to prepare socially responsible teachers of high values and morality, conversant with the unique features of cultural heritage. Unfortunately, however the programmes of teacher education are alleged to be static and stagnant. In spite of many innovations in this area abroad, they are almost static in India; where teacher educators repeat and experiment their own training, which they received earlier upon their students. The existing teacher education model is inherited from British System of education. So teacher education has suffered due to its inability to keep pace with time and to insecure necessary modification in conceptual based theory and practices. The National Policy on Education (1986) and subsequently the Programme of Action (1991 & 1992) felt that the programme of teacher education for various stages need to be overhauled, structured and modernized in its input process and out put to make system quality oriented. The International Commission on Education for 21st century also highlight a similar thought as " A rethinking of teacher education is necessary in order to bring out future teachers precisely those human and intellectual qualities that will facilitate a fresh approach to teaching," (UNESCO, 1996). Quality parameters have already been developed by NCTE, NAAC and UGC like: curriculum framework and planning, curriculum transaction and evaluation, research, development and extension; infrastructure and learning resources; student support and progression, organisation and management; work load allocation and other more criteria for accrediting and assessment of the teacher education colleges.

INNOVATION DEFINED

Foremost in any treatise of innovation is the foundational lexicon or definition that anchors subsequent substantive discussions. Clapham (2003) states that "the word innovate comes from the Latin word ' innovare 'which means to renew, to make new". Therefore, by definition, an innovation can be a renovation of a theme or a variation of an idea. The author further cites Smith (2003) who postulates that a critical component of innovation is "ideation." The notion of ideation suggests credibility to best practice research that in fact is grounded not only on ideation but also on data-based implementation. Kostoff (2003) also suggests that "innovation reflects the metamorphosis from present practice to some new, hopefully, 'better' practice".

PROPERTIES OF INNOVATION

A review of the literature on innovation yields multiple definitions, components, and processes that attempt to distinguish a unique element. Characteristic to all definitions are proximal, distal, and confluent properties of innovation. Rogers (1995) defines innovation in terms of its proximal, distal, and interactive associations by stating that things, ideas, or practices are perceived to be new or novel by an individual or other external entity. The proximal properties include definitions that conjoin to individual or micro perceptions of innovation. The distal properties ascribe a community, or macro, perception of innovation. Thus it can be argued that if an individual learns or performs a task for the first time it may be considered innovative. This also includes tasks that may have been available to the individual yet unperformed. The distal element underscores the value of the perceived task within a community or other external validating entity. Additionally, the confluence of the proximal and distal categories of innovation highlights a dynamic synergy for both personal and public innovations.

Boyer (1997) states "knowledge is acquired through research, through synthesis, through practice and through teaching". Hence, this progression from research to teaching exemplifies the connectivity of innovation and the need for assessment of its outcomes. Hauschildt (2003) posits, "The success of innovation is to a great extent dependent upon the activities and abilities of individuals who enthusiastically support the new product or process". Hauschildt referred to these individuals as champions and promoters.

R. Buckminster Fuller (1981) studied innovations in various industries such as ship building, architecture, and copper mining. He noticed that when half of the industries in a specific area have adopted an innovation, it stops being an innovation and enters a new phase. His notion is based on the distinctions between new practice and accepted practice wherein the majority of an industry is using that method. Thus, an innovation would have to be anything that hasn't reached 50 per cent industry penetration. Generalizing this definition to teacher education, an innovative practice in teacher education would remain an innovation until at least half of the industry has adopted the innovation. Many teacher educator may still practice only one method of teaching, *e.g.*, lecture at the place of cooperative group learning. David Johnson and Roger Johnson (2002) indicate that it can take between two and three years of conscious practice to become proficient in using cooperative group learning so as to gain the research promise of desirable outcomes. In spite of research-based evidence attesting to these desirable outcomes, cooperative group learning remains an innovation, because it has not reached 50 per cent industry penetration in either university or public school teaching. There are many such examples of innovation in teacher education that have yet to achieve the 50 per cent market penetration standard: professional development schools, teaching with educational technology, use of self-study, inquiry-as-stance, service-learning, socio-cultural pedagogical approaches.

INNOVATION IN TEACHER EDUCATION

Innovation in teacher education, like any other context, have two main aspects-'what' and 'how' of an innovation. 'What' aspect of an innovation refers to the substance of an innovation that includes descriptions of new programmes and practices of teacher education? The process aspect of innovation in teacher education includes descriptions of how innovations take place in teacher education. Melvin (1993) calls for more concerted efforts to study the influence of professional studies by faculties of education on actual practice in classrooms and schools.

Describing the teacher as a dynamic innovator since ages in Indian context and innovativeness as the only way towards excellence; Vadhel, Shah and Hathi (2009) states application of innovative practices at three levels-in curriculum, in evaluation system and in management. They recommends more focus to develop the proactive attitude among the students, raise their genuine interest in the curriculum, identify their aptitude and then suggest them the suitable practices.

Sternberg, Pretz, and Kaufman (2003) define innovation as "the channeling of creativity so as to produce a creative idea and/or product that can and wish to be used". So teachers as action researchers can discover innovative curricular, instructional, and management strategies that will effectively benefit their respective classes and may be transported to colleagues.

The concept of newness has been superimposed on the definition of innovation by Goldsmith and Foxall (2003) who posit three different qualities of newness: decency, originality, and similarity. Teacher educators have capitalized on the decency of curricular innovations, for example, by taking the leadership in implementing and evaluating whole-language, student-led individual education programs, and character education. The concepts of originality and similarity are meshed with the various approaches of positive peer culture, cooperative learning groups, and classroom communities. According to Malian and Nevin (2005), multiple sources of influence impact the decisions about what and how teacher educators are expected to operate, including the innovations that are adopted. Some of those sources of influence (such as teacher certification boards) can demand that certain curricula be adopted, specific instructional procedures be utilized, and delineate the conditions under which candidates will be selected for entry into teacher education programs. Other sources of influence include how other professionals are prepared (*e.g.*, case-based or problem-based learning from legal and business preparation, constructivist teaching methods derived from educational psychology).

FACILITATIVE FACTORS SPREADING INNOVATION IN TEACHER EDUCATION

Das, B.C. (2008) has mentioned several factors which facilitate the spread of innovation in teacher training institutes in India. They are awareness and interest, incentive, service and support, leadership role, problem solving approach, prestige value of innovation, and intrinsic value of innovation and evaluation process.

Joshi (1972) and Chaliha (2003) state that a good number of teacher educators those who have gone abroad for higher studies, have brought many new and innovative ideas such as microteaching, Flanders Interaction Analysis Model, Simulation Technique, Internship, and semester system. The awareness creates interest in innovation and its attitude for its adoption and co-operation to other member in their educational ventures. Buch (1973) state that, attitude and academic interest of the schools is a major promoter of diffusion of innovation. In fact proper attitude and support from the institutions are contributory factors for the spread of innovations in teacher education institutions.

Chaliha (2003) observe that, incentive for work of the individual is a favorable factor in the spread of innovations. Incentive is helpful in the acceptance of a creative idea, which an individual receives out of it. Physical facilities and financial support is the most influencing factors to pursue their ideas further. If the outcome of an experiment is satisfying to the innovator, these too work as motivational factors.

Service and support from the community, colleagues and

students are helpful for the spread and adoption of innovations. Support from the Government and other agencies such as UGC, NCERT and Department of Education provides the much financial support for the creation of new ideas. This recognition acts as a big motivational factor for the adoption of creative ideas.

Effective leadership helps in adoption of an innovative idea. Progressive, democratic and dedicated leadership quality of a head of the institution is the most powerful facilitative factors in the spread of innovation. Other facilitative factors are professional growth of teachers, academic programmes, in-service programmes, refresher courses, short term in-service courses, practical trainings, workshops, conferences etc.

Problem solving approach is another helping factor for innovation. The staff meeting also create innovativeness if the approach is problem solving. There are two underlying assumptions-first, teachers work increasingly within a professional group setting as opposed to that of isolated self-contained class room and secondly, teachers perceive themselves as a professional group capable of solving problem and self improvement at higher level of decision making. Chaliha (2003) finds that, teacher education institutions where the academic staff councils make decisions; there are evidences of more creativity and innovativeness. The decision taken through the techniques of problem solving approaches have shown better planning and more involvement of the members.

The acceptance of an innovation, to an extent depends upon the source from which it has been disseminated. Many teacher training institutes in India have readily accepted the new concept of objective base evaluation as the NCTE and National Institute of Education (NIE), New Delhi have propagated the same. Both these bodies command respect in the field of education as ideas propagated by them tend to be more acceptable because the association with such bodies provides prestige to the adopters as well.

The acceptance of an innovation depends on its intrinsic value too. It is likely to be more acceptable if it promises to bring some qualitative improvement and it is line with the traditions of the institutions *e.g.* Block Practice Teaching (Chaliha, 2003) after the experimentation at M.S. University, Baroda caught the imagination of other institutions in India.

The advancement of innovative practices might be enhanced through the development of diagnostic instruments which could be administered, scored and evaluated by personnel in the institute of education. Such procedure as Review meeting and internal reporting by professionals are helpful in identifying the personnel in organization interested and supportive of innovative practices. Review meeting and internal reporting by professionals not only assess the strengths and weakness but also promotes professionalism among members leading to acceptance and innovations.

SUGGESTIONS

Today the pattern of education and its transaction process is changing very fast and innovations in Teacher Education in above mentioned framework is the need of hour. So teachers as action researchers must discover innovative curricular, instructional, and management strategies that will effectively benefit their respective classes and may be transported to colleagues. Following actions are suggested for the spread of innovations:

- Physical facilities and funds should be provided by possible funding agencies.
- The teacher educators should get external exposure and be made in touch with recent trends of their professional world.
- The service and support from community, colleagues, and student teachers, practicing schools, administrators and students should be encouraged.
- Provision of proper incentives to teacher educator for their professional growth.
- Publication and subscription of professional journals should be encouraged.
- Starting Research wing in the university departments and selected institutions.
- An international and interpersonal relation favours innovations, hence encouraged.
- Management should be watchful in maintaining institution to make it innovative.
- Professional training of members of staff.
- Inspiring leadership from head of institution.

- Appropriate freedom and autonomy to teacher educator
- Acknowledged recognition from colleagues and students
- Well qualified staff and organization of in-service and extension programmes

REFERENCES

Boyer, E. (1997). *Scholarship reconsidered: Priorities of the professoriate.* (p. 24) Princeton, NJ: The Carnegie Foundation.

Buch, M.B. (1972). *An Inquiry into Conditions Promoting Adaptability in Indian Schools,* Ph.D. Thesis, M.S. University, Baroda.

Chaliha, B. (2003). *Factors Promoting Diffusion of Innovations in the Secondary Teachers' Training Institutions in Assam,* Unpublished Ph.D. Thesis, D.U.

Clapham, M.M. (2003). The development of innovative ideas through creativity training. In L. V. Shavinina (Ed.), *The International Handbook on Innovation* pp. 366-376. London, UK: Pergamon.

Das, B.C. (2008). Facilitative Factors in the Spread of Innovations in Teacher Education. *University News,* 46 (37) 21-25.

Delors, J. (1996). Learning the treasurer within (Report of UNESCO) of the International Commission on Education for Twenty-first Century), France: UNESCO, Paris.

Fuller, R. Buckminster (1981). *Critical Path.* New York: St. Martin's Press.

Goldsmith, R.E. and Foxall, G.R. (2003). The measurement of innovativeness. In L.V. Shavinina (Ed.), *The International Handbook on Innovation,* pp. 321-330. London, UK: Pergamon.

Hauschildt, J. (2003). Promoters and champions in innovations: Development of a research paradigm. In L.V. Shavinina (Ed.), *The International Handbook on Innovation,* p. 804. London, UK: Pergamon.

Johnson, D.W. and Johnson, R.T. (2002). *Cooperative Research and Training Center.* Minneapolis, MN: University of Minnesota.

Joshi, D.C. (1972). *A Study of Innovations and Change in Teachers Colleges,* Ph.D. Thesis, Udaipur University.

Kostoff, R.N. (2003). Stimulating Innovation. In L.V. Shavinina (Ed.), *The International Handbook on Innovation,* pp. 388-400. London, UK: Pergamon.

Malian, Ida M. and Nevin, A.I. (2005). A Framework for Understanding Assessment of Innovation in Teacher Education. *Teacher Education Quarterly.* Retrieved September, 07, 2009 from http://findarticles.com/p/articles/ mi_qa 3960/is_200507/ai_n14826962/

Melvin, C. (1993). Assessing the contribution of professional studies to professional practice, *Journal of Professional Studies,* 1 (1), 13-15.

National Policy on Education (1986). Ministry of Human Resource Development, Government of India, New Delhi.

Programme of Action (1990 and1992). Ministry of Human Resource Development, Government of India, New Delhi.

Rogers, E. (1995). *Diffusion of innovation* (4th Ed.). New York: The Free Press.

Singh, S.D. (2008). Quality Process Norms for Teacher Education System and Role of Teacher Educators. *University News,* 46 (96) 110-112.

6

Restructuring of Higher Education for Universalisation

Social Perspectives

Baiju K. Nath

Education is one of the intervening variables of social change. The role of Education as an instrument of social change and development is widely reorganized today. Education can bring changes in the outlook and attitudes of people; to change people means to change society. On the other hand society undergoes continuous changes over time. A nomadic society in the ancient past transformed into various forms in the progress of time to learning society, then agricultural society, industrial society and now as information society, (though we call it as knowledge society) because information transferred is in such a faster rate, that it is very difficult to transform into knowledge in short span of time.

There was a time in India, when educational institutions and teachers were engaged in transmitting 'a way of life'. Education was a means of social control than an instrument of social change at that time. But today education aims at imparting empirical knowledge. The new needs in education are strongly based on how we define change in the world as well as what we see as the role of education in relation to that change. Globalization is now reshaping the discourse of education–to create productive worker in a market driven society. So, progressive changes have to be effectively implemented our thinking on educational reform must end into account the public culture in which it functions.

National Knowledge Commission (NKC) of India strongly believes that as resource allocation increases, institutional reforms and organizational changes may become the crucial bottleneck that hamper progress. Rapid changes are taking place in different sectors of the economy, in this scenario education and associated knowledge sectors would need to keep pace with this change to continue to be relevant. We require paradigm shifts in our delivery mechanisms to ensure that we create institutions and structures that are sustainable, have the ownership of the community and are accountable to them.

It is important to begin with the consensus on educational needs which are emerging and the particular forms of knowledge systems which come to be valued with globalization because, without the specifics we are in danger that certain modes of knowledge, certain type of culture come to be treated as common sense, so that they are valued, celebrated and thought of as inevitable and desirable. It can be said that basic literacy brings a society into modern world. But only Higher Education (HE) provokes persons to question the values of everyday life

The famous education expert Martin Trow (1972) divides HE development into three stages: Elitism, followed by Mass and then Universal education, a specialization which has been widely accepted by educationists around the world. In his theory, the most crucial indicator of the three different HE developments is Gross Enrolment Rate (GER), which refers to the share of 18-22 years olds enrolled in fulltime HE as a proportion of the total population in that age group. The cutoff points between each stage are below 15 per cent, between 15 per cent-50 per cent, and over 50 per cent respectively. Many developed countries have achieved a Universal HE level, *e.g.* the US and Germany (Tsang, 2000). The vision of our country also is to achieve universalisation of HE. The National Knowledge Commission suggested Creation of more universities expanding to around 1500 universities nationwide, to enable India to attain a gross enrolment ratio of at least 15 per cent by 2015 (NKC 2006). We are at universalizing primary education through SSA. The pace we are following may not be so fast to reach at the aim in the near future. Hence a reverse processing from the apex to bottom can be tried out. There are about 350 odd universities and 18,000 colleges providing higher education in the country, to about 10 per cent of the relevant age group. This is extremely inadequate in a country where the demographic dividend by way of a young population of about 550 million youth, is a much talked about asset. If we are to achieve a Gross Enrolment Ratio (GER) of 15 per cent and above by 2015, we need to substantially increase the number of higher education institutions (HEIs) in our country.(NKC 2007). UGC expert committee have identified educationally backward districts in India and proposed to set up Model colleges in 370 districts in the Country where enrolment level in higher education is low,

Higher education (HE) in China has been transformed from elite to mass education over the last decade due to commercialisation and funding reform (Yao, Wu & Su 2008). Increased access to HE may not necessarily improve social justice. HE expansion coincided with increasing economic and social inequality. The expansion of HE and rising inequality have caused serious concern as to whether the redistribution of HE resources and opportunities has adversely affected regional and inter-group equality and social justice. Second, HE expansion was associated with a sudden change in public funding, from a model supported by three different government authorities to a co-funding model supported by students and in most cases their parents, the central government fund only 107 national key universities and local governments to be responsible for supporting all non-key universities (Huang, 2005). As key universities in China are concentrated in big cities and some rich provinces, and central ministries other than the Ministry of Education are no longer financing any HEIs, the change in public funding must have disadvantaged poorer prospective students from less affluent regions. Well off urban families are able to afford tuition fees for their children, low income rural and urban families, especially those in inland areas, cannot afford to support their children to study in universities and colleges. High university fees have become a real deterrent to poor families, whereas relatively more opportunities are available to wealthy families, especially those from big cities where entry requirements are significantly lower for local residents than for those outside the cities, giving the former social group unfair access to HE.

The XIth plan (2007-12) viewed to provide flexibility to universities to raise fees accompanied by scholarships, fellowships and student loans. The three focal themes on Indian higher education for the XI Plan are Expansion, Inclusion and Excellence. The extent of HE expansion raises a serious question about the quality and employability of graduates. Due to urban unemployment and social discrimination, HE graduates from some universities are less successful in the labour market (Yang, 2006). The problem of unemployment of graduates, and city migration are the problems in our country also. As poor children are less likely to study in prestigious universities, they suffer further discrimination upon graduation. According to Wu and Zheng (2008), the first radical reform in the late 1990s was the commercialization of HE which led to the emergence of a co-funding model to replace the former funding regime previously supported by the government. Under the co-funding model, students are required to pay tuition fees (from 1999 onward) although those from poor families are entitled to have a certain amount in student loans. The sudden inclusion of private unaided colleges in the field of professional education in Kerala, though helped to raise GER, but crating so many legal problems due to lack of proper legislation, since they causing social disparities.

Rapid economic development has resulted in a rising demand for HE because the labour market, which aims to improve people's living conditions requires more and more university graduates (Yang, 2004). HE expansion not only encourages families to spend their savings on HE, but also stimulates investment in HE related services industries (Zheng, 2006). This is a positive social impact of expansion of HE. Hannum and Buchman (2003) summarize the impact of HE expansion on economic and social development as the following three points:

- It contributes to national economic growth, since better educated Workers create more production.
- It narrows social inequalities by promoting social mobility.
- It promotes the development of a more democratic society.

Based on the theory of Maximally Maintained Inequality, Raftery and Hout (1993) argue that students from advantaged groups are better equipped to make the most of enrolment expansion, as HE expansion widens the gaps between advantaged and disadvantaged classes. Compared to the disadvantaged groups, the advantaged groups are more able and determined to gain access to HE because they are more able to afford tuition fees. Consequently, enrolment expansion increases the disparity between different classes not only for the present generation but also for the future generations (Wan, 2006). The increasing dependence of HE expansion on tuition fees has important social and economic implications, especially on social justice and equality the importance of analyzing the impact of HE expansion on social justice to students and their families from a comprehensive and long term perspective of development. In addition, a suitable regional division in the HE sector is important for initial analysis of resource redistribution. Regional imbalances in medical education would be a limiting factor in providing affordable health care for all sections (NKC, 2007).

Decentralization focused on transferring control and ownership rights from central ministries, except for the Ministry of Education, to regional and city authorities. Commercialization, on the other hand, focused on charging tuition fees to establish a co-funding model between parents and government. (Yao, Wu & Su 2008). For disadvantaged social groups and regions, the expansion of HE is a double edge sword, which creates more HE opportunities, but at the same time, imposes a large financial burden on poor families. Though educational loans are available, the constraints for getting the same and the tendency to keep up with students belong to high social status create social pressure in students of disadvantaged groups. Special assistance scheme should be made to streamline disadvantaged groups. According to the Controller of Entrance Examinations Kerala, only two Scheduled Tribe students were qualified for MBBS admission in Kerala in the year 2008. This shows that even a state with such a high rate of literacy and large number of educational institutions, at least upto higher secondary level the facilities of weaker sections to qualify for professional courses is very limited. Hence, Regional and Social disparities need to be taken care of while preparing plans for restructuring HE. Another alarming social problem that may influence the Indian context is graying of population, especially in Kerala. A prediction on future population remarked that more than 10 per cent of the population may be comprised of old people by 2015 and it might be raised up to 15 per cent by the next five years. Since human resource is the most valuable resource, restructuring of higher education should consider the increased rate of older community also, to contribute for the welfare of the state.

NKC's recommendation to set up an Independent Regulatory Authority for Higher Education (IRAHE) as a single nodal agency to control institutions of higher education would be an effective solution for keeping uniformity amidst of decentralization. In professional education, The NKC 2007, itself not mentioned all professions, due emphasis was given to legal, management and medical profession, but nothing about teaching profession. Since quality teachers are the backbone of any education system, there need to be a national authority for teaching profession and teachers. Scarcity of qualified and experienced teachers is the major problem facing by almost all institutions, especially professional institutions. The suggestions such as outsourcing and adjunct professor may have limited impact in overcoming the shortage of faculties, because a person from outside may not be familiar with the social context of our students as viewed in NCERT position paper on teacher education (NCERT position paper 2.4). Hence a vision for teacher education in a comprehensive and integrated manner is essential on the contrary to view teacher education as a separate faculty. A teacher in any area (engineering, management, medicine, or any other) need to be trained to develop teaching skills for drawing out the best teacher in them in order to get maximum benefits to students. In this manner teaching is more comprehensive and teacher educators should be identified as the immediate stakeholders to be made aware and trained for any positive social change to occur in our country.

"A vision is not a project report or a plan target. It is an articulation of the desired end results in broader terms". (A. P. J. Abdul Kalam). Our former president, reminds us about the power of dreams to frame vision of future realities. India will have a vision 2020 based on our future dreams, in which we realize knowledge as the treasure to conquer the horizons of growth and development through systematic transmission using various tools of ICT. Education is the primary and most effective means so far evolved for transmitting practically useful knowledge from one generation to another. Achieving 100 per cent enrolment of all children in the 6 to 14 year age group is an ambitious but achievable goal for 2020. Do we need a vision on HE by this time?

Knowledge has replaced finance capital as the most important determinant of development. In a remarkable study in mid-1950s, Nobel laureate economist Robert Solow showed that seven eighth of the growth of US from 1900 to 1950 was accounted for by technical progress, while only 23 one-eighth was driven by capital. A study by Denison, on factors contributing to the growth of the US economy from 1929 to 1982, attributes 94 per cent of that growth to factors relating to knowledge generation and dissemination: 64 per cent of this is linked to advances in knowledge generation (*i.e.* Research and Development) and another 30 per cent to advances in education. Better resource management, which is an application of knowledge, is also identified as a more important factor than capital. By realizing knowledge as the most versatile capital planning commission, Govt. of India has now taking prospective decisions on the basis of NKC report 2007. The system of education should be redesigned on the basis of new measures of GDP of a country proposed by Stiglitz, and Sen (2009), which include physical life standards, educational status, health status, involvement in political power, social relations and contacts, favorable environment, and economic and physical protection.

Literacy rates in India have arisen dramatically from 18 per cent in 1951 to 65 per cent in 2001, but vast differences also remain among different sections of the population. Literacy among males is nearly 50 per cent higher than females, and it is about 50 per cent higher in urban areas as compared to the rural areas. Rates are also significantly lower among scheduled castes and tribes than among other communities. Literacy is an indispensable minimum condition for development, but it is not sufficient. in this increasingly complex and technologically sophisticated world. Universalisation of primary education through SSA and the proposed Rastriya Madhyamic Siksha Abhiyan for universal secondary level are hopeful in raising the rate and quality of literates in the country.

This universalisation process would have resulted in huge number of young students who quest for all levels of higher education in the coming decades. "The severe shortage of qualified instructors, and in the light of India's outstanding expertise in the IT industry, the country needs to embark on a massive programme to convert the entire higher educational curriculum into a multi-media, web-based format and to establish accreditation standards for recognition of the distance education so imparted", (NKC, 2007).

Since independence, higher education in India has witnessed many fold increase. The number of universities has increased from 20 to 417, and number of colleges from 500s to 20,667 during the 1957–2007 periods. Access to higher education is measured in terms of Gross Enrolment Ratio (GER), which is about 10 per cent in India, lies far behind to developed countries ranges between 20–90 per cent. The views of the general public and parents collected in a series of detailed public opinion surveys and interview with legislators, business executives, and other opinion leaders about major issues in higher education is an effective way to overcome problems of higher education (Immerwahr Johnson, & Gasbarra 2008).

The areas related to higher education required immediate address are;

- Access to higher education,
- Disparities in access (inter regional and inter group),
- Institutional Quality and excellence,
- Relevant education,
- Academic and administrative governance, and Cost and Funding

The XI plan envisages a target GER of 15 per cent, which is projected to reach upto 20 per cent by 2017. Expansion of institutional capacity by setting up of new institutions is proposed in XI plan (Thorat, S. 2008). Expansion with inclusiveness is inevitable to bridge regional, cultural, economical, and social disparities.

Greater public investment has to be supplemented by greater private investment to enhance access and quality of education to desirable levels in a knowledge society (Panikkar 2008).

A radical reform of the system of Open and Distance Education (ODE) is imperative to achieve the objectives of expansion. Open Educational Resources (OER) must be created online through a collaborative process, pooling in the efforts and expertise of all major institutions of higher education (NKC 2007).

Though the government is ready to set up new institutions, the lapse in setting up of infrastructural facilities will be the most common problem. Hence promoting e-education, through a system of ODE, by exploring Virtual Learning Environment is a viable solution for various issues of higher education, such as access, quality, relevance, governance, cost and time.

REFERENCES

Govt. of India (2007). *National Knowledge Commission–Report to the Nation* Govt. of India (2002). *India Vision-2020. Report: Planning commission.*

Hannum, E. and Buchman, C. (2003), *The Consequences of global educational expansion: social science perspectives*, Cambridge, MA: American Academy of Arts and Sciences. Available to read online: *www.amacad.or*

James. J.W. (2006), Social justice in Chinese higher education: regional issues of equity and access, *Review of Education*, 52, 149-169.

NCERT (2005). *National Curriculum Frame Work 2005*. New Delhi.

Raftery, A. E. and Hout. M. (1993), Maximally maintained inequality: expansion, reform, and opportunity in Irish education, *Sociology of Education*, 66 (1), 4162.

Trow, M. (1972), The expansion and transformation of higher education *International Review of Education*, 18(1), 6184.

Tsang, M. C. (2000), Education and national development in China since 1949: oscillating policies and enduring dilemmas, *China Review 2000*, Retrieved from www.tc.columbia.edu/centers/coce/publications.htm.

Wan, Y. (2006), Expansion of Chinese higher education since 1998: its causes and outcomes, in *Asia Pacific Education Review*, 7 (1), 1931.

Yang, D. (2006), *Higher education opportunities: gaps persist despite improvement*, Beijing: Higher Education Research Institute, Beijing University of Science and Technology.

Yang, D. S. (2004), Analysis of education industralisation, *Nanfang Weekly*, 10 October 2004.

Zheng, Z. (2006), Mr. Tang Min, isn't enrolment expansion a mistake? *Nanfeng Chuang*, retrieved from http://www.sina.com.cn.

Stiglitz, J.E.and Sen, A. (2009). GDP Poor Measure of Growth. http://www.huffingtonpost.com/2009/09/23/stiglitz-amartya-sen-gdp-_n_295764.html

www.wikipedia.com

www.ncert.nic.in

www.ugc.ac.in

7

Interpretation and Reporting of Test Results

Marks vs. Grades

Nityananda Pradhan

The systems of marking, interpretation of test results and reporting pupil progress are designed to serve a variety of functions. They provide information that is helpful to pupils, parents, teachers and employers: Pupils find them useful as a periodic summary of their learning progress. They can pinpoint strengths and weaknesses in learning with implications for remedial action. Parents, teachers, and counselors use the information in guiding and helping pupils make realistic future plans. Administrators use the information to determine promotion or certification. The reports also provide useful information to other schools and prospective employers.

The task of marking, interpreting results, and reporting them in a brief and understandable form to a variety of users (*e.g.* pupils, parents, teachers, counselors, employers) is a difficult one. It becomes especially difficult when a variety of evaluation data, *e.g.* tests, lab work, projects, efforts, work habits, are summarized as a single letter grade (*e.g.* A, B, C, D, F) or mark.

MARKING VS. GRADING

While assessing students' achievement we are invariably interested in three things: (i) How the student is progressing with reference to him/herself; (ii) How the students is progressing with reference to his/her peer group; and (ii) How the student is progressing with reference to criteria set out by the teachers in terms of expected levels of attainment. Currently, this is being carried out by way of awarding numerical marks on an interval scale (*e.g.* 0, 1, 2 ....100) that suffers from a lot of shortcomings.

One of the drawbacks in the present marking system of 101-point scale that runs from 0-100 is the absence of both absolute zero and 100. The zero that is artificially created for the convenience of the users does not represent the nothingness of an attribute, nor does the score of 100 signify the perfection in achievement. This results in variations in spread of scores in different subject areas. This limitation neither allows the comparison of scores from test to test nor from subject to subject.

Another significant imperfection in assessment of students' achievement is inculcation of measurement errors that results from inter and intra-examiner variability, imperfection of tools, sampling of contents, sampling of objectives within the content, arbitrary time limits for answering individual questions, testing situations, etc. Interestingly, some of these errors are identifiable and some are not. The magnitude of such errors is reported to vary from seven to fifteen per cent. In such a situation application of 101-point scale where the individuals are discriminated on the basis of single number right score is inappropriate.

This shortcoming can be overcome if the students are placed in ability bands that represent ranges of scores. These ability bands may vary according to the number of categories one wishes to employ for the classification of students. Each ability range may be designated with a letter which is called a grade. Several committees and commissions in the past, even prior to NPE-POA, 1992, have recommended the use of grades in place of marks.

It is because of the superiority of the grading system over the conventional marking system that several premier institutions of higher learning in India have adopted it successfully. At the school level the Indian Council of School Certificate Examination (ICSCE) has been using grading for a number of years. The central Board of Secondary Education (CBSE) tried to introduce the grading system but had to revert back to making in the wake of adverse public opinion and resistance from the University system. Now the CBSE as well as ICSCE indicate both grades and marks in their marks sheets and system of declaring pass and fail continues in all the Boards.

Use of Grades

In the context of evaluation, grading is essentially a method of using a set of symbols, *e.g.* A, B, C, D, E that ought to be clearly defined and uniformly understood by the students, teachers, parents and all the concerned. Marks are also a type of grades on a very big 101-point scale. A property introduced grading system may not only provide for the comparison of students' performance, but also indicate the quality of performance. The award of grades may serve a variety of purposes, including making decisions pertaining to placement and promotion; and determining the Grade Point Average (GPA) for the purpose of awarding scholarships etc.

Methods of Assigning Grades

Grading may be carried out in a variety of ways: (i) direct grading and indirect grading; (ii) absolute grading and relative grading.

Direct Grading

In direct grading, the performance of learner is assessed in qualitative terms and expressed in terms of letter grades. This method can profitably be used for the assessment of both cognitive and non-cognitive learning outcomes.

Indirect Grading

In indirect grading, the performance of the learner is first assessed in terms of marks and subsequently transformed into letter grade using absolute or relative grading procedure.

Absolute Grading

Absolute grading involves direct conversation of marks into grades irrespective of the distribution of marks in a subject. It is just like categorizing the students into five categories as follows:

Range of marks		*Grade*
75% and above	:	A
60% to 74%	:	B
45% to 59%	:	C
33% to 44%	:	D
Below 33%	:	E

In absolute grading system, the distribution of grades is not predetermined. If all pupils demonstrate a high level of performance all will receive high grades. If some pupils demonstrate low level of performances they will receive low grades. This method of grading has got several advantages. The procedure is simple and straightforward to use. Meaning of each grade is distinctly understandable. One of the limitations of this method is that the distribution of scores is taken on its face value regardless of the errors of measurement.

Relative Grading

Relative grading is knows as grade on the curve. The curve refers to normal probability curve. It is also knows as norm referenced grading. The assignment of relative grades is essentially a matter of ranking the pupils in order of overall achievement and assigning letter grade (*e.g.* A, B, C, D, E). The proportion of As, Bs, Cs, Ds and Es to be used must be determined prior to letter grades are assigned. Grading on the normal curve that has been widely used in the past results in an equal percentage of As and Es, and Bs and Ds. For example, if the students will be divided into five categories, the distribution of grade wise cases would be as follows:

Letter Grade	*Interval*	*No. of cases*
A	1.5 to 00	7%
B	0.5 to 1.5	24%
C	-0.5 to 0.5	38%
D	-1.5 to -0.5	24%
E	-00 to -1.50	7%

Grading on the basis of normal curve seems to be irrational and inappropriate for classroom groups (*e.g.* too small groups to yield normal distribution). The most sensible approach is to set guidelines for the approximate distribution of marks by the teachers. The distribution should be flexible to allow for variation in caliber of pupils from one course to another and from one time to another in the same course. Ranges rather than fixed percentages of pupils who should receive each letter grade need to be indicated as follows:

A = 10 to 20 Percentage of Pupils
B = 20 to 30 Percentage of Pupils
C = 30 to 40 Percentage of Pupils
D = 40 to 50 Percentage of Pupils

E = 50 to 60 Percentage of Pupils

There is no scientific basis of determining these ranges. The decision must be made by the institution taking into account the institution's philosophy, ability and progress in ability of learners in different subjects.

Comparison of Overall Performance: Grade Point Average

Relative grading system allows comparison of students' performance both within the subject and across the subjects. But if we want to compare the overall performance of the students in different subjects, we need to find out a Grade Point Average (GPA) by combining the grades awarded in different subjects. However, for computing the GPA, the grades in all the subjects must be based on relative grading method.

Students	*Grades in Different Subjects*					*GPA*
X	A	C	B	B	C	3.8
Y	C	B	A	A	B	4.2

$$\text{GPA of X} = \frac{5+3+4+4+3}{5} = \frac{19}{5} = 3.8$$

$$\text{GPA of Y} = \frac{3+4+5+5+4}{5} = \frac{21}{5} = 4.2$$

On the basis of GPA, it may be inferred that the performance of 'Y' is better than that of 'X'.

GUIDELINES FOR EFFECTIVE GRADING

In the context of the grading system, careful implementation of the following measures will lead to awarding of grades with high degree of reliability and validity:

(i) Describe your grading procedures to pupils at the beginning of instruction.

(ii) Make clear to pupils that the course grade will be based on achievement only.

(iii) Explain how other elements (effort, work habits, personal-social characteristics) will be reported.

(iv) Relate the grading procedures to the intended learning out comes (*i.e.*, instructional objectives)
(v) Obtain valid evidence (*e.g.* tests, reports, ratings) as a basis for assigning grades.
(vi) Take precautions to prevent cheating on tests, reports, and other types of evaluation.
(vii) Return and review all test results (and other evaluation data) as soon as possible.
(viii) Properly weigh the various types of achievement included in the grade.
(ix) Do not lower an achievement grade for weak effort or misbehaviour.
(x) Be fair, avoid bias, and when in doubt (as with a borderline score) review the evidence. If still in doubt, assign the higher grade.

(*Gronlund and Linn,* 1990, p. 443)

INTERPRETATION AND REPORTING OF TEST RESULTS

The systems of reporting test results are designed to serve a variety of functions: (i) Instructional uses; (ii) Report to Parents; and (iii) Administrative and guidance uses. The progress reports, which are most common at elementary school level, typically include ratings of progress (Marks/grades) in basic school subjects (*e.g.* History, Math., Language). The report forms also include a series of work habits and personal-social characteristics (*e.g.* cleanliness, punctuality, truthfulness) to be checked by the teacher. A more detailed and meaningful reporting system supplement the marks/grades with checklist of major objectives in each subject. In some cases, two marks are assigned to each subject: one for achievement; and the other for effort, improvement, or growth.

Reporting Test Results to Parents

Informing parents or guardians of their children's progress is a basic function of reporting system. The results are commonly reported to parents during a parent-teacher meeting. Although parents have a legal right to all information the school has concerning their children, it should be presented to them in an understandable and usable form. This means avoiding technical jargon and presenting test results to parents in language that is meaningful to them. The meaningful communication of test results to parents includes:

(i) Describing what the test measures.
(ii) Explaining the meaning of the test scores.
(iii) Clarifying the accuracy of the test scores.

Discussing the use of the test results. In general, it is best to keep the explanations brief and simple. Do not overwhelm parents with more test information than they can grasp.

Describing What the Test Measures

In reporting on the results of learning ability test, saying something like "this test measures skills and abilities useful in learning" may be sufficient. If the test contains several scores (*e.g.* verbal, quantitative, and nonverbal), each section of the test may be described in similar general terms. To say that a reading test measures "vocabulary and reading comprehension" or that a math test measures "computation and problem solving" is sufficient. In some cases it may be desirable to describe the test results by objective or item clusters, and these are typically identified on the pupil's individual report form. Parents should be referred to the appropriate staff member if they have questions about scores.

Explaining the Meaning of Test Scores

In making norm-referenced interpretations of test scores, both the meaning of the score and the nature of the norm group should be explained to parents, simply and understandably. Percentile ranks and percentages are widely used in reporting to parents because they are easy to explain and misinterpretation is less likely to occur. Percentile ranks can be interpreted by saying: "On the English language test Geeta scored higher than 80 per cent of the students of the University who appeared the same test". If both percentage scores and percentile scores are used, it is necessary to distinguish between them.

Clarifying the Accuracy of Test Scores

It is important to communicate to parents that all test scores contain some error. The magnitude of such error in case of scoring in a 101-

point scale is reported to vary from seven to fifteen per cent. In this context it is inappropriate to discriminate individuals on the basis of single number right score. It would be appropriate to interpret test scores using confidence bands/intervals. For example, a student is awarded a score 50 and where the standard error of measurement is ten. In this case the true score is likely to be any where between 40 and 60 in two out of three cases; between 30 and 70 in nineteen out of twenty cases; and between 20 and 80 in all the cases. In view of such wide variations, assessment of students' achievement in terms of single number score is totally unjustifiable. It is always good practice to interpret test scores to parents in light of the other available data concerning the pupil.

Discussing Use of the Test Results

The interpretation of test results should be accompanied by an explanation of how the test results are to be used in the instructional programme and a discussion of what action should be taken by both teacher and parents to improve the pupil's learning and development. This discussion, of course, should not be limited to the test results but should be based on all the evidence concerning the pupil's learning and development. The value of test scores becomes clearer to parents when they are communicated with all other information about the pupil.

CONCLUSION

Marks awarded by the Boards or Universities do not reflect the true ability of individual learners. They suffer from a number of imperfections. The long association with numerical marking in examinations has left an indelible impression on our minds. It is becoming difficult to erase this from the minds of students, teachers, parents, and employers, etc. Therefore, to understand the benefits of grading system, one has to come out of this mind-set and think rationally. Once the result is declared in terms of grades, parents' focus will shift from marks to grades and they will not pressurize their wards. Grading in public examinations will directly benefit the students in the following ways:

(i) It will minimize misclassification of students on the basis of unreliable marks.

(ii) It will eliminate unhealthy cut-throat competition among high achievers.

(iii) It will be a greater relief to low achievers when the system of declaring pass/fail is abolished.

(iv) It will provide a chance to improve upon his/her grade in any subject over a period of time without carrying a stigma of fail.

(v) Students will stop committing suicides or running away from homes on failing in examinations.

(vi) The nation will be benefited by sharing human and natural resources by not failing candidates that may be to the extent of 50 per cent or more.

(*NCERT*, 2000, pp. 35-36)

Institutionalization of grading in school system would largely depend upon its acceptability in the tertiary sector of education. The University Grants Commission (UGC), therefore, may be persuaded to work out a strategy for removing the bottlenecks and introduce grades in the university system.

REFERENCES

Anastasi, A. (1988): *Psychological Testing* (6th Ed.), Macmillan Publishing Company, New Delhi.

Gronlund, N.E. and Linn, R.L. (1990): *Measurement and Evaluation in Teaching*, Macmillan Publishing Company, New York.

NCERT (2000): Grading in schools, New Delhi.

NCERT (2001): Using Grades for Admissions, New Delhi.

NCERT (2003): Continuous and Comprehensive Evaluation–Teachers Handbook for Primary Stage, New Delhi.

NCERT (2005): National Curriculum Framework 2005, New Delhi.

Shukla, C. (2004): *Assessment and Evaluation in Higher Education*, Vedams Books (P) Ltd. New Delhi.

8

Shared Learning Through ICT in Teachers Education

Vision T 20

Hemant Kumar Khandai and *Anshu Mathur*

Through various suggestion and recommendation given by elite group/committees have targeted the present system of education, and forced us for the paradigm shift. Though our government is in process of transforming educational system, so as to remove the "Rote method", which is the major traditional system of learning. As per new ideology, to learn and understand should only be the aim of education. Frequent use of technology is one of the key recommendations to work on and we still follow the old model of teacher's education in traditional classrooms where knowledge transmission from a teacher to students based on "instruction approach". The Education experts have found ICT beneficiary in future education of upcoming teachers but it is insufficient to grab it as a "subject" in their curriculum but there should be realism in it. The aim of teacher education is to develop skills and appropriate knowledge among teacher trainees for using and integrating the correct technology in an appropriate manner. Every teacher should know how to use technology, pedagogy and subject area content effectively in their daily classroom teaching. The teacher education program play a great role by providing essential components of teaching process to the teacher trainees who are directly responsible for producing future citizens to the nation. Hence it is essential to develop the teacher education program, which can cater the changing needs of the society, as the change has been universally accepted as essential features of modern life in a society. Information Technology (IT) has caused many changes in the Communication network system therefore teaching at all levels needs to be modern, innovative and concurrent with the latest development to face the emerging changes of the future teacher education system by that the teacher gets transformed into an enriched, dedicated and committed professional. As a course of action effective development of communication skills thru ICT tools in learning must be supported because the individual Human mind is limited and opportunities and expectations are high and endless in this era of becoming superpower.

CONCEPT OF SHARED LEARNING WITH ICT

Shared Learning can be defined as "Groups of people, engaged in intellectual interaction, for the purpose of learning."

The formal definition of learning describes the process as "a relatively Permanent change in behaviour based on an individual's interact ional experience with its environment." As such, learning is an important form of personal adaptation. But we cannot escape the fact that, in order to learn, we need other people. Both formal and informal learning requires human interaction–whether that can be the words of someone written down, media others have created or the acknowledgement from others of our grasp of concepts. So, personal learning also requires others. Use of classrooms as a workplace with sharing, collaborating, exchanging and understanding of knowledge by different ways with students, teachers, B. Ed. *students of other colleges and teachers of other B. Ed. colleges at* a common place. We should begin to create a "shared learning" system. B. Ed. Teachers + B. Ed. Students + Experienced Teachers of various schools + Students of other colleges of Education, with each other build a cluster of educators. *It is a set of persons who embedded into the day-to-day processes of learning, such that team members continuously learn and develop their knowledge, skills and attitude together.*

Shared learning is the accumulation of individual learning. It's a structure that facilitate team learning with features such as boundary crossing and openness, therefore it is important that team members develop open communication, shared meaning and understanding. That will transform learning from an individual to complex with the involvement of persons at all levels of the teacher's education system and Goal of their actions is to enhance their effectiveness as professionals. Therefore it is important that team members develop open communication, shared meaning and understanding and the key role of ICT tools will certainly enrich and assist in the transaction of learning experiences. Learner can access knowledge and information through Internet, Satellite TV, Cable network, Radio and Digital media of various kinds of CD's, DVD's, etc. For teachers to become fluent in the usage of educational technology means going beyond mere competence with the latest tools to developing an understanding of the complex web of relationships among users, technologies, practices, and tools. Teachers must understand their role in technologically oriented classrooms, as good teacher with knowledge, attitudes and skills will turn out the potential of our school children. The slogan of Shared Learning using ICT can be echo all over. In this concept for teacher's education, decentralization of organizational structure is necessary, which allow creation, acquisition, dissemination, and implementation of the knowledge, skills and attitude. We need to transform our classrooms into workplaces in similarity with all equipments to access communication tools as learning medium, with others in form of sharing the knowledge thru various mediums. Tools of ICT to be used are-Mobiles, Computer/Laptop with access to the Internet, Radio, TV, Digital Storage devices (CD's, DVD's, USB and Memory of system), Projector (LCD/OHP), Web/Digital Camera (Audio + video), etc.

DESIGN

1. Techno Friendly Learning

Teachers acquire the skills and knowledge they need to use technology effectively. In the curriculum, application of technology must given priority for professional development of learners. Teacher should be trained in Multimedia techniques more emphasis on IT needs to be given. Uses of various mode of ICT effectively open the door to all kind of opportunities within the group to understand more together. The integration of ICT itself tends to be focused on technology rather than on information communication.

2. Democratic Environment

Environment should be opened inside and outside to exchange different types of knowledge thru tools of ICT. Democratic environment provides a platform open for everyone to participate as a protagonist with his or her own role and responsibility. Solely one can use the technology and can have the knowledge but dispersion of it will result in variety of thoughts and visions. Discussions through interactive communication in a democratic environment will establish the potential of expertise in educator's education. All educators (Teachers/Students) can exchange thoughts/ideas to create a knowledge environment.

3. Collective E-Approach

The most effective method to transfer wisdom/practical knowledge is for the inexperienced to learn through practice under the supervision and guidance of the experienced teachers is in a collective approach. Building relationships and collaborating with others is essential with technology. The growth of every kind of teaching skill depends how teachers share the teaching experiences, express their own practical knowledge related to practice, and create new practical knowledge through audio/video discussions, live telecasts, presentations and observations of storage devices.

4. Dynamic Participation

Learning as a quantitative increase in knowledge. Learning is acquiring information or 'knowing a lot'. ICT can save time and efforts made by learners to get efficiency. e-libraries/laboratories with online lectures will lead the system in future. "Dynamic participation" of all as a community/group in a cooperative and collaborative environment is the key of success of the programme. Everyone will take part with all new gadgets in a techno friendly organization for improvement of oneself and education.

5. Integration of Equipments in Learning

Learning should be integrated with equipments for learners to access all new mediums of communication— Mobiles, TV, Radio, Projectors, CD's, DVD's etc. It will lead the quality of educator's knowledge extreme. In a techno-friendly learning organization, each individual must excel at his or her discipline with equipments and skills. It will allow progressively learning through multiple interactions and therefore progressively build in intelligence among educators.

METHODOLOGY INCORPORATION WITH ICT

Some teachers have made their own perception regarding the complication and difficulty level for usage of technology in today's world. The present technology is so user friendly and easy that their own children/ grand children are able to use the same. Need for good training program for both the upcoming teachers and teacher's educators can remove the mental barrier.

The various technology available and will play the major role are described below:

Technology at the "THUMB"

Mobiles are the latest tools to access anywhere, anytime to get information. Day by day it's becoming the popular mode of communication, even in rural areas users count is increasing many fold. We have already seen one of the commercial on rural education with the message of learning thru mobile lastly *"What an idea sir ji"* Internet through mobile is really mean to "Kar Lo Dunia Muththi Me". In the *Vision* 2020 it is going to be sure success of this mode of receiving/distributing knowledge.

Learning by TV

Television channels like Doordarshan (DD), Etv and Satellite TV and other are telecasting educational programs and Learning programs everyday and with the presence of colleges staff, students. Sometime specific programs can be conducted in two-way communication so that students can get real advantage out of these programs.

Learning by Radio

Redefined approach of FM radio stations are already on air they can be used especially for students. Radio will be established medium through which educational information could be given/ taken with a variety of entertainment programs. Twenty-four hours telecast, easy to available and simplicity will work behind it. Special channel on education; One-way or two-way audio live programs, should be organized for upcoming teachers.

Learning Thru Digital Storage Devices

A *storage device* is a hardware device designed to store information. There are two types of storage devices used in computers; a 'primary storage' device and a 'secondary storage' device. A storage device may hold information, process information, or both. Memory of a computer, CD's, DVD's, USB's, and other audio/video storage devices can be helpful in development of knowledge and to fulfill the need of inquiry of an individual as per needs.

Virtual Clubs of Educators

The Internet has changed the way the world behaves, does business, and thinks. Today, academicians should have the facility of faster and surer access to a much wider range of information through the Internet, not just to read but to talk, print or save or forward to others as might suit their purpose. Internet to be recognized as an essential study tool in all higher education courses in developed countries. We can have the facility of virtual clubs to interact with each other through dialogue in which all the educators of universities, colleges and other educational institutes may appear with their dialogue on related theme.

Unification of Knowledge

ICT can be the medium of sharing knowledge around the globe, which most of the times do not require physical presence of a person. All resources can be unified for the great source of knowledge. Using all experts' knowledge in an interactive way thru Internet or TV/Radio, e-libraries etc will give ample opportunity to learners to understand the subject in different ways. Learning by unification of knowledge will enhance the potential of understanding among teachers.

Online Conversation

Online teaching and learning discussions will increase meaning and understanding of the content and provide more knowledge globally. They should be motivated towards "Dialogue" as it is the latest method of presentation to Generate knowledge leading to development of collective wisdom. *"Dialogue ... is about a shared inquiry, a way of thinking and reflecting together."* The way that it does this is through the four practices (Listening, Respecting, suspending and Voicing) the whole person is "enfolded" in every part of their conversation. This has enormous implications for the potential richness of meaning that we can bring into conversation.

E-Way Presentation

Electronic way of Presentation is the practice of showing and explaining the content of a topic to an audience or learner. It's a better way of communicating ideas and information to a group. It improves understanding and attracts learners towards new knowledge. In teachers education this may helpful in various topics related to curriculum and to break the monotony of the class.

Presentations increase attentive listening and communication skills of an individual, which is required in shared learning.

New Technologies

Now days, there are numerous technologies offered for various communication which are helping in learning programs done thru teleconferencing, web conferencing, web casting, broadcasting, even Internet facility can be given using the same.

Some of them are:

- CDMA/GPRS/Bluetooth (Used in Mobile communication)
- VPN/Leased Circuit/ ISDN (for Wide Area Networking)
- VSAT (for remote and wireless connectivity)

Advantages

- Exploration of Different Learning Paradigms
- Re conceptualization of the Role of Teachers and Learners
- Support to New Interdisciplinary approach,
- Balance Economics and the Quality of Education
- Move beyond standard curriculum and simple notions of efficiency
- Maturity in Communication technology
- Correctness of Communication
- Change in Mode of Teacher Behaviour.
- Import and Export of knowledge is possible.

Disadvantages

- Dependency upon "Basic" Skills of user.
- Cost, infrastructure and maintenance.
- Students often express dissatisfaction with technology-based learning.
- Authenticity, reliability and usability of e content.
- The gaps and overlaps on subject learning will take places
- Personal approach can be missing because of tools.

CONCLUSION

Shared learning is the accumulation of individual learning. It is a structure that facilitates team learning with features such as boundary crossing and openness. It's a way of cooperative and community learning and with the wings of ICT tools; the system will have no limits of sky.

Already it is been felt that there is no alternate other than usage of ICT in field of Education. ICT has become, within a very short span, one of the basic building blocks of modern society. It has profound influence in teaching and teachers education. Today's society is characterized by increased professional specialization changes in marketplaces (local and global are no longer clearly distinguished); and new technologies for information sharing, communication, and collaboration, made possible by Internet technologies and specialized applications. We have several National schemes that run concurrent to a large number of privately led ICT initiatives across India.

In addition there are several ICT in education initiatives across the country and these accounts for a large degree of understanding and awareness about the role that ICTs can play in enhancing the teaching learning process. However, the lack of a concerted, dynamic education policy has continued to hound the ministries of education, increasingly, this new tool–called ICT and its incorporation with shared learning will revolutionize the system. The challenge of curriculum is not only to develop new frameworks, and new educational environments to support the ICT system incorporate with Shared Learning, but also to support by overcoming the limitations of the technologies available at some initiatives that should be underway specifically focus on delivery of the final output and achievement of the ultimate goals.

"A developed India by 2020 or even earlier, is not just a dream. It need not even be a mere vision in the minds of many Indians. It is a mission we can all take up and succeed" A.P.J Abdul kalam in his book–*India Vision 2020*.

REFERENCES

Carlson, S. (2002), *The missing link in educational technology: Trained teachers.*

Chaturvedi, Aditya and Vandana (2009), *ICT in teacher education.*

Dahiya, S. (2005), ICT-enabled Teacher Education, *University News*, Volume 43. Issue 18. New Delhi.

Mahapatra, B.C., *Impact of technology in teacher education programme for social development*-article published in 2009.

Mathur, A. (2010), *Shared learning as a vital approach for teacher education in India.*

Murphy, C. (1997), Finding time for faculties to study together. *Journal of Staff Development.*

Manabu, Satu (2008), Philosophy on the restoration of schools in Japan: The principles and activity system of the Learning Community, *Journal of all India Association for Educational Research.*

9

ICT in Education

Efficacy and Reluctance

Smriti Bhosle

Globalization and innovations in technology have led to an increased use of Information and communication technologies in all sectors-and education is no exception. Technology does and will increasingly change what goes on in classrooms. We have entered into a period of transition towards such change, and it can either happen in a particular way, or it can be energized by growing understandings about how learning, and the job of teaching, might be enhanced as a result.

Information and communication technologies have been powerful enabling tools for educational change and reform. When used appropriately, different ICTs are said to help expand access to education, strengthen the relevance of education to the increasingly digital workplace, and raise educational quality. However, the effective integration of ICTs into the educational system is a complex, multifaceted process that involves not just technology, but also curriculum and pedagogy, institutional readiness, teacher competencies, and long-term financing, among others.

The educational system in developed countries is facing major challenges as a consequence of the revolution of information and communication technology. Relationships in modem societies are transformed by emerging new means of creating, processing, accessing, and transferring information. Information and communication technologies are dramatically altering many aspects of economic and social life: production systems, working methods, and relations, the organization of companies, and the way people communicate with each other are under-going changes throughout the world.

The revolution of ICT is a major challenge for teachers' professional development. They have to learn technical skills adequate to use ICT productively, as well as to instruct and guide the students to use ICT purposefully and generatively. Teachers not only have to become familiar with ICT but also to acquire the pedagogical expertise needed for fruitfully working with new technology-based learning environments. New pedagogical practices have to be explored and developed to facilitate higher-level knowledge acquisition skills the learners need to constructively adapt to the knowledge society. Currently, teachers' lack of technical expertise in ICT appears to significantly constrain possibilities of developing new and innovative computer-supported pedagogical practices.

Knowledge building refers to a process of advancing understanding by setting up, articulating, and answering research questions, searching and exploring information, and generating and evaluating explanations. Progressive inquiry entails that knowledge is not simply assimilated but constructed through solving problems of understanding. The emerging new models of computer-supported collaborative learning promise, with appropriate institutional support, to elicit development of higher-level skills of knowledge processing needed in knowledge society.

ICT FOR IMPROVING THE QUALITY OF EDUCATION

Improving the quality of education and training is a critical issue, particularly at a time of educational expansion. ICTs can enhance the quality of education in several ways: by increasing learner motivation and engagement, by facilitating the acquisition of basic skills and by enhancing teacher training. It can promote the shift to a learner-centered environment and it will engage the student in the learning process. The audio-visual combination if integrated sensibly with the textbook and syllabus, can work wonders in getting across abstract concepts and logics to the student in a short span of time.

The educational effectiveness of ICTs depends on how they are used and for what purpose. Educational videos now encompass multimedia CDs, slide-shows (like PowerPoint), video books, digital story-telling and many other forms that imaginatively combine visuals with text and audio that can be delivered on a range of platforms. Videos can be used in a range of learning environments, such as to enhance learning in classrooms, train illiterate women on basic life skills, teach children from tribal communities, and so on. Various organizations have produced videos on a range of topics including disaster management, child rights, forced migration, adolescent and gender issues and HIV and reproductive and sexual health topics. Commenting on the ability of video to simplify complex subjects and engage children, teachers pointed out topics with strong visual contexts–like scientific evolutionary theories, planetary movements and geographical topography, geographical phenomena, biological phenomena–which can be quite difficult to grasp if taught using conventional methods. The educators often felt that the use of videos as an alien feature outside the regular curricular teaching and thus the challenge is to integrate videos into day-to-day teaching. If ICTs are used, teachers need capacity building to recognize educational videos as an extension of the experiential aspect of learning and not merely as a visual alternative to textbooks.

It was more important to integrate the computer with classroom teaching through Computer Aided Learning (CAL). With the basic understanding on computers generated through Computer Education (CE), the effectiveness of CAL will increase. Computer education is necessary in all walks of life today. To keep pace with the changing world the students need to have basic computer knowledge. For economically weak students, the opportunities of computer education are not possible outside the school/college; though a private course should be provided for them within the educational institution. In addition, to CE, to improve classroom teaching, CAL and TAL (Technology Aided Learning) are extremely important. A lesson if introduced with audio visual media and then taken back to the text book, would prove to be extremely useful in teaching-learning processes.

Impact of ICT on Teaching-Learning Process

It is generally believed that ICTs can empower teachers and learners. With the introduction of ICTs in the classroom, the teacher's role in the learning process becomes even more critical. What can and should change is the kind of role that the teacher plays. The role of students, in turn, also expands. As learning shifts from the "teacher-centered model" to a "learner-centered model", the teacher becomes less of an authority and more the facilitator, and mentor. The teacher's primary task becomes to teach the students how to ask questions and pose problems, formulate hypotheses, locate information and then critically assess the information.

ICTs cannot replace the teacher. Because computer, is only an instrument; the human touch can only be given by the teacher. Further, decisions pertaining what to learn, when to learn, how to learn can only be taken by the teacher. As such, the computer can in no circumstance over ride the place of the teacher in the classroom.

Factors that Prevent Teachers from Using Technology

A number of early studies investigated why teachers do not use computers in their teaching (Rosen and Weil, 1995; Winnans and Brown, 1992; Dupagne and Krendl, 1992; Hadley and Sheingold, 1993). Not surprisingly they found a list of inhibitors:

- Lack of teaching experience with ICT
- Lack of on-site support for teachers using technology;
- Lack of ICT specialist teachers to teach students computer skills;
- Lack of computer availability;
- Lack of time required to successfully integrate technology into the curriculum.
- lack of financial support.

Evans-Andris (1995) summarized three styles of computing use among teachers: avoidance, integration and technical specialization. These styles play a significant role in student access to computer technology. The dominant style of computing among teachers is that of avoidance. Teachers typically distanced themselves from computers and otherwise reduced the amount of time they spent attending to computer-related activities.

Robertson et al (1996) argued that teachers' resistance to computer use was divided into several broad-based themes:

- Resistance to organizational change;
- Resistance to outside intervention;
- Time management problems;
- Lack of support from the administration;
- Teachers' perceptions;
- Personal factors.

There is often a difficulty for teachers who have had some training to be able to use ICT because there are insufficient ICT resources in the institution or there is not enough time to review then and plan lessons incorporating their use.

Teachers must have adequate access to functioning computers (or other technologies) and sufficient technical support. Shifting pedagogies, redesigning curriculum and assessment tools, and providing more autonomy to educational institutions, all contribute to the optimal use of ICTs in education. Besides that, ICT make lessons more interesting and more enjoyable.

Access to computer and the laptop can increase the staff's use of general applications in their work, particularly for administration (*e.g.* class registers and assessment scores). There is a need for adequate and careful training so that teachers become aware of the range of uses and possible benefits of ICT.

One of the most fundamental problems in education reform is that people do not have a clear and coherent sense of the reasons for educational change, what it is and how to proceed. Thus there is much superficiality, confusion, failure of change programmes, and unnecessary resistance.

Willis (1996) argued that the integration of computers into the classrooms is a complex process that involves personal, group, organizational, institutional and even cultural change.

In Short, Negative Factors That Influencing Usefulness is

- Difficulties in using software/hardware
- Need more technical support
- Not enough time to use ICT
- Is too expensive to use regularly
- Insufficient access to the resources
- Restricts the content of the lessons

Factors that Encourage Teachers to Use Technology

Cox et al (1999) carried out a study examining the factors relating to the uptake of ICT in teaching. The results showed that the teachers who are already regular users of ICT have confidence in using ICT, perceive it to be useful for their personal work and for their teaching and plan to extend their use further in the future. The factors that were found to be the most important to these teachers in their teaching were: making the lessons more interesting, easier, more fun for them and their students, more diverse, more motivating and more enjoyable. Additional more personal factors were: improving presentation of materials, allowing greater access to computers for personal use, giving the teacher more prestige, making the teachers' administration more efficient and providing professional support through the Internet. Sheingold and Hadley (1990) conducted a nationwide survey of fourth to twelfth grade teachers in the USA. The three major factors involved in these 'accomplished' teachers' success were:

- Teacher motivation and commitment to their students' learning and to their own development as teachers;
- The support they experienced in their schools;
- Access to sufficient quantities of technology.

In addition, these teachers worked in schools where hardware and access to resources were twice the average, were comfortable with technology and used computers for many purposes. They perceived that their teaching practices became more student centered with the integration of technology in their curriculum and they held higher expectations of their students. Sheingold and Hadley's (1990) study also identified that the source of motivation for teachers to use technology included gains in learning and using computers for their own development as teachers.

Further research (Hruskocy et al, 2000) suggests that teachers' expertise and dedication are necessary for technology integration to occur and students' enthusiasm and talent prompt the process to unfold.

Recent research into pedagogy and ICT in the UK was carried out by Moseley and Higgins (1999). They found that teachers who successfully made use of ICT had the following characteristics:

- A positive rather than negative attitude towards ICT. Teachers who have positive attitudes towards ICT itself will be positively disposed towards using it in the classroom.
- Student choice rather than teacher direction. Teachers who preferred directive styles of teaching tended to rate their own competence as low and made use of helpers with ICT.
- Pupil empowerment as learners rather than pupils receiving instruction.
- A preference for individual study rather than pupils receiving instruction.

IT in classrooms can be associated with significant changes in classroom climate, and teacher and student roles in learning; for example, group-work and collaborative learning activities can be enhanced when IT is used.

In Short, Positive Factors that Influencing Usefulness is

- Regular use and experience of ICT outside the classroom
- Ownership of a computer
- Confidence in using ICT
- Easy to control the class
- Easy to think of new lesson ideas

Constraints/Obstacles

A widespread investment in ICTs in education is probably not possible in most developing countries. It is, therefore, critically important to better understand the costs and benefits associated with ICT types and uses in various educational situations in order to effectively target scarce resources. There is some evidence, for instance, that computers may be most cost-effective when placed in common areas such as libraries and teacher-training institutes.

The lack of computers, TV sets and video playback systems in most schools and colleges and a whole transformation is needed at the grassroots, requiring the collaboration of multiple agencies.

Most of the teachers have both access and training inadequacy and hence, unable to utilize internet and other facilities. Many teachers are reluctant to use ICTs, especially computers and the internet. Some of the reasons for this reluctance include poor software design, uncertainty about the effectiveness of computers in improving learning outcomes, lack of administrative support, increased time and effort needed to learn the technology and how to use it for teaching, and the fear of losing their authority in the classroom as it becomes more learner-centered. These are all issues that must be addressed by professional development programs if educational institutions are to fully exploit the potential of computers and the Internet as educational tools.

Sometimes the teachers have very positive attitudes towards the use of technology in education, but are far less confident about their ability to actually use the technology and do not think that their teacher training programmes prepared them to use technology in innovative ways. Also, that teacher training faculties, although positive about IT, do not have a strong background in integrating that into teacher education courses they teach. Besides that, in many

ICT professional development courses, teachers are not often taught how to revise their pedagogical practices, how to replace other traditional lessons without depleting the curriculum coverage and so on. This means that after teachers had attended a course they still did not know how to use ICT for teaching.

There are three interlocking factors that affect teachers' take-up of ICT. These are institution, resources and the teacher. The educational institution gives little time to teachers to manage and familiarize themselves with ICT (Robertson et al, 1996). Due to pressures of work inside and outside the classroom, timetabling does not allow time for such learning, as well as lack of time, no supportive network for teachers who are not confident enough to take up ICT (Rosen and Weil, 1995; Winnans and Brown, 1992; Dupagne and Krendl, 1992; Hadley and Sheingold, 1993). Thus, institutions seem to be slow in embracing ICT, and there is a resistance to change.

Limited resources within the institutions are a great impediment to the take-up of ICT. Lack of computers and software in the classroom can seriously limit what teachers are able to do with ICT. Limited resources results in lack of computer integration, which in turn results in lack of sufficient computer experience for both students and teachers (Rosen and Weil, 1995; Winnans and Brown, 1992; Dupagne and Krendl, 1992; Hadley and Sheingold, 1993).

Time and equipment are the obstacles to ICT implementation. Simply, when these were lacking or in short supply, successful implementation became difficult.

CONCLUSION

Teachers need to be provided with adequate facilities and training to be able to use those facilities in order to progress in a technology-rich context. An appropriate full-time technical support and significant opportunities for teacher education in ICT use are as necessary as up-to-date equipment if teachers are to move toward curricular integration. The conventional learning skills, such as locating, collating and summarizing information, and identifying connections and contradictions within a body of information, all need to be explicitly moved to the centre of the curriculum. The development of such skills needs to be supported using appropriate forms of software. This requires the explicit teaching of ways of organizing cooperative activities involving computers, whether in face-to-face groups around a single machine, or through cooperation at a distance via a conferencing or email system. In order to do this, teachers themselves need more opportunities and support in using the new technologies in collaborative contexts, so that they can both identify the problems and possibilities for themselves, and find ways to model these activities in their own practice with learners. Finally, when introducing these newer technologies teachers too need time to reflect upon and research what is happening.

REFERENCES

Dupagne, M. and Krendl, K. A. (1992) Teachers' Attitudes Toward Computers: a review of the literature, *Journal of Research on Computing in Education,* 24, pp. 420-429.

Evans-Andris, M. (1995) Barrier to Computer Integration: micro-interaction among computer co-ordinators and classroom teachers in elementary schools, *Journal of Research on Computing in Education,* 28, pp. 29-45.

Hadley, M. and Sheingold, K. (1993) Commonalities and Distinctive Patterns in Teachers' Integration of Computers, *American Journal of Education,* 101, pp. 261-315.

Hruskocy, C., Cennamo, K. S., Ertmer, P. A. and Johnson, T. (2000) Creating a Community of Technology Users: students become technology experts for teachers and peers, *Journal of Technology and Teacher Education,* 8, pp. 69-84.

Moseley, D. and Higgins, S. (1999) *Ways Forward With ICT: effective pedagogy using information and communications technology for literacy and numeracy in primary schools.* London: Teacher Training Agency.

Robertson, S. I., Calder, J., Fung, P., Jones, A., O'Shea, T. and Lambrechts, G. (1996) Pupils, Teachers and Palmtop Computers, *Journal of Computer Assisted Learning,* 12, pp. 194-204.

Rosen, L. D. and Weil, M. M. (1995) Computer Availability, Computer Experience, and Technophobia Among Public School Teachers, *Computers in Human Behaviour,* 11, pp. 9-31.

Sheingold, K. and Hadley, M. (1990) *Accomplished Teachers: integrating computers into classroom practice.* New York: Centre for Technology in Education.

Solomon, C. (1986) *Computer Environments for Children.* Cambridge, MA: MIT Press.

Willis, J., Thompson, A. and Sadera, W. (1999) Research on Technology and Teacher Education: current status and future directions, *Curriculum and Instruction,* 47 (4), pp. 29-45.

Winnans, C. and Brown, D. S. (1992) Some Factors Affecting Elementary Teachers' Use of the Computer, *Computers in Education,* 18, pp. 301-309.

10

Total Quality Management in Teacher Education

Role of a Teacher Educator

Gaurav Singh

Confronted with declining standards, due primarily to expansion in Indian higher education system, the question of quality become critical. Teacher education system is not the exception of it. In the name of development of education for access to maximum, the self-financing teacher education institutions are mushrooming now days. Dubhashi (1994) pointed out that the number of higher education institutions have increased by leaps and bounds; the quantitative expansion has been accompanied by qualitative deterioration. Facilities in self-financing as well as in government/ government aided institutions have been limited and starched to tearing points. Standards have declining enormously. In such situation, one should come forward to think about qualitative up-liftment of teacher education. A famous gift for us was proposed by W. Edwards Daming after World War II in the name of philosophy of total quality management, one step ahead to total quality control. Deming's PDCA (Plan, Do, Check and Act) model is quite applicable in teacher education too.

TOTAL QUALITY MANAGEMENT IN EDUCATION

Deming's philosophy of total quality management provided guiding principles needed for educational reforms (Vachharajani, 2008). "Quality is the totality of features and characteristics of a product or service that bear on its ability to satisfy the stated or implied needs." When we discuss it in context of education, it refers to features of education; which has to satisfy the needs of students, parents and the society at large by developing appropriate knowledge and skill. It includes availability of competent teachers, adequate infrastructural facilities and the likes (Prema, 2004). Quality assurance in education implies ensuring the maintenance of set-standards from the planning stage till the feedback stage of any educational programme.

Deming's four pillars of TQM, *i.e.* synergistic relationship; continuous improvement and self-evaluation; a system of ongoing process and leadership are of equal importance in teacher education too. Some authors have identified the feature as drivers to implement TQM in education as declining enrollment (Rag, 1996), declining quality (Chao and Dugger, 1990) and student dissatisfaction with overall service quality (Mantono and Utter, 1999). Development of internal quality assurance (IQA) in higher education institutions in much needed (Hegde and Shyamsunder, 2008). The efforts and guidelines of NAAC for internal quality assurance cell (IQAC) are quite useful for us (NAAC Manual, 2005).

Kaw (1996), Dean Elumtio *et.al.* (1996), Owlia and Aspinwell (1997) and Aly and Akpovi (2001) in their Surveys and studies at various USA and UK educational institutions reported few benefits due to implementation of TQM philosophy in Educational institutions.

The role of TQM in education is reflected in the views of various educationists and management gurus as it is value addition to education (Feingenbaum, 1951), conformance of education output to planed goals specifications and requirements (Gilmore, 1974; Crosby, 1979), as a unique opportunity to respond global challenges in achieving quality in education (Mukhopadhyay, 2002), as a process and system that will enable colleges and universities to serve better their customers, who include students, business and industry as well as community that they are in (Dean Elomuti *et.al.* 1996).

TQM AND TEACHER EDUCATION

After understanaing the philosophy of TQM and its utilization, author has planed a model for implementation in teacher education too. Present teacher education system is lacking far behind in terms of qualitative inputs and outputs. I think that through applying the concepts of TQM, we can improve a lot to our system and as a teacher educator; I think that in this reformation process, the role of teacher educator is like a catalyst. A teacher educator is most important ingredient of teacher education system. He is equally connected to the policy makers and management of institutions as well as with the customers *i.e.* students parents and society. Author has tried to develop a TQM Model for Teacher Education by utilizing the concept of Deming's PDCA Approach (Figure 10.1).

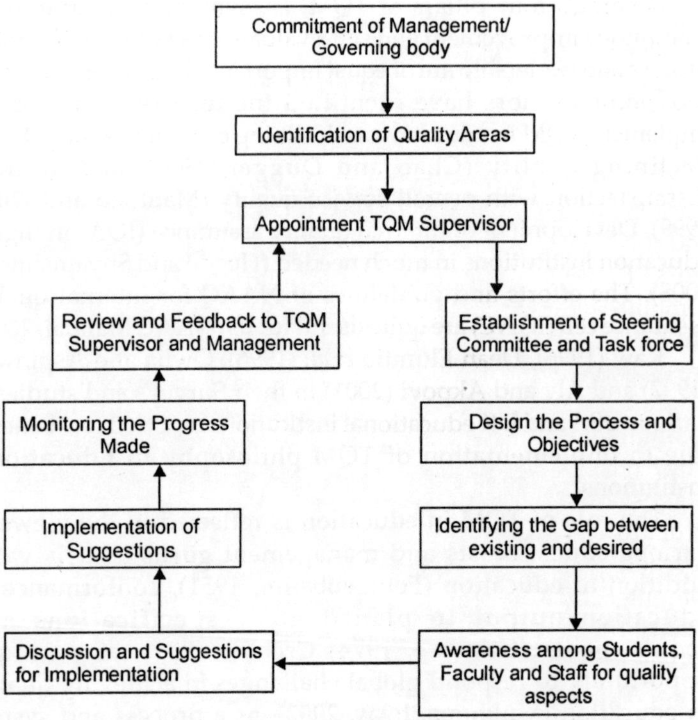

Fig. 10.1: TQM Model for Teacher Education

TQM MODEL FOR TEACHER EDUCATION AND ROLE OF TEACHER EDUCATOR

TQM model for teacher education is an Eleven Step Model. Every step and role of teacher educator in that step is described below:

1. Commitment of Management/Governing Body: It has been observed in various researches that the qualitative downfall in teacher education institutions is largely due to the profit making approach of management of institutions. From the appointment of faculty to ensuring the availability of infrastructural facilities, the loly-pop attitude is most responsible. The brighter side of picture is that some institutions are working extremely well on quality parameters. Such institutions never hesitate to get quality certifications like NAAC Accreditation or ISO Certification. On the other hand, a large number of institutions are hesitating due to lack in facilities or mall practices. The role of teacher educator in he is the key man to develop the mindset of Management on quality issues. He has to show them the right way to be superior in competitive environment of teacher education. Soon the day will come, when only qualitatively sound institutions will run only in long term because quantitative extension is near to saturation. If a teacher educator is able to present the whole scenario is effective and convincing manner in front of management, it will definitely work. I am sure that management will become proactive and committed towards qualitative issues. Ross (1996) rightly pointed out that quality involvement and leadership by top management are essential to the necessary culture of commitment to quality.

2. Identification of Quality Areas: After developing commitment of management, next issue is to identify the areas, in which quality improvements are needed. Teacher educators should suggest the key areas for improvement like quality teacher educators, class room equipments, quality library books, psychology laboratory apparatus and tests, language laboratory, computer and ICT laboratory, innovative teaching methodologies, quality training issues, co-curricular activities, research section, Survey, case study, projects etc.

3. Appointment of TQM Supervisor: It seems to be directly related to management as they have to decide and appoint a TQM supervisor but the suggestions of teacher educators are of utmost importance there. They have to suggest few experienced and quality concern personalities of teacher education to appoint them from external to the institute. One more option is the development of IQAC, in which various teacher educators of the institutions itself can be appointed and their accountability could be set.

4. Establishment of Steering Committee: As per variety of tasks, the steering committees are framed and tasks are distributed among them. Various teacher educators generally head these committees. They also plan their task force, which will look after the regular improvements and problems related to their specific committee.

Committees like library, laboratory, discipline, co-curricular activities; placement facilitation, research groups etc are framed.

5. Design of Process and Objectives: The next step in applying the TQM philosophy is to design the objectives of each steering committee and task force as well as the process of their functioning. To whom they will report, from where they will get help for requirements, how they will proceed, are the issues, on which a teacher educator with his/her committee has to be taken any decision. The proper documentation and its recording are also planned in this step.

6. Identification of GAP: The gap model is very famous in industry for qualitative improvements. The steering committee and task force have to identify the differences between existing facilities in the institutions and the required facilities. During identification of gap, the issues like changing educational world, impact of technology, and availability of funds are to be kept in mind. Better is to make aware to all the stakeholders *i.e.* students, faculties and staff of institutions about the gap issues.

7. Awaring the Quality Aspects: One person cannot introduce quality. It is teamwork. Maintain the quality standards are not possible without awareness and involvement of all related human resources. Faculty, staff and students, all should be well informed about quality inputs and various efforts planned and done by management to raise the quality standards of the institution. Teacher educator is in key role as he is directly in touch with management as well as staff and students. He not only bridges the gap but also play an important role of facilitator and awakener.

8. Discussion and Suggestions: In Total Quality management, discussion is very important for quality inputs. The loop holes in planning, exact areas of implementation, process of implementation, key benefits of quality inputs and their impact on trainee teachers equipped with all necessary abilities and skills for future needs of society are the areas of thorough discussion. Everything is discussed in details so that an error free and smooth implementation should be ensured. The confusion regarding role of various teacher educators, staff members, and students can also be overcome through discussion.

9. Implementation of Suggestions: After discussing, the actual implementation of quality inputs starts. The teacher educators, who are actual implementers, implement the decided task to improve the quality of teacher education system. It may be maintenance of records, innovative teaching methodologies, library management, laboratory management, skill development among trainee teachers etc.

10. Monitoring the Progress Made: Immediately with the implementation, the monitoring also starts. Monitoring of quality processes is the task of task force in-charege as well as head f steering committee. It has been observed that in many cases, quality processes starts at full swing, but as time passes, lathargicity emerges. Some times due to involvement in other tasks or multi tasking working environment, such kind of problems occur. In teacher education, being one-year course, student committees are framed every year. In such situation, regular monitoring has become essential. The steering committees have to look after continuously the quality parameters.

11. Review and Feedback: TQM is not the issues, which once implemented and than to be forgotten. Rather it is a continuous process. The monitoring of TQM activities always provides chances for further improvement. With regular monitoring, the proper feedback can be given to management/ regulatory bodies of teacher education institutions. The feedback can help in designing the process again. Only after actual implementation, one can feel the problem and shortcomings of the system and feedback on such issues help a lot to improve quality in totality *i.e.* Total quality Management.

By applying TQM in teacher education, a lot of improvements can be done. Few are suggested by Mohanty (2008) as decentralization of norm development mechanism, preparation and dissemination of books for library, induction programmes for beginners as trainee teachers, introducing new methodologies, improvement in teaching techniques etc. At last, we want to summarize the discussion as the satisfaction of teachers, students and society can be improved and the teacher education system can bring out the shadows of traditional approaches by using TQM philosophy. The model proposed here might not be the ideal one but it is an initiation to start thought process in the direction.

REFERENCES

Allon B. (1995) A Rose by Any Other Name: TQM in Higher Education, *Quality assurance in Education* 3 (2).

Aly N. and J. Akpovi (2001) Toatl Quality Management in Califotnia Public Higher Education, *Quality assurance in Education* 9 (3).

Chao C.Y. and j.C. Dugger (1996) A Total Qulaity Management Model for Instructional Supervision in Vocational Technica Programme, *Journal of Industrial Teacher Education*, Summer 33.

Cheng Y. C. and W. M. Tan (1997) Multi Tier Models of Quality in Education, *Quality assurance in Education* 5 (1).

Dean E. et. al. (1996) Are Total Quality Management Programmes in Higher Education worth the effort? *International Journal of Quality and Reliability Management* 13 (6).

Dubhanshi P. R. (1994) *Indian System of Higher Education* in N. K. Uberoi Ed. (1995) Professional Competencies in Higher Education, Center for Professional Development in Higher Education, University of Delhi.

Hegde G. and M. S. Shyamsundar (2008) Towards Ensuring and Enhancing the Internal Quality of Higher Education Institutions, *University News*, A.I.U., New Delhi 46 (42).

Kaun P.Y.K. (1996) application of Total Quality Management in Education: Retrospects and Prospects, *International Journal of Educational management* 10 (5).

Majid J. and R. David (1994) Total Quality Management Applied to Engineering Education, *Quality assurance in Education*, 2 (1).

Mohanty S. B. and lakhe (2002) *TQM in Service Sector*, NIEPA Publication

Mohanty S.B. (2008) Ensuring Quality in Teacher Education, *University News* 46 (08).

Montano C.B. and G.H. Utter (1999) Total Quality Management in Higher Education, *Quality Progress*, 32 (8).

Mukhopadhyay K. (2002) *Total Quality Management in Education*, NIEPA Publication.

NAAC (2005) Guidelines for Creating of the Internal Quality Assurance Cell (IQAC) in Accreditated Institutions.

Owelia M.S. and E.M. Aspinwell (1997) TQM in Higher Education Review, *International Journal of Quality and Reliability Management* 14 (5).

Prema P. (2004) Quality Assurance in the Professional Training of Teacher Educators: Challenges and Strategies, *University News* 42 (32).

Ross J.E. (1996) *Total Quality management: tax, cases and Reading*, St. Lucie Press

Vachharajani H. (2008) *TQM in Education: Renewing the Research Agenda*, University News, 46 (13).

11

The Changing Trend in Psycopedagogy

Anjum Ahmed

Psycho pedagogy, a new emerging field, goes beyond the isolated fields of pedagogy and psychology. Formerly used as an adjective as a way of rendering the pedagogical function more psychological, it now exists as a noun, as organized knowledge which, adopting complex thinking, on the terms proposed by theorists, that based on ideas proposed by Prigogine and Marin among others, dare to go beyond their strict fields of study to reflect upon the global culture that today more than ever, is at this level mostly stimulated by the technological advances, that chiefly, allows us to shorten distances. (Carvalho and Mendonca, 2003). Along that line of thinking the theoretical advances in the field of psycho pedagogy seek to know the dimensions that, in an insoluble way, constitute the individual that learns, this active relation being, seeker of the knowledge of himself and the universe.

The building of knowledge takes place where reasons and affection intersect, in tension between cultural diversity and the universality of knowledge: between personal fate and social or historical fate—such tensions being regarded as dimensions, at the same time distinct and inseparable. On the other hand, the construction of knowledge, from this perspective, presupposes that the individual takes a step beyond the acquisition of information to incorporate and manipulate the instruments of questioning; logically assuming that learning is being able to question. For that reason, the individual's pre-suppositions are fundamental when we study the new skills and tools necessary for teachers to act in the current pedagogic environment, in which the use of ICTs (Information Communication Technologies) and distance education and increasingly more widespread. (Salmon, 2002)

What a student learns today is no longer almost exclusively

what a teacher (once the absolute source of knowledge and sole responsible for the transfer of that knowledge) taught him, we surmount the limits of the physical classroom and place learning in other space, such as *cyberspace*.

Such a progress advances involves, as an essential condition, a mentality shift on the part of the parents and teachers, a change in curriculum, as well as the appropriation of and familiarity with, a new language, the digital language, and with new technologies. The so called ICT, defined as computing, learning and range of activities in education, which includes, For example: the use of CD-ROM as source of information, electronic toys and games to develop different skills such as spatial awareness and psychomotor control, email to support collaboration writing and sharing of resources, internet based research etc.

Psycho pedagogy has been pointing out that there is a resistance especially among teacher to embrace this new pedagogical approach and also it has affected every human being facing changes that can shake the paradigms that supports them. Changing the pedagogical field requires a change of attitude, a renovation of pedagogical practices, and a theoretical/practical transformation.

Teachers encounter even more drastic changes and those changes are rapid in nature. Their primary role shifts from dispensing information to facilitating it—not an easy transition for many instructors. Additionally, many faculty members, who were expert teachers in their face-to-face classrooms, now find themselves novices confronting new and intimidating technologies (Berliner, 1988). With increased time demands and continuous teaching engagement, faculty frustration ensues. Instructors also encounter many more technical problems in their electronic classrooms—problems they are often powerless to remedy. Professors must devote much more time to course start-up and management. Online instructors find that their teaching must be much more precise and that ambiguities usually tolerated in face-to face classes present formidable problems in the web-based environment.

The fact that several teachers are not comfortable with e-learning could be in the death of dialoguing because of advent of cyber culture and how is human being supposed to articulate these two different orders, such as the culture of printed materials and of teacher's physical presence and cyber culture? For that to happen, there need to be mentality shift allowing the incorporation of innovations into the pedagogical setting, without cannibalizing it. The way the teacher uses both cultures there will only be balance between them if the teacher can see them as subject to an interrelationship in which their conditions interact without threatening one another and form a new integrated system. The teacher internal flexibility in building his or her course within this different paradigm, as well as the knowledge that it will, be no easy task, is therefore essential. It demands a change in curricula, inner changes in the teacher, mostly in his/her affective, rather than cognitive dimension; time for preparation and specific knowledge of how to work with materials in e-learning, a competency that cannot be acquired without proper guidance and experimentation.

WEB WORLD ADDICTION

Internet as it is seen is so well accepted and appealing to teenagers, keeping them hooked, immersed in it for such long time, while many adults, especially teachers, underestimate and despise it? It is at this stage where the psychology of adolescent comes into being. It is commonly defined as a period situated within mobile boundaries, with childhood on one side and the promise of autonomy in adult life at the other extreme. It is the time of searching and of uncertainty, of establishing new relationships, and of manifestations resulting from new feelings, ways of thinking and behaving. Using the contribution of psychoanalysis, that the web is an environment in which the illusion of user is always present. We know that what remains in the psychic space is the wish to reencounter what has been lived and what has been experienced and it is therefore a representation that replaces the absences. Only that, in that space the absence is not felt as a demand, as a strength that forces arc to keep searching, in the case of Web, the link keeps unfolding in an adventure that gives the illusion of infinite. (Lombard, 2004)

In reality we must admit that the computer, with its programme which accept mistakes and allow redoing, erasing without shame and the Web which never gets tired, seems to always be available and repeat as many times as necessary without complaining both allow the user to have pleasure and satisfaction. Searching on net engines gives them the illusion of exerting their autonomy because they feel as if they are walking with their own feet.

TEACHER CONCERNS AND NEEDS

Collaborative learning and cooperative learning are part of the psycho pedagogical constructivist paradigm, which is considered the central paradigm of post-modern pedagogy (Cartelli Antonio, 2006). These two types of learning must be understood as the maximum expression of individuality, which enters into relationships with others, finding the possibility of complete fulfillment. For this purpose communication is a pre-requisite.

There are teachers who are excellent communicators and very effective at generating learning but who may not be sufficiently able to inculcate in the students aptitude for building through collaborative activity, their own knowledge. Collaboration means 'working together' in the belief that four eyes see more than two, that there is a particular satisfaction in doing something together.

The results obtained by the group through cooperative learning are strongly combined by the overall attitude assumed by a teacher. In the domain of the group, the teacher assumes an autocratic attitude, the students will be very argumentative, they behave as individuals who do not engage with each other and have no interest in the objectives of the group or the activities of the member.

The laissez faire attitude, however, does not produce good results; it generates frustration, due to lack of fundamental rules which inspire the action. The social climate can have a profound influence on the group. A group led by a democratic leader is active, cooperative and creative.

It is safe to say therefore that while learning is an individual set of knowledge and skills, it is the system of social interactions however that we establish in the environment that helps to form it, to keep it efficient and to enrich it. A teacher is a person who, seeing himself or herself as the facilitator of learning, intervenes in the environment and on the environment in order to constantly maintain the educational potential. The problem is to understand how diverse subjectivities, with highly dissimilar experiences, can effectively enjoy a community experience. And this is exactly where the role of pedagogy of didactics and of technology comes in. By acting together, they must indicate the operational solution to adopt. They must tackle the problem of how to enable every individual to recognize the other individuals, their identity, and their specific way of interpreting the world.

In a distributed social situation such as we have, every actor has a significant role and is called upon to perform several actions. This principle is also valid for didactic situations, like e-learning.

The three Macro-action of the Didactic Field are

- *Organization*: Here the teacher acts at two level: *the strategic level i.e,* they articulate the learning plan module and working step and *the distributive level i.e.* to structure personalized learning opportunities and to exploit individual and group resources. Teacher needs a guide to help them organize their work and choose the activity to be successful.
- *Sharing*: at this level, the teacher must speak not only with the students, but also with other member of the staff such as other teachers. In this direction, in some experiences this knowledge and competence-sharing activity includes dedicated online communities (of teacher, of staff, of the course etc). Online interaction in the form of chat, forum, teleconferencing, community etc. completes this process providing important application and re-elaboration opportunities.
- *Evaluation:* In e-learning environment, evaluators is distributed among the staff members. Assessment regarding learning goals; knowledge, competencies, and Meta qualities. Generally it concerns the balance of competencies (ex ante), formative assessment (in itinere) and terminal assessment (ex post). These activities are generally done through in itinerary and final tests and surveys, paper, questionnaires, reports, so on.

Interested and enthused teacher remain committed to e-teaching if their personal satisfaction outweighs the considerable time management and technological demands in course design, development, implementation, and maintenance. Prior consideration should be given to factors such as annual academic evaluations, the teaching role in the tenure/promotion process, and release time for online course development, and should be discussed with appropriate deans and chairs.

Teacher should consult with instructional designers, web masters, graphic artists, computer specialists, and information resource providers (librarians, copyright experts, etc.) to establish realistic course development expectations and to develop key support personnel contacts.

Online focus groups across disciplines will enable teacher to discuss strategies for coping with the additional workloads, to monitor and correct negative influences or attitude changes, to write cross-discipline grants, to determine academic credit and recognition for online course delivery, and to develop assessment and evaluation procedures. One teacher cannot manage so complex an activity. Tutors and mentors are dedicated figures that respectively are interested in evaluation an assessment.

CONCLUSION

To conclude we have to utilize technology in a more humane manner, which implicates two questions: the political question, for which we must maintain the ethical use of certain technologies and the psycho pedagogical question: in the sense of forming more critical and creativeness users, who may make their own opinions about the technologies, not always in accordance with the marketing that is made of them. The teacher needs not just training that enables him to use the ICT, but more importantly, that the condition for an effective change of mentality must be given to him, in order for him to truly incorporate the innovation.

REFERENCES

Berliner, D.C. (1988). *The development of expertise in pedagogy.* New Orleans: American Association of Colleges for Teacher Education.

Biggs, J. (2003). *Teaching for quality learning at university*. (2nd ed). Buckingham, U.K. Society for research into higher education and Open University Press.

Cartelli, Antonio (2006): *Teaching in the Knowledge Society: New Skills and Instruments for Teachers*. Published in UK by information Science Publishing, London.

Carvalto, E.A and Mendonca, T. (2003): *Ensaios de complexidale* 2. Porto Alegre, Salina: htt://inconscient.net/civin.html

Laurillard, D. (1993): *Rethinking university teaching*, London: Routledge.

Lombard, G. (2004): *Psychanalyze du net*. Role of refernce elements. In M.Civi (Ed). *Psychanalyze du net*. Paris: Hachette (w/d). Reteived March 20, 2005.

Salmon, G. (2002): E-moderating, the key to teaching and learning online. London: Kogan Press

Wadhwa, Shalini (2005): *Role of teachers in teaching and learning*. Published by Sarup and Sons, New Delhi.

12

Brain Based Learning

Pedagogical Implications

Noushad Husain

Brain-based learning draws upon the functioning of the brain and takes into consideration the rules of the brain for meaningful learning. According to Caine and Caine (1994), the brain is like our other organs and one of its most important jobs is to learn. It has an unlimited capacity for learning. For learning, the functions of the brain are very important. Brain-based learning is interested in knowing how the brain works and in discovering the ways of maximum learning. Brain-based learning distinguishes between surface and meaningful knowledge. According to this approach, although memorization can be very important, meaningful knowledge is critical for being successful. Making connections among knowledge (including previous experiences) is essential in meaningful learning. In other words, brain based learning is centered on meaningful learning in the context of lifelike, enriching experiences and on providing students with the safety and opportunities to meaningfully learn.

Brain-based learning focus on how the brain learns. Brain based learning includes accepting the rules of brain processing and organizing the teaching according to these rules in the mind for meaningful learning (Caine and Caine, 1994; 1997 and Caine, Geoffrey, Renate Nummela Caine and Sam Crowell, 1999). It is a concept which tells how fusion of the common sense, human experiences and brain researches produce useful tools and principles for classroom environment. It does not give us a map to follow. But it provides us to think the structure of our brain at the stage of making decision. In short, brain based learning is to learn with the brain in our mind (Jensen, 2000).

WHY BRAIN BASED LEARNING

We already learn with our brain. What is the new thing? Caine's answer to the questions that may be asked by the people who have just heared about brain based learning is this: "of course, every learning is brain based but if we say only learning, people may not understand what we have said. People have a brain which is wonderful and has infinite opportunities. So, while we are implying the brain based learning, we are interested in understanding how the brain works best and how we can increase the learning at the highest level and tell these to people (Pool, 1997).

The Aim of Brain Based Instruction

Advocates of brain-based learning have concluded that teaching techniques based on the neuroscience of how the brain learns are effective in producing long-term learning. The aim of the brain based instruction is to pass from memorizing through meaningful learning. It requires these three interactive elements: (1) Relaxed alertness and being ready for easy comprehension (2) Immersion and (3) Active processing (Caine and Caine, 1994; 1997).

1. Relaxed Alertness or being Ready for Easy Comprehension

Two important characteristics of being ready for comprehension are: (a) General Relaxity and (b) Innate Motivation. We need an environment which gives possibility for taking safe risks to increase the learning at the highest level. Sense of safety that accepts a risk at suitable level is a part of being relaxed (Dwyer, 2002). Teachers should start the lesson with open or pair discussion taking several minutes.

2. Immersion

It is the students' focusing on the context. When the wholeness and connecting to each other are inevitable, the students have to use local memory systems to discover the context.

3. Active Processing

To activate the brain of students, the teachers should work with the students purposefully because the students need to connect and innate the knowledge both meaningfully as a character and conceptually harmonious.

HOW THE BRAIN LEARNS

Learning occurs when two neuron communicate with each other. Neuroscientists emphasize that learning occurs when a neuron sends a message to another (Hannaford, 1995, Jensen, 2000, Sprenger, 1999; 2002, Sousa, 2000). Learning engages the entire physiology. Food, water and nutrition are critical components of thinking (Sylwester, 2003). We are "holistic" learners—the body and mind interact the peptides in the blood are chains of amino acids that become the primary source of information transfer. The brain is a parallel processor. Left and right hemispheres work together. Many functions occur simultaneously. Edelman (1994) found when more neurons in the brain were firing at the same time; learning, meaning and retention were greater for the learner.

What Happens to the Brain When Learning Takes Place?

- Learning takes place when *neurons* communicate with each other.
- When neurons receive sensorial inputs they form extensions called dendrites.
- The *axon* is a long thin fiber which starts from a neuron and stretches towards another neuron.
- Dendrites and neurons make up networks.
- The communication between neurons is facilitated by myelin. The point of conjunction is called synapse. The liquids which make neurons communicate are the neurotransmitters.

PRINCIPLES OF BRAIN BASED LEARNING

1. The brain is a parallel processor.
2. Learning engages the entire physiology.
3. The search for meaning is innate.
4. The search for meaning occurs through patterning.
5. Emotions and cognition cannot be separated.
6. The brain processes parts and wholes simultaneously.
7. Learning involves both focused attention and peripheral perception.
8. Learning always involves conscious and unconscious processes.

9. Humans have two different types of memory systems: one system for rote memory and another for spatial memory.
10. Humans understand and remember best when facts and skills are embedded in natural and spatial memory.

CONCLUSION

The exciting learning about brain function and its effects on learning have the potential to revolutionize teaching and learning. Brain research has provided new knowledge about the many ways that humans learn. Brain-based *learning* has resulted from educators and researchers applying the findings of brain research to guide teaching practice. The last decade has seen more systematic implementation of brain-based strategies that emphasize emotion, thematic instruction, differentiated learning, movement, and the use of mental models. As well, changing conceptions of memory, assessment, the learning environment, the biology of the brain, and uses of time have all served to improve student achievement. Brain-based teaching involves the implementation of carefully-designed principles with due consideration of their impact before, during, and after each lesson. For brain-based learning, the following points should be considered:

1. To incorporate brain-based learning strategies teachers should examine current literature and research and reflect on their own personal practice and beliefs before making changes to their professional practice (Caulfield, Kidd and Kocher, 2000; Caine, Caine, McClintic and Klimek, 2005; winters, 2001). When teachers begin to take responsibility for their professional improvement, this will lead to changes in their mental models (Caine *et al.*, 2005).
2. Students' emotional states influence their level of academic achievement. Thus, there is importance of establishing a culture and environment where students feel safe and are not fearful. This is characterized by a state of relaxed alertness where students are not anxious about their surroundings but, rather, open and receptive to new information (Caine *et al.*, 2005). A positive emotional state is essential for the student's ability to acquire new knowledge and helps focus the attention of the individual (Caine, 2000; Caine *et al.*, 2005; Caulfield

et al., 2000; D'Arcangelo, 2000; Pool, 1997; Slavkin, 2004; Wagmeister and Shifrin, 2000; Wolfe, 2001).

3. Learning is enhanced when the environment accommodates the needs of the learner and the instructor. Students need to understand the impact of a lack of sleep, food and water on their biology and how such things impact their brain's ability to learn (Erlauer, 2003; Slavkin, 2004). Students who can participate actively in teaching and learning in the classroom become more excited about their education (Goldberg and Stevens, 2001). Teachers can ensure that their classroom is a rich, stimulating environment, allowing students to become immersed in a complex milieu that stimulates the mind (Caine et al, 2005; Caulfield *et al.*, 2000; Wagmeister and Shifrin, 2000; Wolfe, 2001). They can design a variety of teaching and learning activities that will access the brain's ability to remember visually and emotionally and encourage students to take risks (Caine *et al.*, 2005; Caulfield *et al.*, 2000; Saunders and Vawdrey, 2002; Wagmeister and Shifrin, 2000; Wolfe, 2001).
4. Brain research has discovered multiple memory systems applicable to student learning. Saunders and Vawdrey (2002) suggest brain-based learning involves mastering and sequencing ideas so that learning can be transferred to other situations.
5. "In a brain compatible classroom, assessment both measures achievement and provides motivation" (Goldberg and Stevens, 2001). If teachers wish to establish a classroom in which brain-based learning can thrive, allowing students to create some of their assignments and rubrics for marking. Assessment should be designed to fit the students, not vice versa (Caine *et al.*, 2005). Erlauer (2003) suggests that because students are learning through a preferred intelligence, they should in turn demonstrate their knowledge through a preferred intelligence or learning style. Immediate, constructive feedback increases motivation and makes students aware of how to improve their work.
6. Brain research indicates that the brain does not act as a computer, in a linear fashion, as some educators previously thought. Rather, the brain uses multiple strategies to create meaning (Caine, 2000; Caulfield *et al.*, 2000; Slavkin, 2004).

In particular, the concept of neural plasticity posits that the brain is continually rewiring itself throughout our lives to access new memories and experiences.

7. Students need to access all their abilities to maximize learning. The use of natural movement in the classroom, such as dancing, clapping, manipulatives and role play can help promote students' achievement (Caine *et al.*, 2005; Jensen, 2000; Slavkin, 2004). Brain research suggests that one of the most effective tools to maximize student learning is the incorporation of movement into lessons.
8. Duration of time on task is directly proportional to mastery of a concept. There is the need for students to have time to achieve mastery of a concept or skill before moving on. Another is scheduling regular breaks in the delivery of instruction to allow some time for students to process information and reflect.
9. "If brain-based pedagogy could be summed up in one sentence, it would be, Knowledge should be socially created" (Slavkin, 2004). Erlauer (2003) suggests that "Collaborative learning provides the brain with the means to explore new information, typically in a problem-solving situation". Students and teachers can also work collaboratively to make sense of information. This helps create an environment of relaxed alertness to increase student comfort and ability to focus in class (Caine *et al.*, 2005; Pool, 1997).
10. Thematic instruction encourages students to connect meaningful activities to relevant practice. Through the application of evocative experiences and the relevance of complex situations in which learners are immersed, thematic instruction builds on prior knowledge and enhances comprehension (Caine *et al.*, 2005; Caulfield, *et al.*, 2000; Pool, 1997; Slavkin, 2004; Wagmeister and Shifrin, 2000; Wolfe, 2001). Patterning or chunking information for thematic instruction assists students to mentally 'place' or sort new information in a way that has meaning. This allows for greater internalization and recall of this information can be maximized (Wagmeister and Shifrin, 2000). Teachers can help this process by acknowledging the diversity of learners while focusing on the relationship of students' prior knowledge with the new knowledge to be acquired (Pool, 1997).

REFERENCES

Bruer, J.T. (1999), *In Search of Brain-Based Education*, Phi Delta Kappan, 80 (9), 649-657.

Caine, G. *et al.* (2005), *12 Brain/Mind Learning Principles in Action*, Thousand Oaks, CA: Corwin Press.

Caine, G., Nummela-Caine, R. and Crowell, S. (1999), *Mindshifts: A Brain-Based Process for Restructuring Schools and Renewing Education*, 2nd edition. Tucson, AZ: Zephyr Press. ISBN: 1569760918.

Caine, G. and Caine R. N. (1994), *Making Connections: Teaching and the Human Brain Menlo Park*, CA: Addison-Wesley.

Caine, G. and Caine R. N. (1997), *Education on the Edge of Possibility* Alexandria, VA: ASCD.

Caine, R. N. (2000), Building the bridge from research to classroom, *Educational Leadership*, 58 (3), 59-61.

Caulfield, J. *et al.* (2000), Brain-based instruction in action, *Educational Leadership*, 58 (3), 62-65.

D'Arcangelo, M. (2000), How does the brain develop? A conversation with Steven Petersen, *Educational Leadership*, 58 (3), 68-71.

Dwyer, M. B. (2002), Training strategies for the twenty-first century: Using recent research on learning to enhance training, http://www.tandf.co.uk/journals assessed on February 7, 2004.

Edelman, S. (1994), *Biological constraints and the representation of structure in vision and language*, Psycoloquy, 5 (57).

Elliott, M. (1998), Multiple intelligence and other delusions: Gifted learners in the catholic religious education classroom, *Word in Life: Journal of Religious Education*, 46 (3), 22-28.

Erlauer, L. (2003), *The Brain Compatible Classroom: Using What We Know About Learning to Improve Teaching*, Alexandria, VA: ASCD.

Goldberg, D. and Stevens, J. (2001), *For the Learners' Sake: Brain-Based Instruction for the 21st Century*, Tuscon, AZ: Zephyr Press.

Hannaford, C. (1995), *Smart Moves*, Arlinton, VA: Great Oceans Publishers.

Jensen, E. (2000), Brain-based learning: a reality check, *Educational Leadership*, 57 (7), 76-80.

Pool, C.R. (1997), maximizing learning: A conversation with Renate Nummela Caine, *Educational Leadership*, 54 (6), 11-15.

Saunders, A. and Vawdrey, C. (2002), Merging brain research with educational learning principles, *Business Education Forum*, 57 (1), 44-46.

Slavkin, M. (2004), *Authentic Learning: How Learning about the Brain Can Shape the Development of Students*, Lanham, MD: Scarecrow Education.

Sousa, D. A. (2000), *How the Brain Learns*, second edition, Corwin Press, inc. Thousand Oaks, California

Sprenger, M. (1999), *Learning and Memory: The Brain in Action*, Alexandria Virginia. ASCD.

Sprenger, M. B. (2002), *Becoming a "Wiz" at Brain-Based Teaching*, Thousand Oaks, CA: Corwin Press, Inc.

Sylwester, R. (2003), *A Biological Brain in a Cultural Classroom: Enhancing*

Cognitive and Social Development Through Collaborative Classroom Management, Thousand Oaks, CA: Corwin Press Incorporated.

Wagmeister, J. and Shifrin, B. (2000), Thinking differently, learning differently, *Educational Leadership*, 58 (3), 45-48.

Weiss, R. (2000), Brain-based learning, *Training and Development*, 54 (7), 20-24.

Whitefield, D. (2001), Learning styles-great minds don't think alike, http://cleo.murdoch.edu.au/asu/pubs/tlf/tlf95/whit271.html accessed on July 1, 2002.

Winters, C. (2001), *Brain-based teaching: Fad or promising teaching method* (Report No. SP 040143), University Park, IL: Governors State University. (ERIC)

Wolfe, P. (2001), *Brain Matters: Translating Research into Classroom Practice*, Alexandria, VA: ASCD.

13

Quality in Educational Research

The Policy Implications

D.R. Kapoor

Modern education and emerging trends therein are results of experiments and researches which have led to improvement in the theory and practice of education. University departments, Research Institutes, and specialized centers the world over are devoted today to the task of improving the education by providing research based solutions to the problems being faced by the educators and institutions. Moreover, the introduction of technological innovations such as, the use of computers, e-mail, networks, teleconferencing and new soft ware made possible for the researchers in India to collaborate globally and contribute more effectively towards research in education. Now it is possible to make the entire world's knowledge, or even just a big chunk of it, available to anyone and everyone, anytime, anywhere to compare his or her research findings with others to arrive at logical conclusion. It is now easier for the researchers to view and review a large array of research literature. Such a system could connect research studies not only to related work but to the relevant curriculum materials, state policies, teacher reflections, media reports and support organizations.

Quality in educational research could enable institution and professionals to do things differently and increase the potential for practical improvement in the conduct and/ or organization of learning and teaching. The research output depends largely on the quality inputs in terms of supervisor, scholar and organization. The supervisor (mentor) is the kingpin who is associated with the research programme from beginning to the end. Therefore, competency of supervisor to guide research becomes pivotal. A mentor (supervisor) is required to keep pace with the growing knowledge and strive hard ceaselessly, to meet the international standards in teaching and research.

It is a fact that all phenomena and knowledge have both quantitative and qualitative dimensions. The distinction between objectivity and subjectivity, normally associated with quantitative and qualitative research, is neither accurate nor useful. Standards for quality research, whether primarily designed to gather quantitative or qualitative data, typically emphasize the traits of objectivity, internal validity, external validity, reliability, rigor, open-mindedness, and honest and thorough reporting.

The huge literature on educational research in India demonstrates that there is widespread variation in the standards and conceptualization of quality adopted by the numerous and often competing traditions of educational research.

Questions arise, why do the problems of poor quality of research studies persist? How can educational research improve its quality to produce substantial results in our centers of learning? How can schools be transformed into organizations that have the capacity to continuously improve their practices? How can the use of research knowledge base be increased in the centers of learning? How can educational research be useful to policy planners in devising strategies for the improvement of educational system? It seems necessary to critically examine these issues in the backdrop of researches carried out in the portals of education to find plausible response to our questions.

PRESENT SCENARIO OF EDUCATIONAL RESEARCH IN INDIA

Initiatives

The country has build up a fairly good network of institutional infrastructure for undertaking research in education. National, International and State level agencies such as UGC, ICSSR, NCERT, IIE, CASE, NUEPA and SCERTs and UNESCO, UNICEF, Ford Foundation, and Netherlands Foundations have come up with fair amount of reputation. The international bodies are known to have supported national level large scale research projects. At present there are 250 university departments, 150 PG colleges of education, 87 Centers for Teacher Education (CTE), 35 Institutes of Advanced

Study in Education (IASE), 30 State Councils of Education, Research and Training (SCERT) engaged in educational research.

The experts, educationists, and practitioners in the field of educational research have burnt lot of their energies to build up the knowledge base in the form of 'Surveys of Research in Education'. Surveys of educational research comprise a significant place among NCERT's wide ranging activities. It is a national level organization to advice the government and to act as a clearing house of ideas. The council has served the fraternity of scholars and research institutions by providing reliable information on studies concluded on different aspects of education. The surveys of research in education are useful not only to the researchers, but also to the schools. The Navodaya Vidyalaya Samiti has studied the implications of research findings given in four surveys and prepared reading materials for their teachers under the little of "What research tells to the teachers." The Educational Research and Innovations Committee (ERIC) of the NCERT has conducted five Surveys in Educational Research so far covering the period from 1972 to 2000. 8031 research studies and projects carried out by various institutions in India were included in these surveys. The sixth survey of educational research covered more than 2500 studies carried out by individuals and different kinds of organizations in the country from 1993 to 2000.

The "Encyclopedia of Educational Research' is an impressive document of the research at international level. Researchers and practitioners in India have made use of this knowledge base for the promotion of their research activities. Retrospectively, the period from 1900-1915 was a period during which the ground work was established in statistics and testing. From 1915 to 1940, these procedures and techniques became more wide spread. Most of the standardized research tools and instruments were adapted in India according to local conditions. The period from 1940 to 1990 was witnessed by a large scale expansion in the field of educational research in the world. During this period most of the universities and colleges were established in India and have undertaken research in education. The contributions of educational researches have continued to be quantitative and positivistic.

Poor Out-Put

The terms quality research and quality evidence are related concepts that have been at the center of much debate in academic, professional, and public policy circles. The debate stems from the wide spread belief that the quality of research in education is often uneven and lacking in credibility, making it difficult to make a confident, concrete assertion or prediction regarding evidence for improving practice. (Shavelson and Towne, 2002). However, Research in education has recorded even less respect now than a decade ago. Carl Kaestle (1993) says 'One can argue that the low status of educational research is inevitable, and a matter of concern. Intra-communal disputation has kept us from rallying behind any number of potential consensus statements and speaking with authority. That and a lack of attention to coherent theory building leave us looking balkanized and incoherent, the whole of education, being less than the sum total of its parts. (Hugh-Schoenfeld, 2003).

In general, research does not have much creditability-even among its intended clients, teachers and administrators. When they have problems, they rarely turn to research. Part of the reason may be lack of creditable models of employing educational research to shape educational practice. Part of the reason is that the traditions of educational research are not themselves strongly aligned with effective models linking research and practice. Moreover, the research knowledge base concerning preparation of teachers' in colleges of education is pretty thin.

According to an estimate nearly 10,000 candidates secure Ph.D. annually from Indian Universities. Out of these more than 300 are passing out in the faculty of education but the quality of Ph.D. dissertation, barring exceptions, shows a declining trend, judged by commonly accepted parameters like groundedness, authenticity, explicitness, publication, and citation index etc. (P.K. Rajan, 2006).

Dr. Rais Ahmed and Madulka, studied 9000 theses (ICSSR-Sponsored Study) and found that 78 per cent of the theses failed to make any intellectual contribution, 60 per cent of the research studies were found repetitive, and 80 per cent studies in applied research were found trivial, mediocre, and without any intellectual input.

Unpublished dissertations had not been put to scrutiny to judge the quality of research. Duplication in research work had lead to deterioration in standard. Research reports had not gone through a critical peer-group scrutiny. Moreover, usually research papers were prepared from PhD's submitted to universities. Author could not care to either update it to present it as a suitable research paper.

The paper was read as a summary of the original thesis. A few authors had continued to do research in their chosen field after they obtained their Ph. D. The evaluation process had become quite a casual and non serious exercise, ghost written theses were produced. The quality of Ph.D. had nose-dived to the lowest ebb. The entire negative report ended saying, however the degrees might be awarded. Majority of examiners hardly wrote one or two short paragraphs of general nature. The researchers wanted only degrees. (Dahiya, 2001).

It was thought M. Phil would provide practical orientation in terms of (i) selecting and identifying problems from the priority areas of educational research by developing an ability to comprehend the essentials of reported research; (ii) developing skills analyzing evidence and data in the solution of problems with the help of appropriate tools and techniques; (iii) description reports of finding asked on rigorous application of reasoned criticism;(iv) developing an ability to apply research findings in educational practice. But output at the M. Phil level, in general was marked by mediocrity and poor quality. The student was neither able to comprehend the essentials of reported research nor did he develop competence to apply research findings in educational practice. (Koul, 1991).

Junior Research fellowship was introduced to improve the quality of research in India. Intention was to attract the best talent in the field of research. The data revealed dismal condition. That from 2002 to 2006, less than 1 per cent applicants could qualify in JRF in each session. Out of total 5, 03,132 candidates appeared in JRF test; only 3920 candidates could qualify in the tests during the last five years. In the faculty of education only. 75 per cent could qualify during the same period. Therefore, research area could not attract majorities of brilliant students.

The trend analysis (Surveys of Research in Education) reveals that the discipline of education could not get enriched significantly by new knowledge generated through research. In spite of national efforts to have quality control in educational research, improvement in this direction was not easily visible. Educational researches revealed absence of clear educational perspective, a conceptual framework as the basis of educational research, inadequate understanding of the research processes and inability of research to influence educational policies, programmes or practice. Researchers were limiting them into small isolated themes, like out-hills digging deeper and deeper into just one place which may be part of the bigger world. Much research had been highly pedantic, limited in scope, tentative and jargon dominated. At present both policy makers and academics are shying away from using the research to make any decision for solving educational problems. (Gopalan, 1991).

Researches were found mostly skewed toward quantitative the descriptive survey approach and quantitative techniques of analysis. The qualitative approach could not find adequate place in educational research... Modern qualitative researches which try to arrive at some definite sensible results without standard tools, large samples, advanced statistics or even prior closed design, are becoming more popular in advanced countries, the empire par excellence of standardized tests and massive surveys, albeit with powerful cheeks, which had been conspicuously absent in our system.(Seshadri, 2000). In sociology of education there had been over dependence on the survey method (Sachchidanand, 1997). Indian studies regarding language teaching strategies, showed the use of strategy at a macro level rather than a micro level for language learning.

The teacher education had been the most neglected areas. The research work had been done haphazardly. Most of the researches were ill-conceived, unconnected with the real problems of teacher education. In the absence of empirical research data, no way out had been devised with regard to improving the quality of teacher education. Researchers viewed teacher education in relation to isolated aspects of the total process. (Mehrotra, 1991). Although, it may appear that the research studies have covered all aspects– context, pre-stage, process, product of teacher education-but very vital areas have not been touched. The research referred to in this Trend Report seems to have not even used (leave alone produce) many social, educational, pedagogical and professional concepts, paradigm and theories. The concept of excellence and quality with regards to teachers, teaching and teacher education could not attract attention of excellent, reflective scholars. (Mehrotra, 2000).

Research Studies in educational technology had shown that the larger part of the cake had gone to comparison of methods, media and ETV programmes. The new thrust areas in research which got least attention found were the effectiveness of internal, virtual classroom, virtual teaching and video conferencing.

A review of 1000-1200 papers/articles published in 57 educational research journals reveals that. Research articles on how to write good report and how to improve the quality of Doctoral research in education were rarely seen in Indian research journals. Most of the research papers by Indian researchers could not find space in International journals. The research articles on the quality of report writing, doctoral research, and the parameters of quality in both quantitative and qualitative research had been found the regular feature of the international research journals or review journals in education. (Kapoor, 2008).

Meta-level analysis reports had hardly found a space in Indian educational research journals. Such meta-level reports on various themes such as teacher effectiveness, research and practice, research and professional development, research evidence and policy planning for the improvement of educational system, had generally been found in the International educational Journals.

Bibliographical citations in Indian educational research journals revealed that Indian references in research studies found a little space and most of the references or citations had been found from the advanced countries. It had also been found that no space has been found for Indian references in the international educational research journals. The peer group review of research studies in education has rarely been reported in Indian journals while these are generally figuring in the International journals Moreover, feedback regarding quality of research in education was not available on account of lack of peer-review.

Since January 2002, the editors and editorial board of the Total Qualitative Report (TQR) received 550 original manuscripts from authors living in the United States, Puerto Rico, and 44 other nations from around the world including India. Even though they accept more that 88 per cent of these authors who submit their papers to TQR for inclusion in their manuscript development process, However, editors could publish 36 per cent of their papers in their journal. Two Indian articles could figure in the list. This reflected the little efforts or poor quality of the research skills. *(www.cse.ucla.edu).*

Most of the research studies published in the Indian educational research journals was not available on website. These research articles; meta-analysis, peer group review and review of research studies published in the International Educational Research Journals were found easily accessible on Internet free of cost.

To conclude, a review of researches reveals that the scenario of research in education is very dismal and deplorable. The quality of research output at PhD,, M. Phil. Levels has declined steeply and assuming alarming dimension. The repetitive, ill-conceived, haphazardly conducted researches could not produce any tangible results. Policy planners are not getting substantial evidence to inform their decisions. There is absence of clear educational perspective, a conceptual framework as the basis of educational research, inadequate understanding of the research processes and inability of research to influence educational policies, programmes or practice. The quality of research papers in national and international journals is steadily going down. Moreover, feedback regarding quality of research in education is not available on account of lack of peer-review.

POLICY IMPLICATIONS

The object of research is to find out how to change things, for example, how best to teach children of different abilities, how to pay teacher in order to motivate them, how to deal with the disparities of opportunities arising from class, sex or race, how to solve the problem of children's under-performance in rural schools. If highly qualified, well paid teachers in government rural schools could not make up students progression then it would be policy matter. One of the tasks of research into policy is to formulate these hypotheses and predictions and to test them.(Magee, 1973).

Interactive sessions with policy makers, regulatory authorities, management, principals, and faculty of schools and colleges should be organized to identify issues and problems faced by the stakeholders to find research problems. This would ensure sharing of experiences, selection of relevant research problems and utilization of the findings of research for policy formulation and decision making as well as introducing changes to improve quality of education.

The quality in educational research should be enhanced through a) rigorous research training, The scholars are to be trained to understand the various processes of quality educational research. The scholar should be groomed to understand the importance and need of the research undertaken, *i.e.* how to plan, conduct and evaluate programme in light of policy implications. (b) Pressures on scholars for publications of research articles for research degree or promotion at colleges and universities levels should not dilute quality. (c) Researches should be put to scrutiny by academia and public.

It is time that the research in education should go beyond the captive clientele of students in school and colleges and cover parents, guardians, teachers, social activists and administrators. The multi disciplinary perspective should be strengthened to move socially relevant and policy oriented educational research. The research has to use many social, educational, pedagogical and professional concepts, paradigm and theories.

Research articles on how to write good report and how to improve the quality of Doctoral research in education should become the regular feature of national level research journal. The best research papers by Indian researchers and practitioners should be sorted out and evaluated at high level in the centers of education for publication in the international journals. Meta-level analysis reports on various themes such as teacher effectiveness, research and practice, research and professional development, research evidence and policy planning for the improvement of educational system should find sufficient space in Indian Educational Research Journals.

Formal peer review should be a critical and important mechanism to harness the scholarly potential. Peer review need to be successfully employed as a feedback. There is need for constant attempt to synthesize and reconcile the different research findings, the search for the logical connection between conclusions drawn from different kinds of research, the assessment of the degree of reliability of the research for future policy and practice, the evaluation of the conclusions in the light of the explicitly reported data and methodology, the reporting of the research should be clear and focused.

High quality research can be promoted by creation of a research culture in our university departments of education, national institutions and institutions of teacher education. The teacher should look upon his job more as mission or a vocation rather than a mere means of livelihood. The aptitude, capacity, truthfulness and hard-work on the part of scholar (mentee) on one hand and organizational research culture and policy planning could produce good quality of research The Ministry of Human Resource Development should make substantial funding available for promoting the long–term capacity of the research community through investment in the research infrastructure, the research community, data development, information sharing, and access. The academics need to be encouraged by providing them with time and funds as needed and by flexibility in work load and work assignment.

National and international agencies, autonomous professional associations, and journal publishers should come together to set up norms, standards, and evaluation procedures in order to ensure quality in educational research. Cooperation with journal publishers could lead to the development and monitoring of guidelines or standards for journal publications and professional meetings

There should be National Clearinghouse specifically for research purpose, comprising of apex educational institutions to address the demand of educators, policymakers, researchers. This would help them to get scientific evidence of what works in educational interventions so that they can make informed decisions about what and how to teach. The purpose of the clearinghouse is to provide these stakeholders with an independent evaluative summary about existing research and dissemination of information and instructional interventions that have wide impact on schools and schooling. The National Clearing House should be centrally involved in the determination of what counts as 'quality based research in education.' From its website and professional network, the clearinghouse should solicit suggestions for topics from various stakeholders and identify hot topics from review of existing research and policy directives. The clearing house should focus on the effectiveness of curricular and instructional interventions in a wide range of topics, from 'technology' to 'models of curriculum' to 'formats of professional development.' The clearinghouse has to ensure that the demand of researchers and practitioners with sufficient high quality research be available on specific topics.

The institutions of higher learning engaged in educational research should adopt more objective, scientific, purposeful and more reliable and valid method of evaluation. National and International research community should come together and cooperate to evolve a more integrated and comprehensive model of evaluation based on clearly defined dimensions of quality.

REFERENCES

Alvin C. Eurich (1962). New Dimensions in Educational Research. *AERA, News Letter*, April 1962. 4-10.

Anne Clyde, L. (2005). The Basis for Evidence-based Practice: Evaluating the research evidence. The University of Iceland.

Bleakley, C. and D. MacAuley (2002), The quality of research reports in journals. *British Journal of Sports Medicine*, 36 (2): April, pp. 124-125.

Coladarci, Arthur P. (1954) "Are Educational Researchers prepared to do Meaningful Research?" *California Journal of Educational Research*, 5 (Jan 1954):3-6.

Dahiya, L.N. (2001). Quality of Doctoral Research in India:-Some Monitoring and Control Issues, *University News*, 39 (45) Nov. 5-11,2001.

Dave, P.N. (2007). The Decline in the Quality of Research in Education. *Perspectives in Education*, Vol. 23. No. 1.

Day, A., and J. Peter (1994). Quality Indicators in Academic Publishing, *Library Review* 43 (7): pp. 4-72.

Hugh Burkhardt and Alan H Schoenfeld (2003). Improving Educational Research: Towards a more useful, more influential, and better–funded Enterprise. *Educational Researcher*, Vol. 32, No 9.

John Wlllinsky (2001). The Strategic education research program and the public value of research, *Educational Researcher*, Vol. 30, No. 1 pp 5 -14.

Kapoor, D.R. (2009). *Dynamics of Learning Organizations*. Regal Publications, New Delhi.

Khanka, S.S. (2002). Declining Quality of Doctoral Research in Indian Universities. *University News*, Vol. 40 No. 9, March 4-10.

Michael l. Kamil.(1994). More on the Quality of Educational Research: Respose to Pressley and Harris. *Educational Psychology Review*, Vol. 6, No. 3.

National Research Council (1999). Improving students learning: A strategic plan for educational research and the utilization. Washington, DC: National Academy Press.

P.K. Rajan (2006). *Research in State University*: *University News*, Vol. 44, No. 09.

Reddy, D.O bul. (2000). Supervisor's role in improving the quality of research. Unpublished paper at the National Seminar on Supervision of Researchin Universities. New Delhi.

Robert. E. Slavin (2002). Evidence-Based Education Policies: Transforming Educational Practice and Research–. *Educatonal Researcher*, Vol. 31, No. 7, pp. 15-21.

Shakeel Ahmand (2008). UGC-NET: A measure to Maintain Quality in Teaching and Research. *University News*, Vol. 46 No. 21 May 19-25, 2008.

14

Achieving First Goal of Education for all, Dakar Framework of Action, 2000

Cross State Public Initiatives

D.D. Pandey

Young children experienced a revolutionary transformation in children and educational circumstances during the past half-century (Hernandez, 1998). There has been now an enormous increase in centre based alternative care and early childhood educational experiences for them. The testimony of this fact is evident from the considerable increase in the enrolment figures across all regions of the world (UNECSO, 2003). This revolutionary public favour is perhaps the outcome of generated awareness about the young child potential for early learning and emergent literacy.

Consequent upon recognition of this highly diverse area of learning opportunities varying from centre based pre-school experience to more informal home and community based activities, number of international events has drawn their attention towards to six years. Out of four sets of rights of the child as envisaged in Convention on Rights of the Child (CRC, 1989), the right to education including early education has been included under the broader framework of right to development. Focusing on the principle that learning begins at birth, the World Conference on Education for All (1990) emphasized the need to expand the early childhood and development programmes.

The World Summit on Children (1990) after synthesizing the principles and concerns urged the world societies to work for children's enhanced development and education. At the United Nations General Assembly Special Sessions on Children (UNGASS) on 10 May, 2002, the General Assembly adopted an ambitious agenda for children of the current decade entitled 'A

World Fit for Children'. The Document's declaration and plan of action call on Member States to complete the unfinished business of the 1990 World Summit for Children, and to address the goals and commitments of the MDGs through national action and international cooperation. It stresses a global commitment to sustainable human development, taking into account the best interests of the child, and the universality, indivisibility and interdependence of all human rights including the right to development. Finally, the neglected field of early childhood care and education received further impetus by identifying it as first and foremost goal of Dakar Framework respect of Education for All project. A significant change that has taken place involves putting the agenda of early childhood education at the central to the discussion of all movements (Early Childhood Education Programmes, 1997:41) supported by the UNDP, UNESCO, UNICEF and the World Bank.

Articulating the intent to specifically cater to the needs of 0-6 years old children, the constitution's Eighty Sixth Amendment Act has substituted article 45 (directive Principle of State Policy) to read 'The State shall endeavour to provide early childhood care and education for all children until they completes the age of six years'. The Eleventh Five Year Plan (11th FYP) has also acknowledged the early childhood education as a first step in the educational ladder and reaffirmed its priority for the same adopting right-based approach as advocated in the national policy and charter for children (2003). Under Sarva Shiksha Abhiyan (SSA) too, which is one of the major initiative of the Government of India for universal retention by 2010 in a mission mode, a provision has been made for taking recognition of these facts, NCERT designed national core curriculum framework, 2003 and 2005 has also advocated the introduction of two years early childhood education for all eligible children.

Gaining such momentum has proliferated multi pronged approaches (centre based early childhood education and socialization activities for children, experimentation with new models, convergence with existing system, education for parents and social support for families) to initiate and impart the ECCE initiatives. A miniature picture of such approaches being adopted by various States/UTs is discussed henceforth.

SOUTHERN REGION

Andhra Pradesh

The state has seen a high distinction of improving enrolment figure considerably during the span of 1998/99 to 2007/08. A total of 9574 ECCE centres under SSA/NPEGEL were established in 2001/02, 4972 in 2002/03, 5359 in 2003/04, 11558 in 2004/05, 7277 in 2005/06, 6494 in 2006/07 and 3140 in 2007/08. In the academic year of 2008/09, 8700 ECCE centres (2218 under SSA and 6482 under NPEGEL) are proposed to be established. Similarly as a result of especially designed initiatives for establishing the linkages of pre primary with that of institutionalized based primary schooling, the transition rate has also increased manifold between 1998/99 to 2007/08. The transition rate, which was 21 per cent in 2001/02, got increased to 36 in 2002/03, 41 in 2003/04 and 53 in 2007/08. The massive increase in transition rate may be attributed due to attachment of pre primary section in 22. 95 per cent of primary schools and about 36 per cent of elementary schools in the state. In the Fiscal Year of 2007-08, a total of 3,140 ECCE centres have been established in the state under innovative head of SSA and NPEGEL. The total enrolment in these newly opened ECCE centres are 72,913 with transition rate of 53 per cent. A total number of 13,129 children have been relieved from sibling care by these newly established ECCE centres. Mothers committees have been given orientation on owing up and managing these ECCE centres. So far as pedagogy of ECE is concerned, these newly established ECCE centres have been provided with activity book (Aduthu Padhuthu Module) comprising more than 100 songs and creative and readiness activities. A set of 100 multi colour story cards (Chitti Patti Kathalu) have also been provided to these ECCE centres. Integrated comprehensive multidimensional packages known as Sisu Vikas Karyakrama (SVK) has also been evolved by the state resource centre for the benefit the children. SVK is a developmentally congruent programme for eliminating the pressure oriented mis education that has spread its roots. The programme contains basically ten months schedule offering stimulated environs to 3-4 years age group and school readiness to 4-5 years old children. Concepts identified under the programme have been hierarchically organized keeping in mind the principle of child development encompassing through six strategies namely conversation, games, songs, stories, creative activities and readiness. A comprehensive package has also been developed which inter alia includes worker's manual, programme calendar and 300 activity banks.

The AWWs of the state have undergone through ten days long intensive training programme designed in three phases with a gap of two months in each phase. While the first phase includes three days joint training of AWWs with primary school teacher, the second phase of five days duration is meant for developing the skills for preparing and use of teaching and learning material. The third phase of two days duration is devoted for organising school readiness activities.

So far as teacher education concerning ECCE in the state is concerned, only 12 NCTE accredited ECCE teacher education courses with intake of 595 students are available in the state. These courses are being run under name of Pre Primary Teachers Training (PPTT) Courses. The Department of Home Science and Food Technology of Padmavati Mahila Vishwavidyala, Tirupati also offers a PG Diploma in Pre School Education. The programme is of one academic year duration with two semesters. The eligibility criteria of this course is Bachelor Degree with 45 per cent marks in group. The course contents of PGDPSE includes Growth and Development of Pre School Children, Nutrition and Health, Management of Pre School children, Methods and Materials of Pre School Education, Programme Planning for Pre School Children, Communicative English, Project Work, Administration and Management of Pre Schools, Developmental Programmes for Pre School Children, Home School Relationship and Practice Teaching. The university also offers three months long self financing evening course of certification nature in Child Care and Management (CCCCM). The eligibility criteria of the course include Intermediate in any subject (10+2). The main contents of the course are Growth and Development, Health and Nutrition, Parent Practices and Child Welfare Programmes. Osmania University, Hyderabad–which is one of the oldest universities in the state-, also offers a Post Graduate Diploma in ECE (PGDECE).

Tamil Nadu

Over a period of last two decades, the state of Tamil Nadu has emerged as the prominent site of experimenting countless innovations in ECCE. Though language intervention thorough mother tongue has been scientifically proved as most appropriate way of working with preschool children, however, due to increased urbanization and privatization, the child's learning in English medium schools has now a day's comes out as a legitimate desire even in rural parts of the country. A study in Tamilnadu found that even parents from low-income communities in urban areas sought English Medium private pre schooling for their children once they reached the age of 4 years (M.S. Swaminathan Research Foundation, 2000). The committee appointed by GOI on ECE (2004) also substantiated it by stating that these days socially and economically upward mobile families are often fleeing from public initiatives towards locally available private alternatives in search of so called English medium pre schooling. The rise towards enrolment in English medium schools is happening so fast that a nationwide enrolment in English medium schools has seen a hike of 74 per cent during 2003/04. The growth for English medium schools is witnessed more in southern States, which alone accounts for 60 per cent of the students during the past three years. The three states which top amongst the rest in enrolling kids for English Schooling are Andhra Pradesh, Tamilnadu and Maharashtra.

In order to keep pace with these emerging demands of the community for English medium pre schooling on the one hand and taking into consideration the fact of favouring introduction of second language from very early stage by the pedagogical/ curricular experts, located in the developed and advanced countries, the Government of Tamilnadu had decided to upgrade the AWCs into English Medium Pre Primary Centres. As a supportive scheme for introducing English medium standard 1 since 2003/04, about 20,000 randomly selected AWCs have been upgraded as English medium pre primary schools. In these centres the children are taught the English Alphabets and English rhymes, which help in developing good communication skills. While upgrading, priority is being given to the centres attached with primary schools while upgrading. Further on demand of the community, some English medium AWCs have also been started. The DSW pays the honorarium of the worker and helpers in the upgraded centres. A token money is also being paid from SSA funds. All the upgraded centres have been supplied with play materials worth Rs 1,500/- and kit material for Rs 225/-as a one-time grant. In addition to the honorarium paid, a recurring grant of Rs 1.50 per month per child is given as replenishment and stationary charges. Workers in upgraded centres have been given training on theme-based approach for language development. The duration of AWCs has been extended up to 16.00 hours. The extension of timings helps the elder children studying in primary schools to get themselves free from sibling care. In order to strengthen the pre school education component of ICDS, some of the AWWs have undergone through nursery teachers training also.

All AWCs in the state have been uniform ally painted so as to give a pre schooling look to them. The state is providing lot of emphasis on Integrated Education. All the AWWs of the state have been trained on Early Detection of Disabilities and instructions have been issued to enrol the special children in AWCs. In ten districts of the state (Chennai, Madurai, Coimbatore, Tiruchy, Tiruvanu, Salem, Kanya Kumari, Tiruvallur, Shivganga and Tirunvelli) Early Intervention Centres for infants and young children with hearing impaired have been sanctioned. These centres-which are mainly being run by NGOs-are being managed with support of parents and families. Only those children who are less than 2 years with hearing impairment without any additional disability are being admitted in these centres so that by the time they becomes old, they can develop visual language skills and get ready for admission into 1st grade of regular schools.

The state has unique decentralized pattern of ICDS training. Under this pattern, one trainer has been appointed in each ICDS project for catering to the training needs of grass root level ICDS functionaries. These block/ project level trainers not only impart training but also visit the AWCs to render guidance and to clarify the doubts of AWW/H on the spot. 11.65 per cent of primary schools and 66.70 per cent of elementary schools have attached pre primary section in the state (NIEPA, 2003). The Tamil Nadu Forum of Creche and Child Care Services has drafted an ECE curriculum for the young children (3-05 Years).

The state, since 2004, is implementing an innovative programme known as Developing Parenting Skills on Early Childhood Education (DPSECE). The programme was mainly designed in view of the fact that though parents and teachers are required to function together as partners to help the child learning and grow, however, it was being experienced that whatever was being achieved by the child at ICDS centres were not being reinforced or compensated at home. Not only this, it was being generally seen that most of the time the parents lack the correct perception of outcomes of NFPSE activities being organized at AWCs. Thus, a need was felt to make vigorous efforts by ICDS functionaries so that parents may not only have correct perception of PSE inputs but also may not equate with the learning of reading, writing and arithmetic. Parents were also needed to be educated about the quality of instructions with the child. The major objectives of running DPSECE includes creating awareness on importance of "Parenting"; making the community realize that father and all the members in the community have a role in "Parenting" and just not the mother alone and making Parents/Caregivers realize that the development of children not only depends on proper nutrition and health care but also equally on proper care, love and affection. Under DPSECE strategy, awareness campaigns are being organized across the state in all the Anganwadi Centre's in 2 phases. During these awareness programmes, sensitization on parenting skills is being attempted by the AWWs along with children and adolescent girls enrolled under ICDS scheme. Exhibitions are also being organized to promote their parenting practices. Relation between the cognitive development and the sensory organs are being explained through a poster depicting that five sensory organs are the gateway of the Brain Development. Kolam exercise is also being conducted to sensitize the community on the Neurons and the Networking of the Brain. Towards the end of each awareness campaigns, the parents are also being motivated to take "oath" to follow proper parenting messages concerning ECE and early stimulation.

Karnataka

Besides 54260 ICDS centres and 877 centres being run under Rajiv Gandhi National Creche scheme, 164 Nursery Cum Women Welfare Centres for Schedule Caste Children are also functioning in the state. A total of 6366 children are being benefited by these Nursery Cum Women's Welfare Centres. Though these centres were started by the Department of Social Welfare for the first time in 1958 for the children of Schedule Caste and their families, however, these facilities were later extended to children belonging to Schedule Tribes, Denotified Tribes, Nomadic and Semi Nomadic Tribes also. These centres are mainly located in Scheduled Caste Localities. The sanctioned strength of each centre is 50, consisting of both boys and girls. A Women Welfare Organizer and a conductress maintain these centres. Every year in the month of May, the women welfare oerganizer visits the Schedule Caste houses in the locality and prepare a list of children who are in the age group of 3-5 years. These children are brought to the centre by the conductress from their homes, every day by 9.00 a.m. The organiser -who also works a teacher-, teaches alphabets, rhymes, storytelling etc to the children. These children are given a hot mid day meal at the centre at the cost of Rs 1/ per day per child. The children are also being given two dresses annually, at the cost of Rs 150/ -per child.

In addition to ICDS, the Karnataka Government under the education department runs a scheme of pre primary centres (PPCs) attached to lower primary schools. Each PPC has a teacher and helper. The teacher is at least a matriculate and diploma in nursery teacher training. The PPC is run for the same duration as the lower primary schools (NCERT, 2000).

As per International Standard Classification of Education– which has defined pre schooling at level code of 0 in educational ladder of 1 to 6, the Government of Karnataka, on a pilot basis, has established zero grade system–pre primary units–in 593 schools located in north and south zones of Bangalore city. Being run under financial assistance of SSA, these zero grade pre primary unit's aims at not only to provide school environment but also for attempting to taught alphabets, numbers etc. All children enrolled in these centres are being provided hot noon meal. In order to take care of children, two volunteers have been appointed in each of these zero grade class. Learning tools are also being developed. Based on the response, this pre schooling system is planned to be extended in other parts of the state also. The pre primary sections are attached to as many as 78.43 per cent of the integrated higher secondary schools and 50 per cent of the primary schools. Under the innovative head of SSA, more ECE centres have been planned to open in those areas not covered by ICDS. On the line of mother's groups in Assam, Bal Vikas Mahila Samiti (BVMS) comprising primary school teacher, AWW and community members have been formed to monitor the activities of AWCs.

In order to strengthen the pedagogical aspects of children attending ICDS centres, the state is implementing a blended approach of COPCC under curricular inputs. Under this initiative, the preschool education is being imparted using theme approach. About 42 such themes have already been identified. UNICEF has developed compilation of children's activities called CHUILIPILI (a collection of stories, songs, games in local languages) in partnership with National Institute of Public Cooperation and Child Development (NIPCCD), Department of Child Development (DWCD), experts and NGOs working in the field. The chuilipili kits have supplied in 24790 AWCs. In addition of chuilipili, PSE kit worth Rs 500/-per AWC has been provided.

So far as giving technological inputs are concerned, the IBM has supplied 20 computers in 20 AWCs in the state on experimental basis. The computers are fitted with multimedia kits to utilize their young explorer product to support early childhood educators in order to reinvent education in childcare and preschool setting. The state is in process of installing data maintenance by giving one computer in a circle of 10 AWCs. This will be the nodal point for collection of data for 10 AWCs.

The state government is planning to regulate admissions, fee structure and monitor quality pre schools beings imparted under private initiatives the form of nurseries, play homes, and kindergartens. Hitherto, these schools were free from any sort of regulations. Now, the government plans to enforce the provisions of the Karnataka Education Act, 1983, in all pre primary schools. As a first step, it has been made mandatory for all pre primary schools to register with the Education Department. The Government of Karnataka has also initiated action to make it mandatory even for pre primary sections of the schools affiliated to the two Central boards of CBSE and ICSE to register with the state education department. While ICSE and CBSE schools do not come under the purview of the State Education Act (hence the state has no control over these schools) the government feels that pre primary sections can come under the domain if the Central boards do not regulate them. By enforcing the provisions of the Karnataka Education Act 1983, the government will be in a position to keep a tab on these schools. Further, in order to stop the admission process as early as November, the Government of Karnataka is in process of making it mandatory even for nursery schools to commence their admissions process only during April. These new initiative does not require any amendments to the Karnataka Education Act, Act, 1983 as the provision to regulate pre primary schools already exists in the Act but was not being enforced. The government decision to tighten its grip on pre primary schools has received mixed response from the managements. Like, the new initiatives will not only usher in quality pre schooling but also put to end to the present trend of play homes mushrooming in every nook and corner. It will also ensure that only trained and qualified personnel are recruited in these schools. On the other side, it has been said that why does the government want to mess things up? One cannot compare pre primary centres with other schools. Private managements have termed this more as illegal (Deccan Herald, 2005).

Kerala

The state of kerala is also utilizing many alternatives to impart PSE to the children. These includes 25376 Angadwadi Centres,55 PSE centers being run by the general education department,75 PSE centres being run by PTAs,75 PSE centers attached to government primary schools and 11895 private/NGOs owned PSE centers. Under the scheme of Schedule Tribes Development Activities, the state has set up 43 Balwadis for children between 3 -5 years age group. The Schedule Tribe Development Corporation also runs 14 Nursery Schools. The children attending these ECCE centres are being given free and day meals and dress in addition to lump sum grants. The subject of PSE has been included as the priority area in state plan of action. As per enrolment statistics available for 2002-03, the share of pre primary enrolment to total enrolment in primary schools comes to about 1.12.

In order to enjoy the fruits of the local governance, some of the ECE centers have been transferred to them. Pre Primary centers for visually impaired/hearing impaired/hearings impaired/ mentally challenged are also functioning in the state. The parents of these differently able preschool children have been oriented by the PSE workers on the use of aids and appliances and on required behavioural and attitudinal change towards these children. Access to well train general education teachers, special education teachers, Para professionals, mental health services, and other necessary support is integral to success. Noon Meal support (NMS) is being provided in all PSE centers attached to government and aided schools and recognised special school students. Handbook has been developed for PSE teachers adopting thematic approach and has been distributed amongst Pre School run by government and PTAs. Well designed training inputs have been given to PSE teachers and

AWWs under SSA. Every year, on the occasion of children's day Chacha Nehru Painting competition is being conducted for pre schooling children.

Teacher Education concerning PSE is being imparted by using wide network of the network of three government PSE teacher education institutions, 20 self-financing institutions and 27 AWTCs established under ICDS. The state has largest number of 25 NCTE recognised teacher education courses with intake approved capacity of 977. University of Kerala under Distance Education mode runs a PG Diploma in Early Childhood Care, Survival, Growth and Development (PGDECCSGD). The course has four papers with three units in each paper. First paper concerning Early Childhood Development covers three units namely Developmental Psychology, Developmental Assessment and Therapy and Pre School Education. Paper two concerning Child Care and Nutrition has three units namely Parenting Practices, Child Nutrition and Common Childhood Illness. Third paper on Special Education includes three units namely Theoretical Concepts in Special Education, Young Children with Special Needs, and Montessori Open Education. The fourth paper focuses on Behavioural Paediatrics includes units namely Behavioural Paediatrics, Behavioural Problems and Research Methods in ECD. The eligibility criterion for the course is PGDCCD/ DCCD with Graduation or any graduation with two year experience in ICDS/Social Work. University of Kerala also runs a programme titled PGDDN (Post Graduate Diploma in Developmental Neurology). Though the focus of this programme on neurological aspects, however, it has a separate unit of early Child Development with PSE as one of the essential unit therein.

While the draft curriculum for ECCE centres being run under Education Department is being developed by SCERT, the same for ICDS is being developed by Department of Social Welfare.

CENTRAL REGION

Chhattisgarh

The public mode of providing center based opportunities for ECCE mainly includes centrally sponsored ICDS based 29437 AWCs and to some extent 372 crèches being run under newly launched central initiative of Rajiv Gandhi National Crèche Scheme, designed after merging two schemes of Crèches and National Children's Fund.

1338 Pre Primary Education centres are also being run by Department of Education and Tribal Welfare Department of the state with total enrolment of about 75000 children in these centres. Besides this, 16.80 per cent of primary schools have attached pre primary sections as well. So far as training opportunities for ECCE is concerned, though the state has 10 AWTCs and 1 MLTC running under well designed comprehensive training strategy of ICDS but does not have even a single NCTE recognized teacher-training course. Under business allocation rules, preschool education has been allocated to education department.

For the first time in India, the State of Chattisgarh has also developed a State Policy on ECCE. Under this policy, which has been designed by the state on the initiation of SCERT, the state has made the commitment towards covering all children by the benefits of ECCE by the year 2015. Linkages of ECCE with Primary Education, expansion of ECCE services based on qualitative inputs, emphasis on action research, evolving well designed monitoring and evaluation system, establishment of State Resource Centre and evolving minimum core curriculum framework of ECE are other major concerns of this newly designed state ECCE policy. While emphasizing on training inputs, it has been categorically stated in the state ECCE policy that Pre Primary Teacher Training Institution will be set up in the state to take care of training aspects of ICDS and Pre Primary Teachers and Teachers Educators in the state. In order to address the issue of absence of context/culture specific ECE pedagogy, the state has come out with a Pahal initiative aiming at to provide quality inputs to AWWs for organizing various activities which are helpful in developing different developmental domains of the child. Pahal strategy is basically based on the theme approach. Each identified theme has 8-10 sub themes based upon which the AWW are organizing various PSE activities. Besides this, eight key activities aiming at familiarizing the children with natural environment, different body parts, living and non living things, local culture and social norms have also been detailed out in the Pahal Strategy. Pahal strategy believes in fact that though continuous evaluation of the child is the complex process for AWWs, however, it can be made easier by adopting little efforts and some simpler methods. In view of the fact that ECE in essence is development oriented and not syllabus oriented, the Pahal initiative gives much importance to continuous informal evaluation of the child in terms of all the developmental objectives. The evaluation of the child is being done individually covering all aspects of development and is being carried out through observation of the child's behaviour and responses either on play activities or on work sheets. Realizing the importance of nature walk as a strongest tool to familiarize them to their local environment, the emphasis has been made in the Pahal strategy to take the children to nature walk at least once in two months so that they can relate themselves with the local environment under which they are residing.

Madhya Pradesh

Besides imparting non formal pre schooling through net work of 49594 ICDS centers in the state, the establishment of pre primary centers under the name of Shishu Shiksha Kendra's (SSKs) in 35.33 per cent of primary schools and 45.30 per cent of elementary schools in the state offers the dual advantages of linking ECCE with that of primary schooling and getting the school going children free from sibling care, which in turn, enables them to attend primary schools (NIEPA, 2003). These ECCE centers have been established only in those areas from where demand comes from village education committees (VECs). The contributory role of VECs also includes identification of two women functionaries as per the eligibility requirements, recommending their names to the Zila Panchayat (ZP) and construction of rooms in the primary school premises by utilizing the Z.P funding. Thus active involvement of ZP is a positive feature of this model (NCERT, 2000). Other model of expanding early childhood education in the state includes implementation of UNICEF assisted early childhood education project since 1985. After stressing the need for convergence with ICDS in the decade of nineties, the teachers working in these centres have been placed in District Institute of Education and Training (DIET) for creating separate ECE cell in the DIETs (*op. cit)*. The state has also tried out the school readiness programme throughout the state as part of class one curriculum. This experiment has been done keeping in view of the children who have come to school without any pre schooling experiences.

NORTH WESTERN REGION

Haryana

The responsibility of implementation of goal 1 of EFA concerning universal provision of ECCE, which was primarily with the

Education Department, has now been shifted to Department of Women and Child Development in the State. Under public domain, besides ICDS, which covers 446947 preschool children in the state, the ECE is being imparted by Education Department and two other national level NGOs namely ICCW and CSWB. Under Education Department, nursery classes have been started since 2002, which runs for three hours a day for 220 days in a year. 9273 government primary schools hold such classes in all the 20 districts of the state. Seven government nursery schools are also being run in the state. JBT primary teachers, in addition to their responsibilities of teaching primary classes, also take nursery classes.

Further, the provision of early childhood care and education to children in the early stages of development, prior to entering primary school, has been given special place in SSA initiatives. Under SSA, the initiative of starting a school readiness programme at pre primary level has been envisaged to (i) create enabling environment wherein children can familiarize themselves with school like environment and can get varied experiences, (ii) learn to perform simple tasks, (iii) experience cooperative learning and peer group/adult child interaction through group activities, (iv) make learning more relevant and culture specific, and (v) build a greater sense of social values, personal hygiene, self esteem and confidence (NIPCCD,2008). Under this initiative, PSE centres in the name of Bachpanshalas have been established for preschool children across the state. By the end of FY 2007-08, a total of 800 Bachpanshalas have been established in the state. About 180000 children have been enrolled in these Bachpanshalas. These children are provided supplementary nutrition @ Rs 2 per child per day. In each of these shalas, the social service of a volunteer (10+2 with second division) and a helper (8+ with good second division) is being utilized to create school readiness among children in the age of 3-6 years in school environment. These two functionaries of Bachpanshalas are being paid the honorarium of Rs 1000/ and Rs 300 respectively. These Bachapanshalas, which are located in the premises of the local government primary school in the village, are being run for 4 hours a day for 200 days in a year. All Bachpanshalas are being run under direct supervision of head teacher. The selection of the volunteer and helper of Bachpanshalas are being made with community involvement. The VLEC is first required to send the list of the female volunteers (of the same locality) for short listing to the DLEC, which in turn finally make the selection as per specified eligibility conditions. In case of selection of volunteers, preference is being given to those with NTT and D. Ed. In order to impart comprehensive training in the early child care to the volunteers engaged in the Bachpanshala, a training module has been prepared by group of experts drawn from different educational institutions. The newly opened Bachpanshalas have been strengthened by providing them infra-structural facilities, TLM and play way items. The curriculum of these Bachpanshalas has been made in such a proactive way so as to give them adequate space for carrying out the early educational activities among the peer group. Input provisions have been made so as to transact the teaching learning process in a play way method. Emphasis is laid on the process of learning by making them understand or do things and not to follow the traditional rote learning method. Easy to do exercise book lets and various play way activities which improve learning, applications and social skills of the child, have been developed for use in the Bachpanshalas. While developing such TLM, renewed focus has been given on vocabulary development of the child, impact of local language/dialects, recognition of objects, gradual beginning of counting, alphabets, different social contacts, sounds of letters, recitation of poems and proper muscular coordination etc.

Another mode of ECE in the state includes 480 childcare centers with enrollment of 11209 children spread in ten districts only. One volunteer cum helper (10+2) is recruited in each of this centre getting honorarium of Rs 625 per month. During 2006-07, 652 more centres have been sanctioned to cover remaining 10 districts of the state. Under RGNCS, 758 centers with enrollment of 7275 children are being run by matriculate workers for 25-27 days a month and from 9.00 to 17.00 hours or 9.00 to 14.00 hours depending upon the need. A school readiness programme is proposed by setting up 20 nursery schools in five districts (to be selected on random basis). These nursery schools are proposed to be named as Bachpanshalas located in the premises of local primary schools of rural areas where at least minimum infrastructure of two room and one verandah is to be made available by district level education committee. These schools will initially run under the supervision of head teacher of the school in the first phase of the programme. The programme would be expanded after analyzing its impact on the performance of children. The percentage share of pre primary-to-primary schooling is only 4.0 per cent. In addition, shifting of AWCs to Primary Schools having more than 4 rooms is under process and a regular follow up is being done in this regard by asking the field officers to send weekly progress of shifting of AWCs in primary schools. At present 1800 AWCs have been shifted in primary schools.

The state has the unique advantage of having several experimental programmes in ECCE. These include dissemination of ECCE workbook, training manual and introduction of CHEER project with collaborative efforts of NCERT, All India Radio and Department of Women and Child Development. ICDS has been universalized in the state. Besides setting of ECCE cell in the State Council of Educational Research and Training (SCERT), one lecturer of ECCE has been posted in each DIET so as to monitor and supervise the activities of ECCE in the AWCs. The state has placed high emphasis on training part of functionaries by adopting cascade model. Master Trainers (MTs) and Key Resource Persons (KRPs) have been trained by NCERT and SCERT respectively. These key trainers have trained nearly all the AWWs of the state in the proper ECCE methodology. A comprehensive guidebook for AWWs was developed in the name of Ankur. The manual of Ankur provides weekly timetable from 8.45-12.00 p.m. The manual has thematic approach with 55 identified themes. One theme has to be taken up every week. It also has 37 stories,4 prayers,45 rhymes and 29 riddles for children. Ankur Workbook was developed in 2002 and has pre writing, pre reading and pre arithmetic skills. 20 workbooks per AWC have been provided. No state policy concerning ECE and regulatory framework as in case of Delhi, Chattisgarh or likely to be in Karnataka has been designed. The state has 4 NCTE accredited teacher education courses with intake of 200 students, besides 8 AWTCs and 1 MLTC.

Himachal Pradesh

The early childhood education experiences are being imparted to children adopting triple action mode of involving NGOs, private initiatives and public initiatives under primary schools and state owned ICDS projects. In total 7354 AWCs are being run by the state besides 102 AWCs, which are being managed by NGOs. With the objective of relieving girls from sibling care responsibilities during school time, 2766 ECCE centres have been started in convergence with ICDS. The mapping exercise carried out by ICDS has been used for the purpose of site selection for setting up these ECCE centres. These centres have been set up in UN served eligible areas in accordance with norms for hilly areas followed by ICDS. SSA pays honorarium to the worker @ Rs 500/ per month for ten months together with a kit worth Rs 725/per ECCE centre. SSA and ICDS have jointly developed the training module and all trainings are being conducted by ICDS. One uncommon thing with the state is that due to reduction in entry age in grade one of primary schooling from 6 to 5 years in the state; the AWCs are enrolling the children from 3-4 years age group instead of 3-6 years age group as provisioned in the operational guidelines of ICDS. The community and other charitable agencies like Lions and Rotary clubs not only donate generously the teaching learning material (TLM) in AWCs but in most of the cases also provide rent-free accommodation for them. Further, the curriculum concerning PSE has been designed in the state after having rigorous and brain storming sessions and series of consultations with ICDS field functionaries and principals of private schools. Based on this extensive exercise, teaching learning material in the form of kit–1 and kit-2 have been developed by the state and have been disseminated to all AWCs so that parents are aware of their children learning and development process at AWC level. The sketch of such especially designed PSE pedagogy is basically centered on thematic approach. Care has been taken to put in age specific pedagogical inputs and addressing different developmental domains of the personality. The funds received under SSA have been utilized for this purpose.

So far as implementation status of PSE curriculum is concerned, all AWWs, CDPOs, and DPOs have been given special three days training on this newly devised curriculum. 33 supervisors of selected ICDS circles have been given additional three days training on this new approach of PSE and they have been given 6-9 months to show results, which will, in turn, set the stage for replication of this model in other clusters of the state also. In order to have the stakeholder's participation, VLCCs have been constituted at AWC level by giving representation to mothers of preschool children, members of SHGs, Mahila Mandals and local ward, school teacher, health worker etc. Personal interaction with state officials further provides additional inputs to make the project a great success. In order to assess the impact of this thoroughly designed curricula on school readiness outcomes, pre and post evaluation questionnaire have been prepared. Pre School is the major issue for discussion in VLCC. Regular meeting of the committees is being held on 3 rd of each month throughout the state.

May and November are the designated months when AWC children perform before the VLCC and parents. In Feb, circle level functions of pre schoolers take place. Selected supervisors circles have also been selected as areas of excellence on PSE. In evaluations, besides, ICDS functionaries, VLCC members and parents of children have been involved. Outcome of these special initiatives includes improvement in the skills of field functionaries, incremental trend in enrolment and retention of children in AWCs, increase in awareness level of ICDS functionaries, enriching the environment of AWCs and increase of community participation. The Panchayat Raj Institutions have been involved in selecting AWWs and Helpers in the state. Under innovative head of Sarva Shiksha Abhiyan (SSA), more ECE centres are being set up in those areas which are uncovered by ICDS. In order to take advantages of developing ties with primary schools and better community supervision and monitoring, a proposal is being sent by the state to Government of India for construction of AWCs in the premises of primary schools. The state has developed a prospective plan envisaging preschool attendance certificate as compulsory for admission in primary schools (NIEPA-UNESCO, 2003).

The challenges includes keeping regular track of activities going at AWCs, equipping functionaries with all relevant data/ information/skills, maintaining strong data base of all activities, bridge the gap between available and desired infrastructure, make optimum use of community participation, show the results in time bound manner, ensuring continuity of trained manpower, having strong monitoring system at project/district/state level.

Four per cent of primary schools in the state have pre primary wing with per cent share to total enrolment to about 0.89. There has been not even a one-pre schooling NCTE accredited teacher education courses in the state.

Punjab

Besides ICDS, which is being managed by Deptt of Social Security, and is a major vehicle for providing PSE in the state, the ECCE centres have been opened in formal setting of primary schooling under the aegis of education department. Using the infrastructure of existing primary schools in the State, the Government of Punjab is implementing the scheme of Pre School Education on a pilot basis since 2005-06. In such a path breaking initiative, 1660 pre schools (nursery schools) have been opened all over the state to equip children with school readiness skills and thus setting the stage for having a better start of their educational career. The premise of this PSE scheme under SSA is based on the fact that pre schooling intervention would not only help in improving the quality of education at later stage of life but would also increase enrollment and reduce drop outs in public run primary schools across the state. Under the scheme, multiple benefits of establishing such PSE centres in Primary Schools includes (i) using the entire infrastructure available at the primary school (ii) exposing the preschool children to an educational environment in a formal setting from the beginning (iii) receiving exclusive attention of the teacher and learning school readiness skills in a formal settings (iv) promoting early bonding with the primary schools due to close proximity with them (v) providing preschool going children an greater opportunity for curricular continuity (vi) providing a sense of security among preschool children due to close proximity to older siblings and (vii) increasing scope for the girl's participation in primary schooling as she is freed from sibling care. Some of the key parameters adopted at the PSE centres established under SSA in Punjab includes (i) renovation of ECCE rooms to make them more child centric and appealing with vibrantly painted walls, sketches of animals, fruits etc. (ii) introduction of ECE TLM kit in every centre to teach children school readiness skills through play and activity based techniques (iii) introduction of toys to make play time more attractive (iv) imparting 10 days extensive training to ECE volunteers (v) appointment of one teacher and one helper at each ECCE centre with a monthly honorarium of Rs 800/ and 400/ respectively (vi) functioning of ECCE volunteer and helper's under direct supervision of Primary School Head master (vii) administrative control of the ECCE centre by Village Education Development Committee (viii) hiring and providing honorarium to ECCE volunteers (ix) purchasing of TLM and renovation of ECCE centres through VEDCs (x) minimum enrolment of 20 children in each ECCE centre (xi) Shifting of ECCE centre to a new area if it has consistently less than 16-18 children.

The success of the PSE scheme under SSA lies in receiving overwhelming response from all quarters of the community. There has been a demand from large number of villages to open a pre schooling centre in their primary school and to extend the benefits of the scheme universally to all primary schools. The success of the scheme has been further documented by exploration of 8.5 per cent increase in enrollment during the 2nd year of the programme, which is in sharp contrast of decreasing the enrollment trends in public run private schools in the state. While there were 40,954 children enrolled in ECCE centres in 2005-06, the number increased to 44,435 children during 2006-07. Further the transition of 12961 ECCE children have been made to class 1st of the primary schools in the state. Further, convergence between SSA and ICDS has been established by strengthening 10,375 AWCs through educational and/ or material support and training with approximate cost of Rs 2 Crores.

NORTHERN REGION

Delhi

While the public programme mainly ICDS is meant for children of disadvantaged situation, the pre primary class is available in 39 schools out of 910 government schools and 225 government aided schools. Similarly, out of 1818 MCD run Primary Schools, the pre primary class is available in 919 schools that include 33 independent nursery schools also. In NDMCs run 81 schools (26 primary, 11 middle, 07 secondary, 05 senior secondary, 01 navyug secondary, 05 Navyug Senior Secondary and 03 aided schools), Pre Primary Education is available in 34 schools of which 18 are exclusively pre primary schools. The Pre Primary Education is uniformly of one-year duration in these schools and the minimum age for admission is 4+. In order to cope up with the enormous demand for pre schooling facilities, the private initiative in varied names of Play Schools, Nursery Schools, Kindergarten, Preparatory Schools, etc are targeting the children of middle and upper class families. These non-state or private initiatives impart preschool education through nurseries, kindergarten and pre primary classes. This type of pre schooling is oversubscribed and the competition for spaces in the lead schools is intense, with as many as 300 children competing for a single opening (Prochner, 2002). This phenomenon is not limited to the elite. In fact, it has resulted a bourgeois revolution by the growth of consumer class and more parents who are able to purchase their children a preschool experience (Stern, 1993). Owing to this, most of these schools are not only termed as teaching shops but also being criticized for their ambiguous nature by holding interviews of parents, knowing their economical background etc.

Uttar Pradesh

Besides centrally sponsored scheme of ICDS and Central scheme of RGNCS, the state is currently implementing ECCE Scheme, under which 9208 AWCs centres have been identified for their strengthening within the overall domain of SSA-one amongst the eight identified flagship programme of the Government of India (GOI) for universalizing elementary education and which has succeeded the DPEP. These ECCE centres are located across all 70 districts of the state and run for five hours a day. The AWWs and AWHs of these 9208 identified AWCs are paid an additional honorarium of Rs 250/ and Rs 125/ per month. Each of these AWCs has also been given Rs 1500/ per annum to meet out the contingent expenditure and Rs 5000/ for equipping them with TLM. For establishing convergence of SSA with that of ICDS, state task group with representatives from education, UNICEF, women and child development and health has been formulated. A further input includes agreeing on co-terminus, extended timings of ICDS centres and pro rata additional honorarium to AWWs. Under teacher education initiatives, the ICDS functionaries are not only being trained in AWTCs and MLTCs but also through DIETs on the lines of ECCE workers. In 52 DIETs of the state, ECE resource centers have been established. Besides DIETs, academic support is also being provided by BRCs and CRCs established under SSA and NPEGEL.

Uttaranchal

The state is using the net work of 6639 AWCs and 3356 Government run ECCE centres to impart publicly designed early educational experiences to children. Besides imparting training to AWWs by 18 AWTCs, the state has also employed DIETs to provide specific inputs on PSE to AWWs. Three NTT institutes have been imparting training in ECCE. In order to facilitate government run ECCE centres, the curriculum, student's evaluation cards, activity calendar, books have been developed by leading NGOs and SCERT. Though NTTIs institutes have been recognized by state education board but no mechanism has been set up to recognize private pre schooling. Convergence model of SSA and ICDS have not only yielded high enrolment of older girls in primary schooling but also has decreased repetition and failure rate in grade 1 and 2. 7 per cent primary schools in the state have pre primary sections. NCTE has only accredited one ECCE teacher education course in the state. Acknowledging the critical role of midday meal in increasing enrolment, retention and fostering equity, there is a government order to extend the scheme to cover all ECCE centers.

WESTERN REGION

Gujarat

1463 ECCE centers under NPEGEL component of SSA and 3723 under its innovative head have been opened in those areas where social conditions are difficult and/or state norms do not allow for opening of AWCs and/or the regions, which are located in scattered habitations. These centres, which have been opened by Gujarat Council of Primary Education, have been established in proximity of alternative schooling centres so that issue of sibling care may be attended to a large extent. The workers of these ECCE centers are being appointed with active involvement of Village Education Committees. The concept of toy bank is being implemented with the help of Reliance and Red Cross. In order to address the pedagogical concerns, activity based modules for children have been developed and disseminated. In order to facilitate the use of these modules, induction and orientation training have been imparted twice to all ECCE workers. Other major initiatives includes distribution of gender equity play cards, annual and monthly activity calendar, monthly review meeting of ECCE workers at block level, two days meet at district level for ECCE workers every four months to take stock of the day today functioning and learning based activities. Two state level workshops are held every year with all district gender coordinators to develop yearly strategy and action plans, to discuss issues and problems and to share experiences etc. During the year, Personality Development Workshops were also organized for ECCE workers, during which they were oriented on effective usage of TLM and other educational material provided under SSA. These state initiatives have not only resulted in enhancing the motivation among preschool children towards primary schooling but also have given rise of 9.48 per cent enrolment in standard 1.

Rajasthan

Recognizing the fact that state owned AWCs have the main focus on nutrition, immunization and health care, several initiatives have been taken up to strengthen the non-formal preschool education component of ICDS programme. For instance, the state from its own initiatives and financial resources has appointed one additional AWWs in the name of Sahyogini in all the AWCs. Thus, out of two AWWs, one is being exclusively engaged for imparting pre schooling and other has been assigned the job of attending care issues, which *inter alia* includes supplementation, health and well being etc as well as care of the children in the 0-3 age group in the crèche, if any. Other measures includes strengthening the provisions of ECE, extending the time of AWCs in accordance of primary schools, developing context specific TLM, orientation of ICDS team on TLM and kit material concerning ECE. Under SSA initiative, the operational time of AWCs has been extended to two hours more. The state has also taken several initiatives to impart ECE to children using Infrastructure and resources of primary schools as well. Besides this, annual PSE calendar has been developed to impart four hours pre schooling to 3-6 years children in AWC. All AWWs have been provided five days specialized training by expert trainers. In this five days long training on PSE programme, first specialized trainers demonstrates the PSE activities for them in day one and subsequently, the AWWs performs these activities in sequence during the remaining four days of the training. PSE guidebook, which may be termed as Rajasthan Strategy of PSE, contains the details of integrated day-to-day activities of PSE. This guide book was developed in the year of 2000 with twin objectives of (i) helping AWWs in organsing PSE activities under ICDS and (ii) helping the supervisory staff (District level officials, CDPOs and Supervisors) to ensure during the course of observation that PSE activities are being organized as per desired manner of ICDS scheme. The Rajasthan Strategy of PSE under ICDS is based on PSE annual calendar. The annual calendar of PSE is divided into 12 parts; one part has to be followed in each month of the year. Monthly activities are divided into weekly activities.

With the help of DIETs, an ECE experimental pilot project is also being implemented in nine districts of the State. Each DIET of the state has also adopted 25 AWCs to develop them as Child Friendly Centres (CFCs). Audio CD of ECE songs, rhymes, riddles and an animation film to advocate the concept of ECCE have also been developed in the state with the financial support from the UNICEF. Other innovation, which the state of Rajasthan is trying out includes joint training of AWWs with Primary School teachers, evolving community based monitoring system to strengthen ECE in CFCs and creation of ECE resource faculty and resource centre in all DIETs of the State. 380 Key Resource Persons (180 of ICDS and 200 of DIET) have also been trained in the state on various aspects of ECCE. These Key Resource Persons includes CDPOs, Lady Supervisors, Instructors of AWTCs and MLTCs, Faculty of DIETs and representatives of prominent NGOs.

Maharashtra

Public defined age group for pre schooling in India is 3-6 years but due to sub national system's variation in primary schooling age structure, nationally about 21.8 per cent of 5 year olds are enrolled in Std I class. In States like Rajasthan, MP, Himachal, Uttaranchal and Haryana, the Std I class in 2006-07 has more than 30 per cent of children who represents the age group of 5+. However, this case is not true in Maharashtra where this cohort (5+ age group in Std Class) constitutes a very little proportion of only 3.2 per cent of children. Similarly, the state has the advantage of enrolling more than 90 per cent of all four year olds in largest public based system of pre schooling (ICDS), which is not the case of other northern, western and central states accounting enrollment of less than 60 per cent of 4 years+ children. In view of the fact that PSE activities at the Anganwadi centres are very limited, the state in collaboration with Pratham (a leading NGO) had experimented an innovative strategy known as Shishuvachacn programme in 300 anganwadis located in slums of Pune city in 2004-05. The twin objective of the intervention was to introduce the children to formal education through informal means and ensuring that every child should acquire basic learning skills. Children in the age group of 4.5 to 5 years and children in standard one were covered under the intervention. The duration of shishuvachan was nine months, which came to around 120 days. Typically, around 15-20 children were enrolled in a class. Around 4.400 children participated in the sahishuvachan programme. The programme was conducted in 4 phases of 30 working days each. The programme provided the children constructive activities that enable them to learn reading and number recognition without stress. Besides imparting training to the members of the slum communities to teach basic skills of reading and number recognition to children in the age group of 4.5 to 5 years, the Pratham Shishuvachan teacher used to teach children for one hour at the local AWC. Specially designed teaching learning material was also provided to the children. The parents of the children were so enthusiastic about the intervention that one point of time, they formed their own committee to oversee the programme. The evaluation of the programme showed that the intervention not only helped in increasing children's attendance significantly but also in developing the reading and number recognition skills in just six months.

UT of Daman and Diu

Besides imparting ECE through 97 AWCs, 5 pre primary schools in Daman and 8 pre primary schools in Diu are also imparting PSE to children. 150 children in Daman and 240 children in Diu are enrolled in these schools. The school timings are 8 to 12.50 p.m. The PSE teacher in these schools is being assisted by a helper. The PSE teacher is getting honorarium of Rs 1200/ while helper is getting honorarium of Rs 500/ only. Unlike of 3-6 years as in case of ICDS, the children belonging to age group of 4 to 5 years are enrolled in these centres. These schools are located in government buildings. All AWCs are also running in Government buildings fully equipped with water, electricity and other civic amenities, except five which are in rented buildings. The AWCs are admitting the children from 3-6 years. A proper time table incorporating in door and outdoor games, national anthem, prayer has been given to each AWC. The total coverage under ECCE includes 8716 children (4731 children of 0-3 year's age group and 3985 children of 3-6 years age group). The government is targeting 100 per cent outreach of ECCE by all children with space of 2 per cent each for private and NGO sector. There has been no pre schooling policy in the UT.

NORTH EASTERN REGION

Assam

The centre based early childhood educational inputs are being delivered adopting fourfold modes. ICDS scheme is the largest provider of ECE services in the state. The programme delivers its non formal preschool education component inputs through 36835 operational AWCs located primarily within 223 ICDS projects. The average number of children per AWC attending PSE inputs is 33, which is, though, little higher than national average of 32 but much higher than the NE average regional attendance of 25 PSE children per AWC. Further, as per statistics (as on 29.02.2008) available for ECE initiatives under ICDS, the GPI index of the state comes out to be.96, which is, though equal to national GPI of ECE under ICDS but lower than the GPI for NE region of.97.

The second mode includes 199 pre primary/pre basic schools being run under directorate of elementary education with total enrollment of 746390 children (NER data bank, 2008). All these pre primary/pre basic schools are being managed by single teacher. Besides running these pre primary/pre basic schools, pre primary section has also been established in other schools. As such, 44.95 per cent of all type of such schools (primary, elementary and senior secondary) has attached pre primary section as well. Segmental statistics further shows that little more than half of total primary (54.53%) and senior secondary schools (52.05%) and six out of ten of each elementary school has attached pre primary section in the state. The percentage share of enrolment in pre primary classes to total enrolment is 17.59, 9.39, and 13.75 respectively in primary, elementary and senior secondary schools (NUEPA, 2007). The state has now developed a vision document, known as State Vision, 2025, envisaging to start pre primary classes in all the provincial and government schools (Government of Assam, 2009). For the accomplishment of this task, sizeable portion of primary teachers from all districts have been trained in ECE methodology so that they can take care of children of pre primary classes as well. The third mode of delivering the services includes Balwadis, which are being run by NGOs with support received from State Social Welfare Advisory Board. As per ASER survey 43.3 per cent of children (3-6 years) are attending AWCs, while 22 per cent of children are attending the pre primary inputs being provided under education department. 14 per cent of children in the age range of 3-6 years in the rural areas of the state are not receiving any type of PSE inputs.

Under erstwhile DPEP initiative, the ECE centres were established in the state under the name of Mukulikas and were generally been located in those areas which are uncovered by ICDS.

Community ownership of running the centre was witnessed from the fact that village education committees (VECs) and/or Mahila groups were managing the centre either by operating the same or by helping the ECE worker in preparation of TLM. Mukulikas were being run by locally recruited two ECE personnel known as Malini and Sahmalini. Academic support to these personnel was provided by block level resource personnel and through exposure visits. The experts worked out the appropriate curriculum involving principle of joyful learning and its monthly plan of transaction was used to be shared with Malini/Sahmalini in the cluster meetings held monthly. Further, review of TLMs, attendance, enrollment and decision about theme of the month also occupied the point of discussion in the agenda of the monthly meetings. MOU was also been signed between Deptt of Social Welfare and Deptt of Education regarding utilization of services of AWWs and resources of AWCs for running the pre primary classes. As per MOU, about more than 1500 AWWs were looking after the children of pre primary classes in addition to her own job responsibilities (Pandey, 2005). Thus AWW after opening her own AWC from 7.00 to 9.00 a.m. also operated pre primary classes from 9 to 12 p.m. or even 1.00 p.m. As a token of appreciation, the AWWs were paid an additional honorarium of RS 300/ and annual TLM grant of Rs 500/. The AWWs of pre primary classes underwent through training module jointly developed by NCERT and SCERT both. The activity books for children were also developed in local languages of Assamese, Bangla and Bodo. AWWs are being trained in phased manner to work as community based rehabilitation worker. Two Supervisors in each ICDS project have been identified to work as Multipurpose Rehabilitation Worker for early childhood disability detection and intervention.

Arunachal Pradesh

ICDS is the biggest public provider of ECE intervention in the state. In total, 85932 children are receiving non formal preschool education inputs from 4277 AWCs located across all districts of the state. The average number of children per AWC attending PSE inputs is 20, which is much lower than both the figures of national average (32) and the NE average attendance of 25 children per AWC. The GPI index of ECE under ICDS of the state comes out to be 1.00 showing the parity between both the sexes of boys and girls under ECE in ICDS. As per DISE data, little more than half of all type of schools

(56.10%) has attached pre primary sections in the state. DISE data further stipulates that percentage of all type of schools having Pre primary section has increased during recent past from 41.10 in 2005 to 56.10 in 2007. As a result, the percentage share to enrolment in pre primary classes to total enrolment has also got improved from 24.22 per cent at primary level in 2005 to 35.55 per cent in the year of 2007. As per DISE statistics available for 2006-07, about 60.92 per cent of primary schools, 43.68 per cent of elementary and 20.05 per cent of Sr. Secondary schools have attached pre-primary section in the state (NUEPA, 2007). In similarities of these two broad indicators, during 1991 to 2001, the pupil teacher ratio (PTR) has also improved in the state at pre/primary level from 50:1 to 34; 1. These average figures, however, only tell us a part of the story. There are significant interstate variations in the pupil teacher ratio. For example, in 1991, at the pre primary school level, the number of students per teacher in Dibang valley was 66:1 while in Tawang it was 34:1. In 2001, the highest and lowest pupil teacher ratio was observed in East Kameng (61:1) and West Kameng (19:1) at pre primary/primary level (Government of Arunachal Pradesh, 2006). The number of pre primary schools in the state is 57 with enrolment of 37,111 children (20,772 male and 16,339 female). The GPI index for children enrolled in these pre primary schools comes out to be.78, which is far below than the GPI of ECE under ICDS. As per ASER survey 32.67 per cent of children (3-6 years) are attending AWCs, while 22.57 per cent of children are attending the pre primary inputs being provided under education department. 26.16 per cent of children in the age range of 3-6 years in the rural areas of the state are not receiving any type of PSE inputs.

Manipur

In consonance with the national picture of ICDS, centre based non formal preschool education inputs are the biggest public provider of ECE intervention in the state. In total, 146734 children (74248 male and 72486 female) are receiving NFPSE inputs from 4605 AWCs located across all districts of the state. The average number of children per AWC attending PSE inputs is 19, which is much lower than both the figures of national average (32) and the NE average attendance of 25 children per AWC. The GPI index of ECE under ICDS of the state comes out to be.97 which is, higher than the GPI of national level and equal to GPI of NE region. As per DISE data, every seven out of ten schools (of all types) in the state have attached pre primary section. Segmental analysis of this broad indicator further put in for the fact that in just contrast of other north eastern states, number of such senior secondary schools (77.43%) are much higher than such primary (49.80%) and elementary schools (41.18%). Due to continuous emphasis being placed under SSA, DISE data further stipulates that percentage of all type of schools having pre primary section has gone up to 46.19 per cent in 2007. The percentage share to enrolment in pre primary classes to total enrolment is 17.17 for the year of 2006-07 with percentage share of 25.47 per cent in primary schools followed by 12.74 per cent in senior/higher secondary and lastly with 12.43 per cent at elementary school level (NUEPA,2007). As per ASER survey 34.97 per cent of children (3-6 years) are attending AWCs, while 24.32 per cent of children are attending the pre primary inputs being provided under education department. 16.14 per cent of children in the age range of 3-6 years in the rural areas of the state are not receiving any type of PSE inputs. So far as the qualitative inputs to strengthen the ECE inputs in the state is concerned, all Block Resource Centres including Districts Coordinators have been given training on PSE. Need based PSE training has also been imparted to all AWWs in the state. Development of data bank of PSE is on the cards (SSA, 2008). Pre Primary teacher education programme in Manipur is at the initial stage. There are more than seven pre primary teacher training institutes in Manipur which are functioning under control of private agencies. However, these institutions are developing day by day and contributing a lot in the field of pre primary education (Paul and Malemnganbi, 2008).

Meghalaya

As in case of other NE states like Arunachal Pradesh, Nagaland and Sikkim, the state of Meghalaya has also seen a quantitative jump in both the facility and enrolment based indicators of PSE under formal mode of educational ladder. As per enumeration made under DISE data, the percentage of all type of schools having pre primary section has increased from 68.22 in 2005 to 71.42 in 2007. As a result, the percentage share to enrolment in pre primary classes to total enrolment has also got improved from 26.87 per cent in 2005 to 29.55 per cent in the year of 2007 at senior secondary level and from 40.57 per cent in 2005 to 46.08 per cent in 2007 at elementary level. Currently, 85.39 per cent of primary schools, 78.95 per cent of elementary and 77.43 per cent of sr secondary schools have attached pre primary section in the state (NUEPA, 2007). As per ASER survey 33.2 per cent of children (3-6 years) are attending

AWCs, while 25.18 per cent of children are attending the pre primary inputs being provided under education department. 22.70 per cent of children in the age range of 3-6 years in the rural areas of the state are not receiving any type of PSE inputs.

The average number of children attending AWC (42) is much higher than the national average (32) and NE average attendance of 25 children per AWC. The GPI index of ECE under ICDS of the state comes out to be.99 showing the near parity between both the sexes of boys and girls. The GPI index comes out to be much higher than national and NE regional GPI index of.96 and.97 respectively. The NCTE has recognized only one course of teacher education concerning ECCE known as NTT with intake of 40 students located at Government normal training centre, Tura.

Mizoram

So far as imparting ECE inputs under formal schooling system is concerned, the state of Mizoram is running behind compared to other NE states of Nagaland and Sikkim. Though only little of 30.48 per cent of all type of schools have attached pre primary sections in the state, however, the state has seen tremendous improvement on this broad indicator of ECE under education department during the recent past. While only 20.03 per cent of all schools and 19.27 per cent of primary schools, 69.11 per cent of primary and upper primary schools, 77.27 of primary with upper primary and Sec/H. sec schools had pre primary sections in 2005, the figure rose to 35.67 per cent of such primary schools, 77.43 per cent of such elementary schools and 79.41 per cent of such sr secondary schools in 2007 (NIEPA,2005 and NUEPA, 2007). The percentage share of enrolment in pre primary classes to total enrolment has also gone up during these three past three years. The DISE statistics shows that the such percentage share, which was 6.98 in primary schools, 27.00 in primary with upper primary schools and 22.50 for primary with upper primary and sec/ higher secondary schools in 2005 has gone up to 16.40 per cent in primary schools, 30.58 per cent in primary with upper primary schools and 28.71 per cent in primary with upper primary and sec/ higher secondary schools (op ciit). Under PG course of Education, ECE is being offered by Mizoram University as one of the optional paper for the students (Mizoram University, 2009).

The average number of PSE children per AWC is 17, which is much lower than the national average and NE regional average of

25 PSE children per AWC. The GPI index of ECE under ICDS of the state comes out to be the same as that of the state of Meghalaya (.99). The GPI index comes out to be much higher than national and NE regional GPI index of.96 and.97 respectively. As per ASER survey 57.25 per cent of children (3-6 years) are attending AWCs, while 14.35 per cent of children are attending the pre primary inputs being provided under education department. 14.32 per cent of children in the age range of 3-6 years in the rural areas of the state are not receiving any type of PSE inputs.

Nagaland

The stage or ladder of education system in Nagaland is slightly different from the central pattern. All Government Primary Schools (GPS), which are 1442 in number, have one year pre primary class attached to it. Thus, a primary school has five classes from pre primary to Class IV and middle school has classes from V-VIII with or without primary section attached (Government of India, 2008). 95.34 per cent of Primary Schools, 91.11 of elementary schools and 95.20 per cent of sr secondary schools have attached pre primary wing in the state. So far as share of enrolment in pre primary to total enrolment is concerned, it has come highest for primary schools with 41.14 per cent followed by 20.32 per cent in sr secondary schools and 17.42 per cent in elementary schools (NUEPA, 2007).

The state has not only extended centre based pre primary inputs in quantified terms but has also focused on quality of teacher education as well. With the approval of the State Cabinet vide O.M. NO. CAB-2/2008 dated 31.07.2008, the Government of Nagaland has formulated the State Policy for Recruitment of Teachers at different levels of education including PSE. The said policy has been formulated as per the guidelines issued by NCTE, Delhi. As per this State Policy for Recruitment of Teachers, the essential qualification to become preschool teacher includes 10+2 (pre university degree) with preschool teacher education or diploma in ECCE. The Governor of Nagaland vide office policy circular NO EDS (A)-5/2002 dt. 27.10.2008 has given relaxation of such policy in respect of candidates who do not possess the prescribed qualification with the condition that appointment of a person shall be allowed without having such required professional qualification. However, the shortlist candidate has to give an undertaking that he/she will undergo the professional course and clear it within two years failing which his/her services will be terminated. Till such time, she/he will obtain the qualification, the appointment shall be adhoc, on fixed pay. These candidates shall be eligible for regular absorption only after when he/she will attain the required professional qualification. During a period a candidate shall go on professional training, the vacancy caused shall be met through re deployment and not through substitute appointment. Those appointed candidates, who may not get the opportunity of undergoing such professional courses in DIETs, may take the admission to acquire the professional qualification from any of the recognized private institutions and the course fee will be subsidized by the Government to the extent of 50 per cent. This relaxation will be valid from 27th Oct, 2008 for a period of three years. The relaxation has the approval of the Cabinet vide OM No CAB -2/2008 dt. 31.7.2008.

The centre based ECE inputs under ICDS is being provided by 3194 AWCs. The total enrolment in these AWCs is 116653 (59230 male and 57423 female) with GPI index of.96. The average number of PSE children per AWC is 36, which is little higher than national and much higher than NE regional level figure of 25 PSE children per AWC.

Sikkim

The early childhood education services are being delivered adopting fourfold mode. ICDS scheme is the largest provider of ECE services in the state. The programme delivers its non formal preschool education component inputs through 988 operational AWCs located primarily within 11 ICDS projects. The average number of children per AWC attending PSE inputs is 33, which is little higher than national and NE regional average. As per statistics (as on 28.02.2008) available for ECE initiatives under ICDS, the GPI of the state comes out to be.96, which comes to be at par with national GPI and lower than the GPI of ECE under ICDS for NE region. The second mode includes 739 pre primary/pre basic schools being operated under directorate of elementary education. The total enrolment in these Pre Primary Schools is 23615. One pre primary school, which is in control of Central Government, is also running in the state with enrolment of 80 children. There are three Government Aided Schools with 385 students. There are 351 private pre schools with 12406 students in the state. Besides running these pre primary/pre basic schools, pre primary section has also been established in other schools. As such, 44.95 per cent of all type of schools has attached pre primary sections. Segmental analysis further shows that only 54.53 per cent of Primary schools,, 59.98 per cent of elementary schools and 52.05 per cent of senior secondary schools are having pre primary section in the state. The percentage share of pre primary to total enrolment is 17.59 per cent for primary level, 9.39 per cent for primary with upper primary level and 13.75 per cent for primary with sr/higher sec level (NUEPA, 2007). The average number of children attending AWC (13) is much lower than the national average.

In total 855 preschool teachers are serving in Government Schools out of which 350 are trained and 505 are untrained. Thus, clearing the backlog of pre primary teachers has become a major concern in the state. In about 80 per cent of private schools, majority of teachers are untrained. In Government schools, the children are being admitted on the basis of age and the residence certificate. The age for admission in private schools varies from 2 and half years to three years while in government Schools, the age of admission is 4+. The duration of pre schooling in Government schools is one year while it is two years in private schools (LKG and UKG). The medium of Instruction is English, second language is regional or mother tongue and the third is Hindi. Most of the children attend school from the long distance of about 2-3 km. The teachers working in government schools are known as school mother. The main idea behind this nomenclature being that, the person appointed at this level should be motherly, a mother in school who cares for and nurture the child in the best way possible (Rasaily, 2008). Cooked Mid Day Meal is served to all children of Sikkim up to primary level. Though central norms includes serving MDM to children of only class 1-5, however, the pre primary children are also included as pre primary classes are attached to primary schools and children of this level also deserves cooked MDM. This is being done to as added incentives to foster more enrolment and to curb dropout rates (Government of Sikkim, 2008). There is no tuition fee from Pre Primary Stage till degree level in the state. Sikkim State Plan of Action, for Children has been prepared. The education department has been granting scholarship of SC/ST and OBC populations living below poverty line from LKG to Class IV @ Rs 360/ per student per academic year (*op. cit*).

Tripura

Besides imparting non formal preschool education through a wide net work of 7351 ICDS centres in the state, the Deptt of Social Welfare has also introduced 823 Social Education Centres with enrolment of 42,268 children run exclusively from state funds and are providing services similar to ICDS (Government of Tripura, 2008). The workers of these centres have been designated as Social Education Organizer and are class III employee of the state government. Forty per cent of AWWs are being absorbed in these centres on seniority basis (Pandey, 2005). The GPI of ECE under ICDS comes out to be.97 and the average number of children per AWC is 17, which is much lower than the national and NE regional average of PSE children per AWC. Though the percentage distribution of schools having pre primary section has increased in primary schools with 2.18 per cent of such schools in 2005 to 2.95 per cent of primary schools in 2007 and 4.10 per cent of primary with upper primary schools in 2005 to 5.96 per cent of such schools in 2007, however, surprisingly such distribution has come down in case of primary with upper primary and sec/higher secondary schools with 11.30 per cent in 2005 to 5.81 per cent schools in 2007. The percentage share of enrolment in pre primary classes to total enrolment has also come down during the past three years in the state. Such figure which was 2.49, 2.74 and 2.53 for primary, primary with upper primary and primary with upper primary and sec/ higher sec level respectively in the year of 2005 has come down to 1.77, 2.27 and 1.51 for primary, primary with upper primary and primary with upper primary and sec/higher sec level respectively in the year of 2007 (NIEPA, 2005 and NUEPA,2007).

Summing Up

After going through various public initiatives taken up by *north, west and centrally located States* of the country for expanding the coverage and strengthening the quality inputs of centre based pre-schooling, it may be summarized that operational approaches are basically comprised of three fold efforts. These include pre-schooling under formal mode of primary and elementary education, strengthening ICDS based pre schooling and regulatory mechanism to put check and balances on different aspects of pre schooling. Within the broader framework of *first* category, the approach includes SSKs in MP, Bachpanshalas in Haryana and ECCE centres in Gujarat and UP. Likewise, attachment of pre primary sections in primary schools (Chhattisgarh with 15.96 per cent, Haryana with 54.75 per cent, MP with 38.04 per cent, Maharashtra with 36.18 per cent, Delhi with 39.04 %) and elementary schools (HP with 72.77 %, Haryana with 29.62, MP with 49.36 Uttaranchal with 27.29%) also comes under this category. *Second* strategy includes strengthening ICDS based pre schooling. The multi pronged thrust of this approach encompasses two worker model with one exclusively for pre schooling as in case of Rajasthan, involvement of DIETs in imparting training to AWW as in case of UP, MP, Uttaranchal, Rajasthan and Haryana, Shishuvachasn programme in Maharashtra, involvement of community in monitoring of pre schooling services like in HP, Rajasthan, provision of training and supply of teaching learning material by utilizing the SSA funds available under innovative head and the like. The *third* strategy includes regulation of admissions and age structure as being underway in the state of Delhi.

Similarly, after going through various public initiatives adopted in the recent past for universal provision of ECE inputs in different *states of NE region,* it can be safely inferred that the quantitative expansion of ECCE facilities, particularly in terms of ICDS centres with full coverage of all community development blocks and ECE under Education Department, has been phenomenal. Though, most of the NE states are seem to be doing very well in this regard (UNESCO, 2009). However, the actual outreach and coverage per AWC is far below than the national average. There is tremendous disparity in covering ECE children per AWC across the eight sister states of the region with Arunachal Pradesh (20), Assam (33), Manipur (19), Meghalaya (42), Mizoram and Tripura (17), Nagaland (36), Sikkim (13). In order to understand the variations in the level of participation of children in ICDS based ECE inputs, additional data concerning various socio-economic and developmental aspects and to different dimensions of community life and development viz.–demographic, social, cultural, political and economic are needed to be generated (*op. cit*). Another point, which deserves to be mentioned over here, is strengthening the linkage between ECE and primary education programmes. Though, many states of NE region have established pre primary section in primary, upper primary and senior/higher secondary schools, but some states like

Tripura is lagging behind in this facility based indicator of expansion of ECCE services across the state. Apart from quantitative expansion of centre based ECE inputs, there have also been efforts to create alternative models of the same. The effort made in this direction particularly in the state of Tripura by opening of Social Education Centres and in Assam by opening of Mukulikas is worth mentioning. In addition, there have also been attempts to create convergence between ongoing programmes of ICDS and ECE activities, especially for qualitative expansion of the scope of ICDS programme as in case of Manipur and in Assam. In spite of all these efforts, the challenge in expanding the ECCE facilities to all children is enormous as many of the preschool children residing in rural areas of NE region are not attending any centre based inputs of ECE either from ICDS and/or from schooling based pre primary inputs/other alternative models.

In case of states located in *southern region of the country*, it may be summarized that operational approaches are basically comprised of three fold efforts. These include experimentation with alternative models, convergence with ICDS and regularity mechanism to put check and balances on different aspects of nursery education. Within the broader framework of former category, the approach includes setting up of zero grade Pre Primary Centres and Nursery Cum Women Welfare Centres for Schedule Caste Children in Karnataka and ECCE centres under SSA/NPEGEL in Andhra Pradesh and Kerala. Likewise, attachment of pre education sections in primary and elementary schools in all the four states of southern India also comes under this category. Second strategy includes convergence with ICDS. The multi pronged thrust of this approach encompasses synchronisation of timings of AWCs with that of primary schools like in Karnataka, location of AWCs in or near primary schools like in Andhra Pradesh and provision of training and supply of material for strengthening the quality of ECCE component of ICDS like in Andhra Pradesh, Karnataka, Tamilnadu and Kerala. The third strategy includes regulation of admissions and age structure as being under way in the state of Karnataka.

In conclusion, it may be stated that though various States/UTs located in northern, western and central zone of India are striving hard for ubiquitous presence of qualitative pre schooling interventions, yet we have to keep in mind that it should not be done in separation of contextual sensitivity. In fact, there is a need of undertaking micro level planning employing case-to-case method so that access of ECCE by all eligible children is ensured far ahead of two declarations; A world fit for Children and Dakar deadline of 2015 (Pandey, 2005).

Abbreviations Used

ASER	-	Annual Status Education Report
AWC	-	Anganwadi Centre
AWW	-	Anganwadi Worker
AWTC	-	Anganwadi Workers Training Centre
BRC	-	Block Resource Centre
CSWB	-	Central Social Welfare Board
CDPO	-	Child Development Project Officer
CRC	-	Cluster Resource Centre
DIET	-	District Institute of Education and Training
DISE	-	District Information System for Education
DPEP	-	District Primary Education Programme
DWCD	-	Department of Women and Child Development
DSW	-	Department of Social Welfare
ECE		Early Childhood Education
ECCE	-	Early Childhood Care and Education
GPI		Gender Parity Index
GPS		Government Primary School
ICCW	-	Indian Council for Child Welfare
ICDS	-	Integrated Child Development Services Scheme
LRG	-	Local Resource Group
MDM	-	Mid Day Meal
MOU	-	Memorandum of Understanding
MLTC	-	Middle Level Training Centre
NCTE	-	National Council of Teacher Education
NER	-	North Eastern Region
NGO	-	Non Governmental Organisation
NCERT	-	National Council for Educational Research and Training
NIEPA	-	National Institute of Educational Planning and Administration
NIPCCD	-	National Institute Public Cooperation and Child Development
NTT	-	Nursery teachers Training
NCTE	-	National Council of Teachers Education
NUEPA	-	National University of Educational Planning and Administration
PG	-	Post Graduate
PTA	-	Parent Teacher Association
PSE	-	Pre School Education
RGNCS	-	Rajiv Gandhi National Crèche Scheme
SCERT	-	State Council of Educational Research and Training

SSA - Sarva Shiksha Abhiyan
TLM - Teaching Learning Material
VEC - Village Education Committee

REFERENCES

Deccan Herald (2005), Pre Primary schools to be leashed.

Early Childhood Programmes: Setting the pace for learning (1997), Education for All Bulletin No. 28. Available at www2.unesco.org/efa.index.html.accessed 1st sep, 2002.

Government of Assam (2009), *http://www.assamgovt.nic.in* accessed on 15.01/2009 at 2.52 p.m.

Government of Arunachal Pradesh (2006), Arunachal Pradesh Human Development Report. Itanagar.

Government of India (2008), Report on Monitoring of Financial Management and Procurement Relating to SSA in Nagaland. Conducted by Institute of Public Auditors of India.

Government of Sikkim (2009), Education in Sikkim. *http://www.sikkim.nic.in* accessed on 13.01.2009. at 5.00.p.m.

Government of Tripura (2009), Social Education in Tripura. http://www.tripura.nic.in accessed on 15.01.2009 at 3.27 p.m.

Hernandez, D.J. (1998), Economic and Social Disadvantages of Young Children: Alternative Policy Responses. In Barnett, W.S. and Boocock, S.S. (Eds) Early Care and Education for Children in Poverty: Promises, Programmes and Long Term Results. State University of New York Press. 185.

Hindustan Times (2007), Top City Schools in Nursery Trouble.

Mizoram University (2009), *www.mzu.edu.in* accessed on 15.01.2009.

National Council of Educational Research and Training (2000), Early Childhood Care and Education in DPEP—I. An Assessment Mimeo, New Delhi.

National Institute of Educational Planning and Administration and United Nations Educational, Scientific and Cultural Organisation (2003), Different Approaches for achieving EFA—Indian Experience, Mimeo, New Delhi.

National Institute of Educational Planning and Administration (2003) Elementary Education in India-Where do we stand, New Delhi.

NER Data Bank (2008), *http://databank.nedfi.com/index accessed on 15.01.2009* National Institute of Educational Planning and Administration (2005). Elementary Education in India. Progress Towards Universalisation of Elementary Education.

National University of Educational Planning and Administration (2007), Elementary Education in India. Progress Towards Universalisation of Elementary Education.

Pandey. D.D (2005), Expanding Early Childhood Education: Cross State Experiences. *Research Reach-Journal of Home Science*. Vol. 4. No 1. Jan 2005. pp. 1-8.

Paul. S and Malemnganbi. Kh (2008), Teacher Education in Manipur. *Journal of All India Association of Educational Research*. Vol. 20, Nos. 1 and 2. March and June, 2008. pp. 61-2.

Rasaily, Anjali (2008), A Study of Curriculum Load on Pre Primary Children in Sikkim. Unpublished.

Sarva Shiksha Abhiyan (2008), http://www.ssamanipur.nic.in accessed on 20.09.2008 at 8.00 p.m.

Stern, R.W. (1993), *Changing India: Bourgeois Revolution on the Subcontinent.* Cambridge, Cambridge University Press.

Times of India (2007a), Nursery Admission Creates New Castes.

Times of India (2007b), Government Appeals, Settles for 3.5 years.

UNESCO (2003), Education for All: Global Monitoring Report, 2003, Chapter 1.

UNESCO (2009).

http://www.padmavatiwomen-univ.org/prospectus0809.pdf accessed on 10.11,.2008.

http://www.osmania.ac.in/ accessed on 10.11.2008.

www.dwcd.kar.nic.in_english/ICDS accessed on 13.11.2008.

www;//sw/kar.nic.in/edn_files/edn schemes accessed on 13.11.2008.

www://kerala.gov.in/dept_st/index accessed on 10.11.2008.

www://indianews.net accessed on 28.08.2007.

15

Strategic Transformation of Business Education

The Mentor's Vision

Mrs. Vani N. Laturkar

SCENARIO OF BUSINESS EDUCATION IN INDIA

Today, business education system exists as a part of a large system—the Global system. Change in any part of this system certainly gives a cause-effect relationship. The globalization has given only one message, "we can run, but we cannot hide, we can either be relevant or victim of change. The choice is ours. Which means doing away with old, traditional conservation patterns, old standards and relevance to new improvements?"

Surely an academic discipline like management, as old as hundred years, should not be allowed to be a casualty through negligence, self-complacency and indifference on the part of various officers and authorities of the academic world. In fact every academic faculty and discipline aims at achieving the welfare of the society. But it is hardly remembered that policies and values once laid down could never be true forever. Thus all the programme framed by these authorities should be viable tested on following parameters:

(a) Need based as per time, place, people, etc.;
(b) Self renovating through additions, modifications, curtailments, Extensions, updates and up gradations;
(c) Generative of new ideas, opportunities, methods, techniques and Attitudes;
(d) Catering to the growth of the faculties such as intellectual, moral, Cultural and aesthetic needs.

It is rightly said—unless the ship changes its course, it is sure to collide against the lighthouse which cannot shift its position and is meant to guide ship to avoid collusion! Same must not happen with the business education programme too.

The management experts have come to a consensus that to be competitive, one needs to be aware of Economics, Environment and Ethics. But does it really means chasing latest technologies and mechanical fundamentals only? There are no two opinions about keeping oneself updated with latest information and other technologies, but is it the ultimate aim we aim at? Has anybody quantified the speed of change? Is anybody able to predict its direction? An appropriate incidence can be stated over here:

A barber refused to shave a customer. When asked about the reason, barber clarified, "We no longer provide this service as the business in this line is very low. Today we found that women keep boy-cuts as latest fashion while men grow their hair. So just now we have changed our saloon from a barber's saloon to the beauty parlor for hair-settings. This is according to the choice of customer who is the ultimate God."

Whether the management students produced today are wise enough to prove them readily adaptable and rational decision-makers? The institutes may be providing campus placements to them, but how far it could give a back up in life to those being placed? Possibly, the answer is not much pleasing. Then where is the Gap?

It is the need of the hour to make Zero-base budgeting in management programmes. And the moment one does so, he will find that though practical orientation is the ultimate choice, but it is creation of such management graduates who can think in wise terms by their own based on cautious ethical values being exercised even in worst circumstances. In short, it is the commitment of the producers of these graduates, that is their teachers, who have to devote themselves in nurturing the programme of business education in such a way that it creates a perfect fruit fit to demand always. For this, let us peep into a theory called Learning Tree concept which could help the management institutes in finding solutions to all these problems.

TRANSFORMING MANAGEMENT FACULTY INTO FACILITATORS

"The Indian philosophy supports teaching; Japanese philosophy finds its base in training while a Socratic philosophy involves facilitation as its main parts".

Mentoring and nurturing the students has its roots deeply engraved into ancient gurukuls "guru-shishya parampara". The profile of a guru used to be more of a mentor and of student-a mentee in spite of being a pure teacher and a taught.

Truly, nobody can work with absolute perfection all at a time. However, management teachers can become facilitators by producing such students who have capability and willingness to stand to the expectations of all. They dare to dream without aiming at readymade placements from their management institutes. They plan for starting their own business unit where they could employ people with them. Possibly, the biggest irony of business education institutes are of quality education on one side and campus placement to all the students at all times on the other. This could be solved by this philosophy. Though the idea seems to be theoretical, if one looks into ancient scriptures of this country like Vedic and Gurukuls philosophies, the same will directly hit your heart agreeable to mind and heart both.

MANAGEMENT FACULTIES-TURNING INTO A FACILITATOR

Think of your own values and character as a teacher. Have cautious sensitivity that values in educational sphere are going down. A facilitator could very well inculcate values in students through role models, practicing them consistently, keeping time and commitment to works and accepting the fact whole-heartedly that students learn more from what they see rather than what they hear or read.

A facilitator is one who develops the thinking and learning capacity of his student. He is never a problem-solver instead he makes the student to open-up the hidden threads of natural behaviour by focusing on cause-effect relationship. Sharing of knowledge is the crux of this scenario where he shares even the questions creation session with his students. Facilitation can be explained in a simple fashion by the use of learning tree concept.

The Learning Tree: It is a device of facilitating the teaching function. The concept of learning tree necessarily is based on the *"being concept"*—the passion and presence of mind and heart desiring of *serving the students*. It calls for having a attitude of gratitude of thanking in heart everyone who has placed you in this teacher's dignified position.

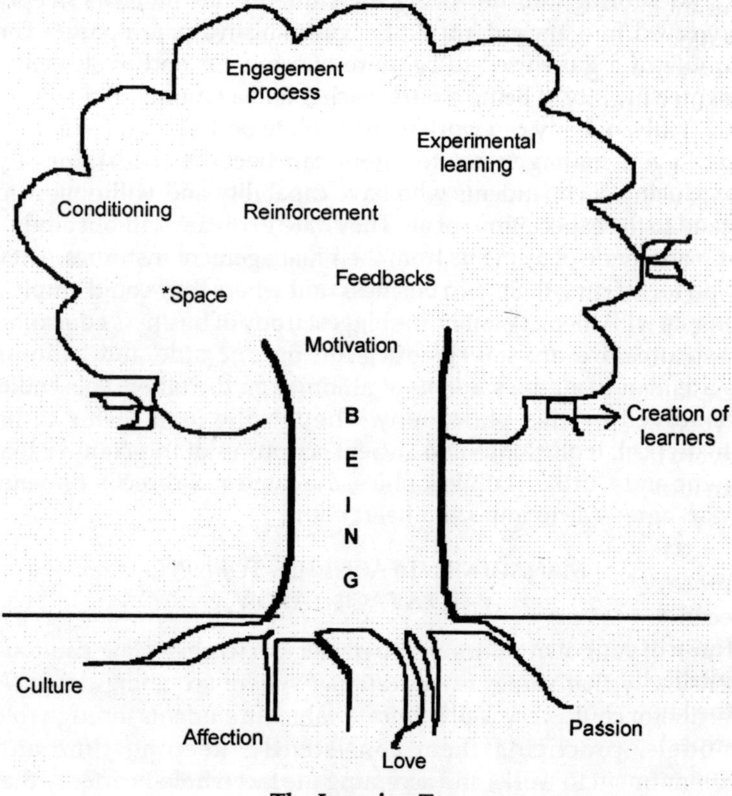

The Learning Tree

**space: providing space to students to mould the teachers learning while teaching.*

Learning tree is a theory which works in parity with the theory of nature. A seed being sown is nurtured by nature but reaps qualitative fruits only if specific and scientific efforts are taken on it. Students are like seeds, to be developed with deliberate efforts. Any negligence on this part leads to spoiled genes ultimately making long term destruction to the individual and his organization and possibly by the time it is being realized, the things are out of control. Learning tree concept is a deliberate nurturing of management professionals through a facilitation function. Facilitation is helping the person in developing to his ultimate capacity. A management course student is like a raw seed with high potentials. He needs a favorable environment in his educational institute where he is treated as one for whom the set-up is meant for. The student has to be cared with affection, love, cultural outlook and passion which make deep impressions in his mind and heart throughout his life. They grow as fast as a healthy plant as a result of proper motivation, feedback, reinforcement, engagement, conditioning, engagement process and a freehand to have experimental learning in the programme itself. This ultimately results in a healthy fruit which can withstand the competitive world with capacity to sow their seeds and create more plants like them.

This theory could be easily initiated through an engagement process from the first session itself. A proper combination of convergent and divergent thinking process helps in evoking the thought, clarifying the expectations about what is to be achieved, explaining the how's and why's of it and enlisting the norms of when and in what way to reach to it. To put if more specifically, every facilitator indulges himself as well as students while creating an understanding of any topic or subject in this engagement process as a part of learning tree.

The non-technical subjects give a wide scope of using this process. In subjects like organizational psychology, communication, economics, students could evoked by attracting their attention towards latest happenings which they can think of with a normal intelligence and a meager experience. Common sense literally means the knowledge of basic-time-tested and which never change. Their expectations could be aroused by making them think about why's and how's of those happenings and defining and explaining what is the particular aim of understanding this concept currently discussed in class. The norms will act as tracks on which the discussion and thinking should flow so as to reach to final understanding of various parameters targeted in the earliest part of session.

Possibly one may argue that this process can be used effectively in social sciences and arts but for technical subjects like accounting and finance, statistics, engineering and medical it is hardly possible. Let it be clarified at this point that no good teaching can be without attentive and desiring students. One has to use AIDA model in this sphere too *i.e.* attracting, arousing interest, creating desire and putting one in action. It is all about your devotion and involvement in this profession which matters.

A teacher of finance, say while dealing with technical topic like working capital management of corporate, could also use this engagement process:

Evoke: Hey, you all are here, May I ask you a personal question? Amit, how much cash you keep in your wallet every time at an average (cash management) or who according to you is best inventory manager in your family? (Mother) or your friend is ready to buy your old mobile but on credit, what will you do before deciding on the issue? (Receivables management)

Expectations: How and why cash, inventories and receivables are managed in personal and corporate life? Concretizing the aim of understanding management of cash, inventory and receivables and how they create an operating cycle.

Explain: Discussing about the concept as students understand by their common/logical sense and how the same is applied in a company.

Enlisting: Putting down the functions, nature, scope and limitations of all the aspects involved in working capital management and ending with concluding remarks about the whole session.

This example itself proves that a technical subject to get learned easily if the students get interested in understanding it. It is nothing then "putting them on fire", igniting the fire of curiosity leading them to the path of clarity of thought and expression.

FROM TEACHING TO TRAINING TO FACILITATION

As such *facilitation demands listening rather than talking*. Facilitator strategically plans his teaching-training-facilitation programme. A business education teacher as a facilitator is never expected to give advice as his right, on the contrary effective listening has to be the crux of this relationship. In majority cases, if the subject is conceptually clear in the mind of the student, the problem or confusions will be solved by wise solution thoughts flashing the mind of the speaker while he clarifies his thought for expressing his problem.

A facilitator is required to do homework on what his clients need? If a management teacher starts thinking of himself as a trainer and final as a facilitator, he will find, that *there is a gap, everything is not so good,* then where to improve? In spite of making this function complex by putting it as a theory, general perspectives could be focused to make it simple:

- How to differentiate, yourself in clatter of management education institutes with large number of faculties?

- Position yourself-whether you are a part of Gyanmandir or an educational factory or somewhere in between?
- What is your focus-quality or quantity?
- Are you accountable for quality of management degree holders you produce?

HOW TO BECOME A FACILITATOR

Once it is clear in heart that for merely passing of information from books to students is the right of libraries and not of teachers, the idea of becoming a facilitator automatically works over there. The qualities of a facilitator get so deeply embedded into the personality of a teacher that the integration and internalization of these concepts are reflected in his routine behaviour in a very natural way. The Learning Tree theory could be very-well applied in business education programmes. What is needed beforehand is:

- Knowing the subject both at micro level and macro level.
- Making use of internet, journals, engagement process and various facilitation methods.
- Believing that the learners have to be created who can discover the knowledge by themselves as the ultimate fruits of the learning trees.

The learning tree theory necessarily comprises of well-planned presentations, deductive or inductive methods of discussion, case studies, role play and simulation, management games, on the project training or learning, demonstrations and some minor methods like playgroup exercises like debate, quiz, brainstorming, synectics, group discussions, attribute listings etc. Keeping the ultimate target of reaping quality fruits serves the purpose.

SUMMING UP

Truly said by paying money you cannot change attitude. No norms are needed to be forcefully applied by universities, AICTE, UGC or any other law to transform teachers, especially the management teachers as they do have awareness of competitiveness needed in these times to sustain themselves as well as their products. It is only peeping in our own divine soul which could feel the soul of others too.

Transformation of business education teachers as facilitators ought to apply this cognitive dissonance theory called Learning Tree which demands a mental conflict in the minds of teachers about what they believed, what they do and what they ought to do. One simply needs to look from the eyes of students and the sky will be clear.

REFERENCES

Chakrawal, A.K. (2005), Business Education in Changing Scenario, *Asia Pacific Business Review*, Vol. 1, Jan.-June 2005, p. 93.

Doyle Brian and O'Neill N. Vincent (2007), *Mentoring Entrepreneurs: Shared Wisdom from Experience*, Prentice Hall of India, pp. 3-7.

Dudeja, V.D. (1999), *The Progressive Manager and Corporate Excellence*, Kanishka Publishers, New Delhi, pp. 14-16.

Laturkar, V.N. (2002)-"T.A.: The Road For Core Teaching Competency", First International Conference, All India Association of Teachers Educators, Rajghat, New Delhi. Collin Beard and John P. Wilson (2007), "Experimental Learning", Viva Books, pp. 17-19.

Patil, V.T. (2002), "University Curricula vis-à-vis National Needs and Global Trends: The Indian Experience", *University News*, Vol. 40 (10), March 11-17, 2002, p. 18.

16

Quality Concerns in Higher Education

Geetika Agarwal

Higher education occupies an important place at the apex of the educational pyramid and helps developing the cream of the society–a select group of individuals–physically, intellectually, emotionally and socially. Higher education is universally recognized as a major driver of economic and social development, in both more and less affluent countries.

Defining quality in education is a massive challenge since it deals with the most sensitive creation on earth–human beings. Industrial products are finished goods–take them or leave them. Nothing can be done once they are finished. Service is here and now. You can look for better quality only next time. Education has no such finished product, nor even the graduates. They are on the way 'to be'. Education only charges the human propensities to evolve and unfold it till the last breath, a process that covers the human journey from 'womb to tomb'. Human beings continue to learn, and evolve, 'to be'. Education facilitates this very evolution of the individual.

CONCEPT OF QUALITY

Quality is a highly debatable theme. Quality has been the goal of an eternal quest through the corridors of human history. It has been the driving force for the entire human Endeavour. Quality is the inspiration for transcendence from the mundane to the higher realms of life. It is the source of craving behind the unfolding human civilization through ages immemorial.

According to the Oxford English Dictionary, the notion of quality includes all the attributes of a thing, except those of relation and quantity. The British Standards Institution (BSI) (1991) defines quality in functional terms as the totality of features and characteristics of a product or service that bear upon its ability to satisfy the stated or implied needs.

The assurance of quality and standards of higher education is now widely recognized as a fundamental pre-requisite requirement, if we are to be confident that the huge potential benefits of higher education for individuals, economies and societies will be achieved. Looking at the importance of quality, there is an urgent need in the country towards the development of knowledge and understanding of the practice of quality assurance in higher education.

The realization of uniformity in quality standards has been one of the major challenges before the higher education planners, as well as the other stakeholders in the country. The basic theory of the service quality management explains that the problem of quality variation is due to the human oriented nature of the higher education services. However, in the present era of knowledge driven society, one needs to delve deep into the problem to identify and explore the real factors behind quality variation, both in the output as well as the process.

In Indian higher education system, a number of positive measures have been initiated by the various higher education regulating agencies including the Assessment and Accreditation Council of University Grants Commission (NAAC-UGC) and National Board for Accreditation of All India Council for Technical Education (NBA-AICTE). The experience shows that despite all these initiatives, the fundamental objectives of quality, as conceptualized by these agencies.

When it comes to the efficiency and effectiveness of the quality management system, as used in higher education there are a number of questions or areas, which need immediate attention of all the concerned. The present paper aims to explore the critical issues relating to the quality concerns in the higher education institutions of the country.

1. Infrastructure

Paradoxically, India being the largest country of illiterates takes the credit of operating one of the largest higher education system in the world. At the time of independence it had only 19 universities and 636 colleges with a student enrollment of about

1, 06,000 in 1947. Despite the constraint of resources, the quantitative expansion has been highly spectacular in the post–independence period. Our literacy has been constantly improving over the years (36.17 in the 1970's 52.19 in 1991 and 65.38 in 2001). We have more than 300 universities, deemed universities, thousands of colleges, hundreds of engineering colleges, IIT's, IIM's, medical colleges and scores of agricultural universities and equally large fund crunching science and industrial councils, scores of national regional laboratories and many other such units. These deliver their products in large numbers, who need employment. It has produced a mismatch of supply and demand. The largest educated middle class is faced with the nightmare of unemployment and unemployable graduates even in science, agriculture, engineering, social science and medicine.

The higher education services by its very basic nature have direct impact on the all sectors of environment in both societal as well as in task environment. Even a minor change in the higher education structure may trigger a corresponding major change in the environment and may further be subjected to the change itself due to the changes in the environment sector(s). This bi directional flow of impact makes the higher education structure very complex as compared to other service sector organizations.

These trends are the indicators of how the important factors in the higher education environment of the country are changing. In order to develop an effective quality management system of higher education, it should be linked to the overall strategic planning framework of the institution.

2. Curriculum

The higher education in our country suffers from many defects as far as curriculum is concerned. Excessive stress on theory takes precedence over the practical aspect and forces the students away from the real life. The syllabus lacks integration between general and skill-oriented vocational education. The recent trend of entrance tests have no relevance with the course content taught in the classes. The syllabus for any level should be designed in consultation with the teachers teaching at that level and should be realistic and inter-disciplinary. Academic programmes should be integrated and students with varying interests should be accommodated in it. There should be enough space for everyone involved: teachers, students

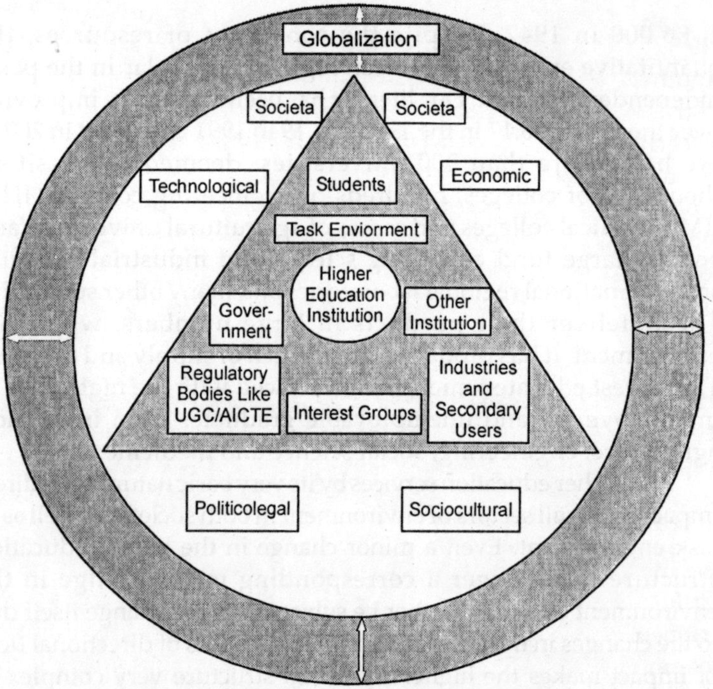

Fig. 1: Framework for Environmental Analysis

and parents. The feedback provided should be constantly acted upon. The courses should breakdown the monotony of the traditional courses; they should be both innovative and job-oriented. In regard to the choice of subjects, there should be number of options available to the students. Computer-friendly gadgets like VCDs, DVDs, CD-ROMs and floppies can be utilized to produce study materials and reduce the burden of students. Computers can also be utilized to access relevant materials from the internet, help students have direct contact with the teachers via e-mail, voice-mail and chatting, produce computer generated presentations to accompany lectures, use real current databases for research and conduct video-conferencing sessions with students from abroad. The best brains can be utilized for the production of self-instructional and audio-visual material in different languages.

3. Methods of Teaching

Another rapid change that is taking place is in the domain of instruction and pedagogy, and educational technology. Methods of teaching should be highly diverse. Lecturing will no doubt linger. But techniques like discussion, role-play, field work, laboratory experimentation, simulation and gaming will move rapidly to the centre stage. The mode of instruction should emphasize student constructed knowledge and interactive nature of learning. Emerging educational technology like telecommunication and computers will reshape practically entire spectrum of teaching methods. This technology factor will take over in rapid strides and encourage autonomous learning. Instead of just remaining at the receiving end, the students will be expected to assume increasing responsibility for managing their own learning.

4. Teachers

The most important component of the instructional process is the teacher who cannot be replaced from the instructional situation irrespective of the developments in the media and ICT. In order to determine the quality of the instructional processes one of the main marks will have to be with respect to teacher's behaviour and competence. There are 3 main areas of teacher's competence:

- Professional knowledge and understanding,
- Professional skills and abilities, and
- Professional values and personal commitment.

The benchmarks of a good teacher are: communicate effectively, using a variety of media, to stimulate pupils and achieve the objectives of lessons, employ a range of teaching strategies and justify their approach, set expectations and a pace of work, work effectively in co-operation with other assistants in the classroom. Teachers should be trained regularly through academic staff colleges to improve the effectiveness of their teaching and classroom performance.

5. Administration and Management

The emphasis laid on academic freedom of institutions of higher learning by public bodies such as the UGC and the Knowledge

Commission of India is quite welcome, and timely. The creation of more autonomous colleges, clusters of autonomous colleges and central universities is the beginning of the long expected academic freedom from the affiliating system. An autonomous college is free to start a new degree or post-graduate course with the approval of the Academic Council of the college. Such courses shall fulfill the minimum standards prescribed by the university/ UGC in terms of number of hours, curricular content and standards, and the university shall be duly informed of such courses. The charter of academic freedom, articulated in terms of the National Policy on Education is broadly indicated in the 11th plan guidelines and it includes the freedom to:

Determine and prescribe (the colleges) own courses of study and syllabi, and restructure and redesign the courses already offered in order to suit local needs;

Prescribe rules for admission of students accommodating the reservation policy of the state government;

Evolve methods of assessment of student performance, conduct examinations and notify results;

Use modern tools of educational technology to achieve higher standards and greater creativity; and Promote healthy practices such as community service, extension activities, projects for the benefit of society, neighborhood programmes, etc.

This academic *panchsheel*, if one may so call it, has far reaching enabling implications to address academic, social, pedagogic, global and quality concerns of higher education in India, if only institutions could be diligent to perceive and internalize them in their own systems of operation.

CONCLUSION

It is never too late to mend. If the system of higher education is not improved in response to the need of the hour, the preamble promise of justice-social, economic and political, equality of status and of opportunity, liberty of thought, faith and worship will ever remain fulfilled. The aim of higher education should be necessarily broad and dynamic. The universities and colleges of today must work not only for promotion and dissemination of knowledge but also for generation of knowledge. They must promote humanism, reasoning, tolerance, critical thinking and search for truth. They are expected to achieve new knowledge, understanding, good leadership qualities and equality for their students. Higher education should aim at socialization and democratization in true sense of the word.

REFERENCES

Arya P.P. (2006), *Higher Education and Global Challenges Systems and Opportunities*, Deep and Deep Publications, New Delhi.

Mohanty Jagannath (2003), *Current trends in higher education*, Deep and Deep Publications, New Delhi.

Saraswat R.C, Tripathi S.K "Analysis of Emerging Environment and Quality Challenges in Higher Education: A Value-chain Approach", *University News*, 47 (03), January, 2009.

http://www.minuteman.org/topics/tqm.html

17

Taxonomy of Interactive Domain of Educational Objectives

S.S. Chaugule

Taxonomy of educational objectives is a classification of educational objectives in terms of learning outcomes. It is a hierarchical classification of human growth in a given domain of development. It means that learning at the highest level of objectives is dependent on having attained lower level of objectives. It helps to understand the sequence and organization of human knowledge and skills in a hierarchical level and its development. It also helps to define and evaluate all round development of the students and educational standards of a school.

Taxonomy of objectives is divided into three domains, a Cognitive Domain, an Affective Domain and a Psychomotor Domain. Cognitive Domain was prepared and published by Dr. Benjamin. S. Bloom, an educational psychologist at the University of Chicago, in his book namely, Taxonomy of Educational Objectives: The Classification of Educational Goals. In 1956 and again in 1965, the Cognitive Domain includes those objectives that deal with the recall or recognition of knowledge and the development of intellectual abilities including new creation as Aderson added it afterwards,. Cognitive Domain includes Knowledge, Comprehension, and Application, Analysis, Synthesis, Evaluation and New creation.

The Affective Domain was prepared by Krathwohl, Bloom and Masia and published in 1964 in 'A Taxonomy of Educational objectives, Handbook II'. The objectives of the Affective Domain describes changes in interest, attitude, values, the development of appreciations and adjustment. Affective Domain includes Receiving, Responding, Valuing Organization and Characterization.

Renowned Educationalist, W.N. Dandekar in his book 'Evaluation in Schools' second edition, 1986 mentioned that Dr. Dave, Head of the Department of Curriculum Development, NCERT, and New Delhi has proposed taxonomy in the Psychomotor Domain. It pertains to the motor skill area of a child. He also mentioned that the feasibility of developing Psychomotor Domain is being studied by a group at the University of Illions under Dr. Elizabeth Simpson, in 1972. Though, this taxonomy was in the form of working hypothesis, we use it as a classification of educational hierarchical objectives of a Psychomotor Domain for a child development. Psychomotor Domain. As Dr. Dave classified, includes Imitation, Manipulation, Precision, Articulation and Naturalization.

Argyle M. in his book, 'Social Interactions', Methuen: London in 1969 and Rockham, N and Morgan, T in their book 'Behaviour Analysis in Training', McGraw Hill: UK in 1977 tried to classify the interactions into two groups like Verbal Interactions and Non-verbal Interactions. But they had not succeeded to frame the Taxonomy of Objectives of the Interactive skills, which is very clearly Prof. Prakash M. Deshpande mentioned on page number 27, in the book namely 'Instructional System Design' in 1993. The members of the Evaluation Committee of this book were Prof. B. N. Kohl, Prof. B.K. Passi, and Prof. M. D. Agrawal. Therefore, this part of developing taxonomy was in vacuum and needs to develop.

1. NEED OF DEVELOPING A NEW DOMAIN

Education is the process of all round development of a child. What is the all round development? When we consider the cognitive domain, we try to develop the knowledge and its application and lastly one can create a new knowledge if cognitive domain is fully developed. It means he is a knowledgeable one.

When we consider the affective domain, we try to develop the emotions, control over the emotions and study which is good and which is bad. It helps to become a ethical person. It means through the affective domain, we try to develop the person with characterization.

When we consider the psychomotor domain, we try to develop the skills of motor Activities, the manipulation of activities and lastly to perform the motor activities with naturalization.

All round development of child, thus, includes creating a knowledgeable person, the person with characterization and the person who performs his motor activities naturally. Then, the question arises, why the meritorious students or characterized persons do not get success in the society. why the child whose psychomotor domain is developed gets the job like worker only. We have the various examples found in the society that a person without education or having less education gets a success in life, for example Vasantadada Patil of Maharashtra who became Chief Minister of the State, thrice.

Therefore, it is necessary to search for developing taxonomy for a new domain like Interactive Domain so that educated people should be able to get a success in their lives and also they are respected.

2. INTERACTIVE DOMAIN

Meaning of Interaction

> *'Interaction is a kind of process of action that carried out when two or more objects have an effect upon one another through its sub processes like assimilation, co-operation, competition and conflict process using verbal and/or non-verbal communication skill, observation skill and inquisition skill as a response of its effect.'*

After reading this definition, we may put out the features of the Interaction below for studying the definition in detail

Features of the Interactions

1. Interaction Requires two or More Persons

Interactions require two or more persons. A person himself can't interact himself. Introspection is differ from interaction. The presence of another person is always prerequisite for interaction. Therefore at least two persons are required for the interaction. More than two persons are always helpful for the interaction.

2. The Effect of the Interaction is Seen on Each-Other

Only the presence of two or more persons is not enough. The effect of interaction.

On each other or one another has to be seen. If the effect is not seen on each other or one another, the communication is not completed; therefore, interaction is also not completed. Therefore, for the development of interaction, the effect of it on the persons involved in it has to be seen.

3. Interaction is a Process

Interaction is a process. It has a beginning and has an end. Since beginning, to achieve its end, it goes through many stages, achieving certain objectives. Sometimes a person assimilates something at the time of interaction, sometimes co-operates, sometimes compete with one-another and sometimes conflict with each other. This process goes on communicating to, observing to and inquisitive into as a response to each other or one-another. It has many hidden factors in it. At the time of developing interactions, one has to study all these things.

4. Components of Interactions

Interaction consists of three main components or skills as follows:

Communication: Communication is the heart of the interaction. If there is no communication, there is no interaction at all. While interacting, communication takes place in many different shapes like—

(i) Oral Communication,
(ii) Written Communication,
(iii) Communication. With Body Movements and Gestures.

Oral communication depends upon the *Speaking Skill* whereas written communication depends upon *Writing Skill*. And thus, for developing the communication, one has to develop speaking skill and writing skill also. Wherever interactions take place, communication always exists in any of these forms. Therefore, communication is the important component in the process of interaction.

Moreover, the communication always consists of the content *i.e.* the matter that to communicate. Therefore, one has to develop the *Listening Skill, Reading Skill, Library Skill and also the Research Skill.* These skills help to collect the information.

Communication also involves the Media *of communication*. Therefore, it needs to develop the *Technical Skill* also. *Computer literacy is always welcome for choosing the media.*

Communication always involves *Feedback*. If the feedback is as desired one, the interaction strengthens and if it doesn't, the interaction lessens. Therefore feedback is also considered the necessary part of the interaction process.

Observation: Observation is the eyes of the interactions. Without observation, one is not able to develop the interactions. Many things of a child development is based on how he observes the others, therefore, observation always helps a child to develop interactions. A child learns attitudes, language, values or behaviour of another person or a group of persons and incorporates them into his own personality. If one wants to develop interactions in a child, it needs him to develop the observation skill especially for the non-verbal interactions.

Inquisition: Inquisition is the feet of the interaction. Our most interactions are made due to our inquiry. The inquiry we make leads to the interaction. We get much information from others. It is needed only to inquire of the information from them. One has to have the inquisition skill for the purpose. Many times, observation of the behaviour of others needs some clarification to attach the meaning to that behaviour. Many new things can be visible because of this skill. Therefore, for the development of the interaction it also needs to develop the inquisitive skill of the child.

5. Social Factors in Interaction

There are four types of social factors or sub processes involved in the Process of interaction as follows:

Assimilation Process: Child learns many things, and shapes its attitudes, learns a language and sticks the values, or gives the values to the behaviour of another person or persons and thus the process of assimilation takes place which is the one of the most meaningful process in education A child uses observation component at the time of assimilating something. A child learns something and makes use of what he has learnt. Interaction helps to assimilate values, languages, and behaviour of other persons and helps to shape the attitudes

Co-operation Process: There are always exchange of thoughts, ideas and goods of transaction at the time of interactions. When the children try to achieve similar or identical aims or objectives, there needs co-operation. In co-operation, there is a sharing and synthesis of thought, energy and often resources. Better interactions are always based on co-operation of each other. In this process, communication component is always used.

Competition Process: Interactions always involve competition along with co-operation as children follow different ways to achieve the same aim competing with others. Therefore, this competition factor always is a part of interaction. Here, the observation and communication are the components observed keenly. It is because a child observes others and tries to compete over them. Moreover, according to feedback, it tries to decide its ways to compete.

Conflict Process: Conflict is the attempt of one or more persons to attain identical aims through elimination of competitors, where the emphasis is on the persons in the competitive process and not on the aims to be attained, It means conflict does not involve well-defined causes or clear aims but is simply a highly emotional battle between the two or more persons involved in the interactions. This battle always goes to prove the influence of one another observing the situation.

6. Interactions in Schools

School situation creates many sorts of interactions. They are given Diagramacally as follows:

A Child	A Child	A child interacts with another child.
A Child	Children	A child interacts with children in the school.
A Child	A teacher	A child interacts with a teacher.
A Child	Teachers	A child interacts with teachers in the school.
Children	A teacher	Children interact with a teacher.
Children	Teachers	Children interacts with teachers in the schools.
A Child	Head Master	A child interacts with a Head Master.
Children	Head Master	Children interact with a Head Master

7. Classification of Interactions

The classification of the interactions will be as follows.

1. Verbal Interactions

2. Non verbal Interactions
3. The Combination of the Both *i.e.* Verbal and non Verbal Interactions

Argyle M., Rockham, N and Morgan, T have classified the Interactions into two groups as follows.

1. Verbal Interactions
2. Non-verbal Interactions

Verbal Interactions: Verbal Interactions are the interactions, which are made verbally. It consists of proposing and suggesting something supporting to something, giving information, seeking classification etc.

Non-verbal Interactions: Non-verbal Interactions consist of bodily movements and gestures used for the interactions. Bodily movements consist of movement of eyes, hands, body posture etc. and Gestures consist of facial expressions of a person.

Verbal or Non Verbal or Combination of the Both: Though Argyle M., Rockham, N and Morgan, T have classified the interactions into two groups, *they* can be made through verbal or through non-verbal or through the both. Through the both means interactions can be made verbally and non-verbally at the same time. Therefore the classification is extended and interactions can be classified into three categories adding one as the combination of the both *i.e.* Verbal and Non verbal Interactions.

The third classification is slightly different than the first two because it involves the first two and their combination at the same time. The process of combination goes without thinking but naturally. When we say something verbally, our body movements and gestures add the meaning into our saying. If we do not get the meaning of body movements or to the gestures, the meaning of only saying may catch different meaning. Therefore the combination of the both is necessary for interactions.

8. Most Interactions are the Verbal and Non Verbal Interactions

If we take the *happenings* of the Interactions of all the three categories, most of the interactions fall under the third category *i.e.* under verbal and non-verbal interactions. In a very few situations, interactions can be made having using one of the categories of the first two. A dumb child interacts with using non-verbal interactions or interactions that take place through phone, etc. But most of the interactions involve both verbal and non-verbal interactions at the same time.

9. Interactions can be Developed Through School Education

All round development of a child is the aim of School Education. Development of the skill of interaction is a part and parcel of all round development of a child. Therefore it needs to develop the skill of interactions of a child. It is possible to develop the skill through the School Education. It requires a systematic taxonomy of acquiring the skill of interactions.

10. Interactions can be Classified in the form of Taxonomy

As it is already mentioned, taxonomy of interaction is not developed yet. Argyle, M., Rockham N., and Morgan, T. had classified the interactions into two categories, and classify them into a taxonomic form. But they had not succeeded as Dr. Prakash Deshpande, (1993) mentioned it clearly. They had not mentioned the definite skills required for developing the interaction skill. And also hierarchical criteria were not also followed. But it is possible to fix the sub skills of interactions classifying them into Verbal Interactions and Non verbal Interactions. It is also possible to fix their hierarchy and put them in the taxonomical form for the development of the skill of Interaction.

In Short, Interaction is a Kind of Action that Occurs as two or More Objects Have an Effect Upon One Another

3. IMPORTANCE OF DEVELOPMENT OF INTERACTIVE DOMAIN

As we have seen, an Interaction process involves three components as communication, observation and inquisition and four sub processes as assimilation process, co-operation process, competition process and conflict process. These three components and four-sub process of interaction process are very important for all round development of the child.

It is because while interacting to one another a child has to.:

1. Learn the communication skill and use it properly,
2. Develop the observation skill and make use of it for shaping the attitudes,
3. Learn to inquire of for seeking information,
4. Learn and change the behaviour and views as it gets the feedback using listening skill,

5. Learn to use library and references,
6. Learn to develop speaking skill and writing skill,
7. Learn to use technical skills especially computer skill
8. Learn to analyses and interpret the information for drawing conclusions.
9. Learn to assimilate the good habits, attitudes, languages, values etc. and shape the behaviour,
10. Learn to cooperate each other and develop collectively.
11. Learn to compete each other for achieving the scarce material and the same objective,
12. Learn to attain the identical aims through elimination of competitors and influence on the others.
13. Learn to adjust with the situation,
14. Learn to lead and guide the society, and
15. Learn to perform non-verbal interactions naturally while performing verbal interactions.

Unfortunately in the present system of education, only cognitive domain, affective domain, and psychomotor domain are considered to be developing in the schools. The cognitive domain is through which we can create a knowledgeable person who can use his knowledge for the betterment of the society. For the purpose, he needs to interact with the people in the society. Therefore it needs to acquire the skill of interaction. The affective domain is through which we can create a characterized person who inherits good values in him. But if he has not succeeded to spread these values in the society, they are of no use and here again requires the interactions. The psychomotor domain is through which we can create a person with certain skills who perform his task accurately, at ease and without mistake. This task of him can be valued with reference to the society where it again requires the interactions. Thus, the development of the skill of interaction is very necessary and important for development of all round development of a child.

It is because the person without having general education gets respect and importance in the society. Therefore, it needs to accept the fourth domain as the Interactive Domain to develop all round development of a child initially in the schools.

4. OBJECTIVES OF INTERACTIVE DOMAIN

Interactive Domain consists of two types of interactions.

1. Verbal Interactions, and
2. Non-Verbal Interactions

Both these two types of interactions go through all the three components namely communication, observation and inquisition and four sub processes or factors namely assimilation, cooperation, competition and conflict as mentioned above. More than that a person sits on his thoughtful sitting and tries to socialize his views or adjusts with the society performing the proper body movements and gestures naturally.

Objectives of Verbal Interactions

(i) To frame or express a opinion of about the subject under consideration.
(ii) To give the support for the opinion expressed.
(iii) To listen to or to consider the opinions of others on a given subject.
(iv) To collect more information or to seek explanation for lessening the differences.
(v) To express the differences of opinions if any
(vi) To understand the opinions of others by exchanging thoughts and views with one another.
(vii) To frame or disclose the final opinion after considerations of other opinions.
(viii) To modify the view and rest on thoughtful sitting.
(ix) To adjust with the others or socialize the opinion

Objectives of Non-Verbal Interaction

(i) To identify a person whom non-verbal interactions are related to.
(ii) To recognize the relation with the person who comes in contact with.
(iii) To decide to maintain the distance.
(iv) To perform body movement or gestures properly.
(v) To perform body movements and gestures without pre-planning and rest on easy Sitting.
(vi) To perform body movements and gestures naturally.

These all objectives are derived from three components namely communication, observation and inquisition and four sub processes or factors namely, assimilation process, co-operation process, competition process and conflict process.

5. TAXONOMY OF INTERACTIVE DOMAIN

As a renowned educationalist W.N. Dandekar (1986) mentioned, 'taxonomy is a hierarchical classification of the objectives of the given field. It can become a means of understanding the sequence and organization of human development. One of the most important purposes of a taxonomy is to establish accuracy of communication regarding instructional objectives and related matters.'

Considering this, a Taxonomy of Interactive Domain can be given as follows:

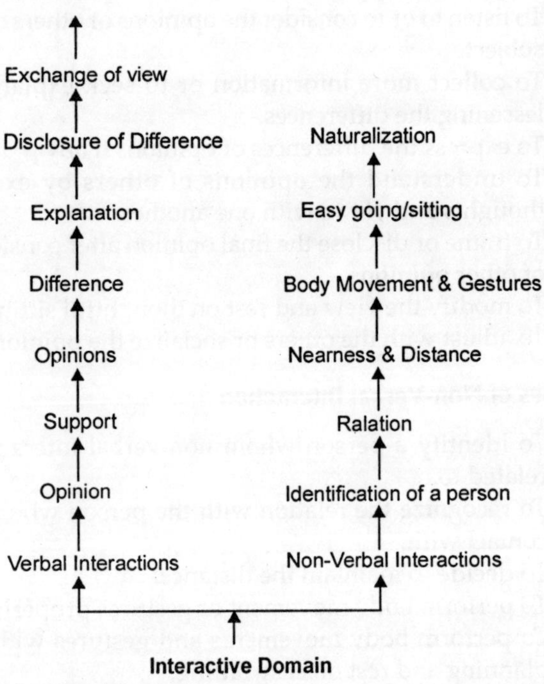

1. Verbal Interactions

When one wants to develop, verbal interactions, one has to express his views or opinions first and lastly his views or opinions can be adjusted or socialized as per the need of the society or lead the society to follow him. The objectives or sub skills are linked with one another sequentially. All these objectives or sub skills are explained in detail below:

(i) *Opinion: (The Skill of Expressing Views or Opinions)*: The first step of verbal interaction is to express ones views or opinions Therefore every teacher has to keep in mind that, he has to assist the student to express his views, or opinions. For example, he can ask the class whether elections be held to select the monitor or follow any other ways. He can ask the students one by one. Thus, he can make the students to express views or opinions. For forming the opinion on any subject, one has to assimilate something without which he cannot express his opinion. And there requires an observation skill and a communication component to assimilate something. Reading references or researches are also helpful for forming one's opinion. Therefore to express ones opinion is the first step of developing verbal interactions.

(ii) Support: (The Skill of Providing Support to the Opinion Expressed): It is not enough only to express one's opinion but it is also necessary to give support with any reasons behind it for one's own opinions. If a student says, elections should not be held in the class or school, he has to give the reasons for his support. Thus, to develop or to produce the evidence or documents or the reasons for support of his own opinions is the second objective of developing verbal interactions. Here he strengthens the communication component so that one should understand the opinion of him with proof. Here also he uses the references or researches that he read.

(iii) Opinions: (The Skill of Acquiring the Opinions of Others): A student should not stick with his own opinion only. He has to consider opinions of others also. To know the opinions of others are also very important objective in developing the verbal interactions. The opinions of others may differ of his own. But it is necessary to learn to acquire the opinions of others. Therefore to develop to acquire this skill in school is necessary at the time of developing all round development of a child. Therefore to listen to others is also very important objective in developing the verbal interactions. It is some sort of feedback he receives while acquiring the opinions of others. For the purpose, he develops the listening skill and to express the views on certain issues.

(iv) *Difference (The Skill of Critically Studying the Opinions)*: To know the opinions of others is not enough in developing the verbal interaction of a child. It is necessary to find out the difference between the opinions of others and of one's own opinion. It needs to study the opinions of others with critically. Therefore, it is considered the skill of finding the difference is the next objective for developing verbal interaction of the child. Here, the child thinks of the feedback he receives on his views or opinions. He analyses the opinions. He may use the computer for the purpose. Thus, technical skill is also used.

(v) *Explanation (The Skill of Acquiring Information Giving the People Respect)*: When there is any difference found in the opinions, it needs to take explanations from the persons concerned about the reasons of the difference. To take an explanation means to try to find out the reasons and lesson the difference of opinions. Here a child respects the opinions of others: Here, communication and inquisition components work at the time of seeking explanation. Thus, explanation is fifth objective in the development of the verbal interaction of a child.

(vi) *Disclosure of the Difference: (The Skill of Developing Critically Thinking and Confirming Oneself)*: After receiving the explanations, it needs to think critically the various opinions expressed and study them thoroughly. And if a student feels, his opinion is correct, he has to present his opinion in that way because by this act, a student develops his critical thinking, enjoy freedom and present individuality. Here the process of assimilation and also competition take place. Therefore, this objective is considered the sixth objective of developing verbal interactions of a child.

(vii) *Exchange of Views: (The Skill of Exchanging Thoughts)*: After critically studying the opinions of others when he feels that his opinion is based on strongly build evidence, he has to exchange his views to others. He has to seek criticism on his own opinion. Study it and convey if any differences remained again to the concerned. Get the opinions of them and study again over it. It is better to communicate it again to the concerned and thus, the process of exchange of views must go on for developing the verbal interactions of child. Here, the components of communication and inquisition and the process of assimilation, competition and conflict take place. A child learns to attain the identical aims through elimination of competitors and influence on the others. Therefore, this objective is considered as the seventh objective for the purpose.

(viii) *Thoughtful Sitting: (The Skill of Resting on Thoughtful Sitting)*: The next step of developing the verbal interaction of a child is 'thoughtful sitting' It is the stage which is built after due consideration of the opinions of others, giving respect to the opinions of them and exchanging the various controversial views with them. Here a child builds and confirms his views or opinions very thoughtfully and reaches and rests on the thoughtful sitting. Therefore, this objective is considered the eighth objectives in developing verbal interaction of a child.

(ix) *Adjustment/Socialization: (The Skill of Adjustment and/or of Socialization)*: A person should not limit his thoughts to himself only. He has to socialize the thoughts. When he succeeds to persuade the others for accepting his thoughts, he succeeds to prove that he has developed the verbal interactions in him.

Sometimes a person is not able to transform his thoughts into society or succeed to persuade others to accept his thoughts. Then there needs the person to trade the path lonely or to go with the others adjusting himself. Many times, adjustment with the others is better for such type of a person, which leads his life without any trouble. Therefore, for developing verbal interactions of a child the last step is the adjustment or the socialization of the thoughts of persons.

When one sees somebody insulting our national flag, one has to stick to the opinion that the person must be punished though others opinions are differ in that situation. Here, no adjustments. It needs to pressurize the authority to punish the concerned one. But sometimes, it needs to adjust the situation. Here, the components of communication and the elements of assimilation, cooperation, competition and conflict take place. Therefore, it is considered the last step of achieving the verbal interactions.

2. Non-Verbal Interactions

The other part of the Interactive Domain is Non-Verbal Interactions. When one wants to develop non-verbal interactions, one has to identify the person whose related non-verbal interactions will be carried out first and lastly the interactions should be carried out naturally. These two objectives are linked with other objectives sequentially. All these objectives are explained in detail below.

(i) *Identification of a Person: (The Skill of Recognizing the Persons)*: In the process of developing non-verbal interactions, it is necessary the presence of other persons. One has to identify this person. It is because we change our non-verbal interactions according to him. If he is our class-mate, we have different interactions than if he is our teacher. Therefore it is necessary to see who this person is, his age, gender, his position whether he is a teacher or a head-master, and also whether he is from insider or outsider of the class, school or village etc, Our non-verbal interactions depends upon who this person is Here, the component of observation works. Therefore identification of a person is the first objective in the development of non-verbal interactions

(ii) *Relation: (The Skill of Strengthening the View)*: It is not enough only to identify the person. But it is also necessary to see what his relation with him or her. If he or she is closely related to us, we behave differently than the one who is not so closely related. The relation of students with the class teacher and with other teachers is also different. The relations of a boy with his mother and with a teacher always differ. Here also the component of observation skill works. Therefore, to observe the relationship is considered the second objective in developing the non-verbal interactions of a child.

(iii) *Nearness and Distance: (The Skill of Keeping the Distance)*: Nearness and Distance are the physical factors considered after identification of a person and taking his/her relation into account. It is necessary to have this object in developing non-verbal interactions because we keep distance while dealing with girls than boys; with head-master than teachers, with teachers than class-teachers, etc. When a teacher goes near to a student, he maintains closeness to him and removes fear out of his mind, and creates love and faith in him. Non-verbal interactions depend upon this physical distance. Closely related persons always keep nearness to each-other whereas distance is always kept if they are not so related to each other. Here, the process of assimilation works as the person assimilates the relationships and keeps the distance or goes near to him or her. Therefore, this objective is considered as the third objective in developing non-verbal interactions of a child.

(iv) *Body Movements and Gestures: (The Skill of Performing Body Movements and Gestures)*: Non-verbal interactions are nothing but body movements and gestures of a person the body movements and gestures of any person are performed after identifying a person who meets him and knowing the relationship with him which affects for deciding the distance, if any, while dealing with him. We can blink the eyes or clap on the shoulder while talking to the friends but not to the teachers or to the headmaster. We can easily touch to the persons who are close to us while talking to them but we can't touch the persons of the opposite sex if they are not close to us. Our body movements and gestures are determined as per the distance we keep with one-another here, the process of assimilation works as the person assimilates the relationships. Therefore, this objective is considered as the fourth objective in developing non-verbal interactions.

(v) *Easy Going or Sitting: (The Skill of Performing Body Movements and Gestures Easily)*: Body movements or gestures should be performed as per the persons we meet. It should be performed easily. When we meet our teacher, our body movement and gestures must be reflected showing the respect to him, or her. Likewise to the elderly person or person's. When we meet our friends, one should guess that we are meeting our friends observing our body movements and gestures. This type of development is necessary in the process of acquiring non-verbal interactions. Therefore easy going or sitting is considered as the fifth objective in developing the non-verbal interaction.

(vi) *Naturalization: (The Skill of Performing Body Movements and Gestures Naturally)*: Naturalization is the last step of developing non-verbal interactions of a child. It is because any body movement or gesture should be performed naturally. There should not be pre-planning for the performance. One should not think while in contacting the teacher about the body-movement and gestures. They have to come out at ease and without any special efforts. Non-verbal interactions should come out naturally. Therefore, it is considered the last step in developing the non-verbal interactions of a child.

In Short

The interactive domain helps to develop the following main skills and sub skills into a child through its four sub processes.

Main Skills

1. The Communication Skill,
2. The Observation Skill, and
3. The Inquisition Skill,

Sub Skills

1. The skill of expressing views or opinions.
2. The skill of providing support to the opinion expressed.
3. The skill of acquiring the opinions of others.
4. The skill of critically studying the opinions
5. The skill of acquiring information giving the people respect.
6. The skill of developing critically thinking and confirming oneself.
7. The skill of exchanging thoughts.
8. The skill of resting on thoughtful sitting
9. The skill of adjustment and/or of socialization
10. The skill of recognizing the persons.
11. The skill of strengthening the view.
12. The skill of keeping the distance.
13. The skill of performing body movements and gestures.
14. The skill of performing body movements and gestures easily.
15. The skill of performing body movements and gestures naturally.

Sub Processes

1. Assimilation Process
2. Cooperation Process
3. Competition Processes
4. Conflict Processes.

6. ALL ROUND DEVELOPMENT OF A CHILD

The all round development of a child or the behaviour of a child has now four domains as given below.

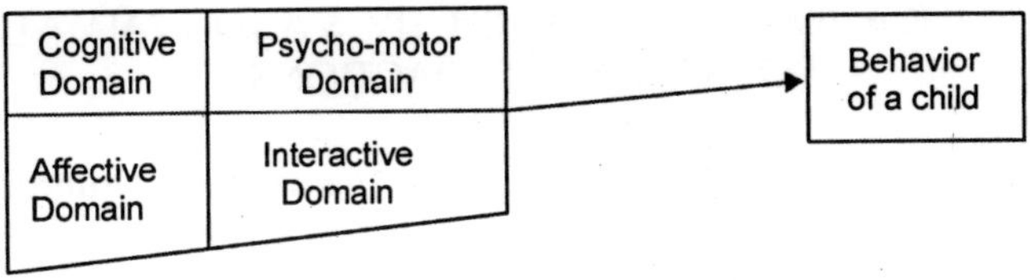

A diagramacally we can present all the four taxonomies as given below.

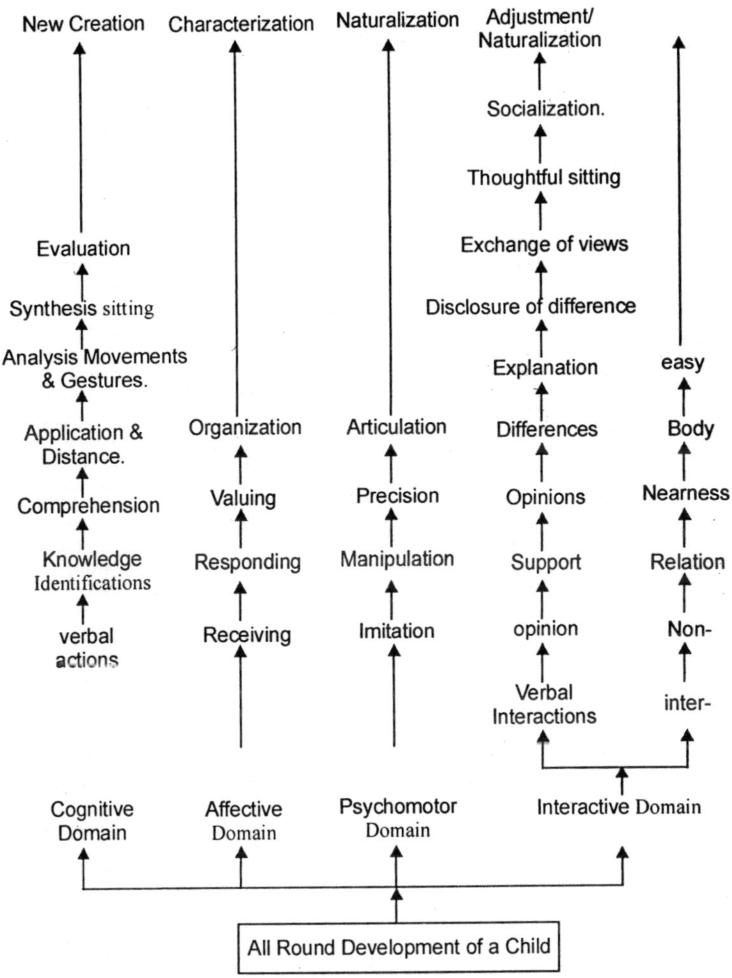

7. SPECIFICATIONS OF THE OBJECTIVES AND EVALUATION OF VERBAL INTERACTIONS

Like other domains, the objectives or the skills of 'Interactive Domain' are needed to be written in the statement form and their specifications are also needed to be written as per the evaluation point of view. It will help one to test whether the objectives are achieved or not.

Domain	*objective*	*Related Information*	*Statement of objective*	*specification*	*Evaluation*
Interactive Domain					
Verbal Interactions	*Opinion*	Expression of opinion	To express the opinion on the given subject	Student expresses his opinions on the given subject/s	1. What is your opinion on this Issue? 2. Present your Opinion.
	Support	Provision of sources for support	To give a support for the opinion expressed	Student gives support for his opinion.	1. On what ground do you say this? 2. Give support for your opinion.
	Opinions	Considerations of other opinions.	To consider the Opinions of others on a given subject.	Student considers the opinions of others on a given subject.	1. What are others opinion on this subject? 2. Take the opinion of others on this issue.
	Explanation	Additional Information	To collect more Information on the issue in hand.	A student collects more information taking explanation from others on the given subject.	1. What information do you collect after seeking the opinions of others? 2. Do you need additional information to study the opinions of others? Have it?
	Difference	Expression of Differences	To express the differences of opinions if any	A student expresses the differences of opinions if any.	1. What differences do you find in various opinions you collect on the issue in hand? 2. Do you think the differences are minor or major? Why?

Domain	*objective*	*Related Information*	*Statement of objective*	*specification*	*Evaluation*
	Exchange of Views	Exchange of views & thoughts	To understand the opinions of others by exchanging thoughts and views with one another.	A student exchanges his views and thoughts with one another to understand the opinions of one another.	1. Do you comm.-unicate your opinion to others? 2. Have others communicated their opinions to you? 3. What others think about your opinions and what you think about their opinions?
	Disclosure of difference	Presentation of confirm opinion	To develop a critical thinking, enjoy freedom and present individuality and also to assimilate something in the process of competition.	A student develops his critical thinking, enjoy freedom and present individuality. He also assimilates something in the process of competition.	1. Have you studied all the differrent opinions of others? 2. Is your opinion different from them? In what sense? 3. Have you disclosed your opinion to the concerned? 4. Have you learnt something after studying the differrences? What is that?
	Thoughtful Sitting	Definite Final opinion	To frame the final opinion after considerations of other opinions	A student frames a final opinion after Consideration the opinions of others and exchange the views with one another.	1. What is your last opinion on the issue? 2. Have you had a thoughtful sitting on this issue?
	Adjustment/ Socialization	Co-ordination	To adjuct with the others or socialize the opinion	A student tries to socialize the Opinion or to adjust with the others.	1. Do you firm with your opinion or want to change it? 2. If you are firm, how you will persuade others to follow you? 3. If you are not, do you want to adjust with other opinions? Why?

8. SPECIFICATIONS OF THE OBJECTIVES AND EVALUATION OF NON VERBAL INTERACTIONS

Non-verbal Interaction	Identifi-cation	Identification of a person.	To indentify a person whom non-verbal interactions are related	A student identifies the person whom non-verbal interactions are related	1. Who is she? Do you know her? 2. Who is he? What is his name? Do you meet him before?
	Relation	Recognition of the relation between the two.	To recognize the relation with the per-son who comes in contact with him.	A student recognizes the relation of him with the person who comes in contact.	1. Is seta your sister? , Mother? Classmate? Friend? 2. How do you call Shreeshant By his nick name, Shree? Or as Shreeshant? Or as a Teacher? Or as a Daddy?
	Nearne ss & Distance	Distance Maintenance	To decide to maintain the distance or to go near.	A student keeps a pro-per distance thinking of relationship	1. When your friends are sad how you will consol him? 2. Do you keep distance in bowing down your parents? Why?
	Easy Sitting	Easy going of body mov-ements and gestures	To perform body move-ments and gestures ea-sily without pre-planning.	A student performs body move-ments and gestures easily with-out pre-planning.	1. Observe the reactions of your classmates when any new announcement is made in the class and note it into observation book. Do you think any one of you reacted it with pre-planning? 2. How do you convince that you are not pre-tending but your body movem-ents and gest-ures were easy going?
	Naturali zation	Absence of pretendency	To perform body move-ments and gestures	A student performs his body move-ments and	1. Find out the pre tendency of your classmates particularly body

	naturally.	gestures Nat-urally and easily without Thinking.	movement and gestures made in the class before your teacher and note it in your observation book.. 2. Descibe one movement you observed in the class or in a family where body movem-ents and gest-ures are not done naturally but are done with pre tendency.

9. SUMMING UP

Interactive Domain is very important domain in developing all round development of a child. A child learns to develop its observation skill, communication skill and inquisition skill going through the assimilation process, the cooperation process, and the competition process and through the conflict process and through many sub skills of verbal interactions and non-verbal interactions.

But the interaction process was not properly analyzed and put it into the objectives or the skills. The taxonomy of the objectives of this domain was also not properly made before. This was the vacuum remained in developing a child in the schools. It is an effort made consciously to structure the objectives hierarchal so that a teacher can develop this domain of a child in a school for fulfilling all round development of a child.

REFERENCES

Anderson and others (2001). *A Taxonomy for Learning, Teaching and Assessing: A Revision of Bloom's Taxonomy of Educational Objectives*, New York: Longthan.

Argyle M. (1969). *Social Interactions*, Methuen: London.

Bhatia Kamala and Bhatia Balder (1986). *The Philosophical and Sociological Foundations of Education*, Doaba House, Booksellers and publishers,1688, Nai Sarak, Delhi 110006.

Bloom, B.S. (1972). *Taxonomy of Educational Objectives Handbook* I: *Cognitive Domain*. Longman: London.

Dandekar, W.N. (1986). *Evaluation in Schools*, Shrividya Prakashan, 250 Shaniwar, Ashtabhuja Marg, Poona 30, India.

Deshpande, P.M. (1993). Instructional Systems Design, YCM open University, Nashik Maharashtra. India

Dave, R.H. (1969). Taxonomy of Educational Objectives and Achievement Testing, in *'Developments in Educational Testing'*, Vol. I. University of London Press, London.

Harper and Harper (1992). *Preparing Objectives examinations—A Book for Teacher Students and Examiners*, Prentice Hall of India Private Limited, New Delhi 01. India.

Krathwohld, D.R. Bloom, B.S. Masia B.B: (1972). *Taxonomy of Educational Objectives, Handbook II: Affective Domain*. Longman: London.

Mager, R.F (1975). *Preparing Instructional Objectives*, Fearon publishers: Belmont, USA.

Pandit V.K. (1978). *Teacher Education Curriculum–A Framework*, National Council of Teacher Education, New Delhi. India.

Patel Rambahi N. (1989). *Educational Evaluation: Theory and Practice*, Himalaya Publishing House, Mumbai. India.

Rackham, N. and Morgan, T. (1977). *Behaviour Ayalysis in Training*, Mc Graw Hill; Uk.

Romiszowski; A.J. (1982). *Designing Instructional Systems*, Kogan Page: London.

Skinner, B.F. (1957). *Verbal Behaviour Appleton-Century*. Crofts: New York.

18

An Achievement to a Challenge in Open Distance Education

A Case Study—YCM Open University

Mrs. Rucha Gujar

Education is no longer merely a means of transmitting traditional values and models of already existing social structures. Increasingly, it is becoming an agent of social change promoting new knowledge, new values and new ways of improving the human conditions. Education has ceased to be an exclusive domain of the chosen field. Its doors are now open to the general population in countries throughout the world. A democratic ideology is replacing a former elitist mentality. To happen this open and distance education systems has come forward.

The concept of 'Open and distance education' originated from the need to extend learning opportunities at various level to people who did not have access to traditional modes for various reasons for example, economic, space and time restrictions related to job and family responsibilities or distance from educational centers. In case of underdeveloped and third world countries distance education has offered a great hope for development because of its capacity for educational innovations for reaching wide audiences at various educational levels and for providing learning opportunities at costs that are lower than traditional forms. It is based on the concept of learning as a continuing or lifelong process that provides for ongoing cultural and professional development, increase technical skills and encourage the general public to keep abreast of current topics as well as scientific and technological advancements.

WHY PROFESSIONAL PROGRAMMES THROUGH DISTANCE EDUCATION?

Professional education in its various forms plays a significant role in the socio-economic development of a population. "Professional education consists of a number of interrelated fields, programmes and curricula with the primary objective of preparation for gainful employment. In the past professional education was concerned with trades and skill-oriented occupations. Now it is used in a wider sense. Jack Foks consider professional education as "demonstrated and acknowledged development of knowledge, skills and attitudes necessary for a place in the workforce at levels ranging from pre-trade to Para-professional".

The advantages of offering professional and technical courses through distance mode said that regarding quantity, the number of seats available in professional and technical education centres might not be sufficient to ensure the required supply. Because of high cost involved in establishing centres of professional and technical education, governments often find it difficult to expand professional and technical education through conventional methods. This problem can be overcome with professional and technical education through distance education, which is cost effective as it makes use of most of the existing infrastructure facilities. Further, because of the time free and space-free nature of distance education, it can reach many thousands of students at a time when it cannot be reached by mere traditional methods.

Y. C. M. OPEN UNIVERSITY: SCHOOL OF CONTINUING EDUCATION

Distance education programmes were initiated in India in 1962 mainly with the objective of receiving pressures on the universities and also to provide opportunities for employed persons to pursue education. The Yashwantrao Chavan Maharashtra Open University (YCMOU) was established in 1989 through Act XX (1989) of the Maharashtra State Legislature. The University has gone a long way in pursuit of excellence in education and has received the Award of Excellence in 2002 from Commonwealth of Learning, a non-profit organization established by the States of British Commonwealth.

In this university the school of continuing education was established in 1989. This school is committed to provide access to education to all sections of people through relevant courses in formal and non-formal stream. The mission has been to respond to the developmental needs of the society by offering need-based vocational/technical and professional courses to larger and larger segment of population, and in particular to the disadvantaged groups such as those living in remote and rural areas including working people, housewives and other adults who wish to upgrade or acquire knowledge through studies in various fields.

The School developed various technical and professional certificate, diploma and degree programmes till today. The fields are Lathe operator, Fitter, Plumber, Mason, Domestic Wireman, Radio-Tape Mechanic, Two wheeler mechanic, Industrial Painting, Computer Hardware Maintenance and Network Technologies, Industrial Security, Beauty Parlor Management, Information technology, Fabrication, AC Refrigeration Maintenance, Four Wheeler Mechanic, Electrician, Cosmetology, Air Travel Management, Hotel Management, Environment Sciences etc. In addition a number of special programmes of the school were used in the training of various strata of the disadvantaged groups.

In recent years our country and the whole world has provided more concentration on the tourism as a profession. Accordingly the need of trained manpower raised in the hotel management, tourism, catering operation and the allied all skills. Looking into this need the school of continuing education of YCMOU developed and launched the B. Sc Hotel and Tourism Management programme (HTM) in 2006. The YCMOU is the first Open University to start the innovative degree programme in Hotel and Tourism Management through distance mode of education.

NEED OF RESEARCHER'S STUDY

Previously some studies were carried out in programme evaluation for agricultural, B.A., B. Com. and Beauty Parlour Management programmes in YCMOU. But the professional programme B Sc (HTM) of degree level is launched through the distance education for the first time. Due to its novelty it becomes essential to evaluate the programme through pilot study at least on some essential fronts. The opinions of the counselors can play a decisive role in evaluation and subsequently improving the quality of implementation of the programme. There was no path already set to implement such type of programme, which could be followed. Hence investigator has developed a questionnaire on the all aspects related to the programme and carried out a pilot study on the sample of 30 counselors of B Sc HTM programme. In this paper the researcher have presented the findings, conclusion only with the objectives: 1. To study the appropriateness of the construction, the study material, the syllabus, the evaluation pattern and the quality of the counseling sessions at study centres of the B Sc HTM programme of YCMOU. 2. To examine the effectiveness of the various services from various involved sections/divisions of the university of B Sc HTM programme.

As this study is based on the views of the counselors mentioned in the questionnaire limitations are framed for this study—the opinion expressed through the questionnaire is considered only as the base for drawing the conclusion for the necessary improvements in the programmes.

This is a pilot study. It suggests some remedial measures related to counseling needs, the quality of learning material, to improve the quality of implementation. The outputs of the study may recommend some changes useful for the better implementation of the programme.

The school has collected the feedbacks from the 30 counselors (teachers) of the B Sc (HTM) programme at the active study centers.

The single questionnaire is developed for collecting the information from counselors of the active study centers. The questionnaire consisted of 31 questions. The questions were designed on the following dimensions: the construction of the programme, appropriateness of the content and the study material, the services from various sections of the university, the quality of counseling sessions etc. The data is analyzed by using simple percentage method. The data drawn from different sources is arranged and tabulated as under.

Table 18.1: The Construction of the Programme

Opinion	*Number of Counsellors*	*Percentage*
OK	26	87%
Revision required	04	13%

From the data in the table no 1 it is confirmed that the construction of the programme is OK. This is reported by the 87 per cent of the counselors of the programme. But considering the

13 per cent counselors opinion it is recommended that the revision shall be carried out at least after the three years because the concepts in such professional programmes are continuously changing.

Table 18.2: The Study Material of the Programme

Opinion	*Number of Counsellors*	*Percentage*
OK	24	80%
Difficult	06	20%

The data from the table 18.2 reports that majority *i.e.* 80 per cent of the counselors observed the study material *i.e.* text books of the programme is OK for the understanding of the students but 20 per cent counselors felt it difficult. Hence to remove the all hurdles in the teaching–learning process the accurate difficult topics shall be located and revised.

Table 18.3: The Syllabus of the Programme

Opinion	*Number of Counsellors*	*Percentage*
OK	25	83%
Difficult	05	17%

The data from the table 18.3 reports that majority ie 83 per cent of the counselors observed the syllabus of the programme is OK for the understanding of the students but 17 per cent counselors felt it difficult.

Table 18.4: The Response from the School Persons to the Queries of the Counselors

Opinion	*Number of Counsellors*	*Percentage*
In time	25	83%
Late	04	13%
Very Late	01	4%

Regarding the response from the school the data confirms that majority of the times, the school persons are prompt in replying to the counselors for any sort of queries and difficulties. Late or very late response from the school faculties for some times may be due to the busy schedule for other new programme developments.

Table 18.5: Services from the Stores of the University (for the Receipt of the Study Material)

Opinion	*Number of Counsellors*	*Percentage*
In time	02	7%
Late	25	83%
Very Late	03	10%

The data from the table 18.5 reports that majority of the counselors get the study material very late from the stores division of the university. This further creates the nuisance to the study centers because the students are aggressive in getting the material in time. The school shall provide some thoughtful solution to overcome this problem.

Table 18.6: Services from Registration Section of the University (for the Receipt of Student Registration Lists)

Opinion	*Number of Counsellors*	*Percentage*
In time	18	60%
Late	10	33%
Very Late	02	7%

From the table 18.6 it reveals that around 60 per cent of the counselors at study centers get the enrolment lists in time but 33 per cent of the counselors get lat. The reason for this may be the late submission of the admission forms to the registration section by the study center counselors.

Table 18.7: Services from the Examination Section of the University

Opinion	*Number of Counsellors*	*Percentage*
In time	19	63%
Late	11	37%
Very Late	00	0%

From the table 18.7 it is clear that 63 per cent of the counselors get the services from the examination section in time but 37 per cent of the counselors get late. The services regarding the examination section are sensitive issues hence the examination division must review the schedule and planning for the timely services.

Table 18.8: Response from Regional Centres

Opinion	*Number of Counsellors*	*Percentage*
Co-operative	20	67%
Non-cooperative	10	33%

The data from the table 18.8 confirms that 67 per cent of the counselors experienced the cooperative behaviours from the regional centers of the university. But 33 per cent of the counselors report the non-cooperative behaviours from the regional centers. In this regard the student services division must take the review for all 8 regions and shall provide the appropriate man power to the regional centers from where the smooth services are not provided.

Table 18.9: Do you Read the Objectives of the Course Before Teaching?

Opinion	*Number of Counsellors*	*Percentage*
Yes	23	77%
No	7	23%

The data from the table 18.9 indicates that majority of the counselors read the objectives of the course before teaching. This helps the smooth conductions of the counseling sessions.

Table 18.10: Are all Courses included in the Programme According to the Objectives of the Programme?

Opinion	*Number of Counsellors*	*Percentage*
Yes	23	77%
No	7	23%

The data from the table 18.10 indicates that 77 per cent of the counselors have the opinion that all courses included in the programme are according to the objectives of the programme.

Table 18.11: Are the Contents in the Textbooks Appropriate to the Objectives of the Course?

Opinion	*Number of Counsellors*	*Percentage*
Yes	23	77%
No	7	23%

The data from the table 18.11 indicates that 77 per cent of the counselors observed the contents in the textbooks appropriate to the objectives of the course. According to the opinion of 23 per cent counselors, some of the topics from the text books required to be edited properly and shall be included more appropriate to the programme and the concept.

Table 18.12: Is the Flow of Content in the Textbooks is Sequential and Appropriate?

Opinion	*Number of Counsellors*	*Percentage*
Yes	25	83%
No	5	17%

The table 18.12 indicates that 83 per cent *i.e.* the majority of the counselors found the flow of the content in the textbooks is sequential and appropriate.

Table 18.13: Is there any Gap in the Chapters According to the Need of Content of the Course?

Opinion	*Number of Counsellors*	*Percentage*
Yes	5	17%
No	25	83%

The data in the table 18.13 indicates that 83 per cent of the counselors found the study material *i.e.* the text books with continuous and appropriate flow of the content.

Table 18.14: Appropriateness of the Study Material for the Self Study

Opinion	*Number of Counsellors*	*Percentage*
Appropriate	24	80%
Not appropriate	6	20%

The data from the table 18.14 indicates that 80 per cent of the counselors found the study material appropriate for the self study. The 20 per cent of the counselors suggested that some of the portions are not written in details and found insufficient.

Table 18.15: Framework of the Textbook in Concern With Topics framing

Opinion	*Number of Counsellors*	*Percentage*
Good	6	20%
OK	20	67%
Not satisfactory	4	13%

From the data in table 18.15 it reveals that 67 per cent of the counselors found the framework of the textbooks in concern with the topics framing OK and 6 per cent found good. But the 13 per cent of the counselor found this aspect not satisfactory.

Table 18.16: Understanding Level of the Language in the Textbooks

Opinion	*Number of Counsellors*	*Percentage*
Good	6	20%
OK	20	67%
Not satisfactory	4	13%

The table 18.16 indicates that 67 per cent of the counselors found the language in the textbooks OK for the content understanding by the students. 20 per cent found good. But 13 per cent of the counselors found the language not satisfactory for the understanding.

Table 18.17: Illustrations and the Examples in the Text Book

Opinion	*Number of Counsellors*	*Percentage*
Good	4	13%
OK	21	70%
Not satisfactory	5	17%

The data in the table 18.17 indicates that 70 per cent of the counselors found the illustrations and the examples in the textbook OK, 13 per cent found good. Regarding this aspect 17 per cent of the counselors expressed their dissatisfaction.

Table 18.18: Overall Understanding Level of the Programme

Opinion	*Number of Counsellors*	*Percentage*
Easy	20	67%
OK	08	27%
Difficult	02	6%

The data from table 18 reveals that 67 per cent of the counselors found the overall understanding level of the programme easy, 27 per cent counselors found OK and 6 per cent of the counselors found difficult.

Table 18.19: Computer Availability at the Study centres

Opinion	*Number of Counsellors*	*Percentage*
Yes	23	77%
No	07	23%

From the table 18.19 it is clear that 77 per cent of the counselors observed the computer availability at their study centres, but 23 per cent of the counselors didn't found the enough computers at their study centres.

Table 18.20: Do you Teach and Complete all Practical's of Your Course?

Opinion	*Number of Counsellors*	*Percentage*
Yes	28	93%
No	02	7%

The data in table 18.20 indicates that 93 per cent of the counselors complete all practicals of their concerned courses. 7 per cent counselors could not complete all practicals due the reason of absenteeism from both sides *i.e.* by the students and the counselors.

Table 18.21: According to your Opinion, is the Content of the Programme Outdated?

Opinion	*Number of Counsellors*	*Percentage*
Yes	01	3%
No	29	97%

Table 18.21 indicates that 97 per cent of the counselors observed the content of the programme relevant to the present needs.

Table 18.22: Need of the Training Programme for the Counselors

Opinion	Number of Counsellors	Percentage
Yes	23	77%
No	07	23%

The data from the table 22 indicates that 77 per cent of the counselors felt the need of orientation training programme for them by the university every year because such professional degree programme implementation is the new concepts in distance education.

Table 18.23: Attendance of the Students to the Counseling Session?

Opinion	*Number of Counsellors*	*Percentage*
Good	27	90%
Bad	03	10%

From the table 18.23 it is clear that 90 per cent of the study centres have good attendance of the students on their study centres but 10 per cent of the study has not.

Table 18.24: How the Practical Sessions are Organized?

Opinion	*Number of Counsellors*	*Percentage*
GroupWise	28	93%
Collectively	02	7%

The data in the table 18.24 indicates that 93 per cent of the study centres are conducting the practical's for the students in proper m anner*i.e.* group wise but some of the study centres are conducting the practicals collectively because they have fewer enrolments.

Table 18.25: Do the Students Raise Difficulties/Questions While Teaching?

Opinion	*Number of Counsellors*	*Percentage*
Yes	15	50%
No	15	50%

The data in the table 18.25 indicates that only 50 per cent of the counselors reported that the students ask difficulties and sessions can be conducted in an interactive way. But 50 per cent of the counselors reported that students are not interested in interaction. Hence they teach the portions and after that if the students have difficulties they ask later on.

Table 18.26: Do you Get Co-operation From the Study Centre Administrative Staff?

Opinion	*Number of Counsellors*	*Percentage*
Yes	29	97%
No	01	3%

The data in table 18.26 reveals that 97 per cent of the counselors get the full co-operation from the study centre's administrative staff.

Table 18.27: Do you Get Salaries in Time?

Opinion	*Number of Counsellors*	*Percentage*
Yes	28	93%
No	02	7%

In the table 18.27 it is clear that 93 per cent of the counselors receive their salaries at proper time. 7 per cent of the counselors don't receive the salaries in time. This dissatisfaction may be the reason for absenteeism for conducting the counseling sessions.

Table 18.28: Appropriateness of the Evaluation Pattern of the Programme

Opinion	*Number of Counsellors*	*Percentage*
Yes	30	100%
No	00	0%

From the data in the table 18.28, it is clear that the evaluation pattern of the programme is found appropriate by the all counselors.

Table 18.29: Do you Face any Difficulty from the Study Centre?

Opinion	*Number of Counsellors*	*Percentage*
Yes	01	3%
No	29	97%

The data in the table 18.29 indicates that 97 per cent of the counselors don't have the difficulties from the study centre. But the 3 per cent of the counselors face some difficulties. As they have reported in their open feedback, they are facing difficulties mostly related to the salaries and hence they are dissatisfied with their work.

Table 18.30: Do you Have any Difficulty With Study Material?

Opinion	*Number of Counsellors*	*Percentage*
Yes	22	73%
No	08	27%

From the table 18.30 the data indicates that 73 per cent of the counselors found that that the study material *i.e.* the textbooks shall be edited properly and shall be updated at least after three years.

Table 18.31: Do you Face any Difficulty from the Students?

Opinion	*Number of Counsellors*	*Percentage*
Yes	04	13%
No	26	87%

The data from the table 31 indicates that majority of the counselors don't have any difficulty from the students.

FINDINGS

1. Majority of the counselors of the B Sc HTM programme found the construction, the study material, the syllabus of the programme OK and relevant to the present needs.
2. Majority of the counselors reported the services from the school very prompt, services from stores late, services from the registration and examination section OK and the cooperative behaviour from the regional centers staff.
3. Regarding the programme construction in detail the majority of the counselors reported that as they read the objectives of the course before teaching, they found the courses included are according to the objectives of the programme, appropriate content in the text books, appropriate flow of the content, study material appropriate for self study, framing of the books, language in the books, illustrations and examples in the book and overall understanding of the books are OK.
4. Regarding the management at the study centers majority counselors reported that their study centers are equipped with the computers, the practical are mostly completed, good attendance of the students for the counseling sessions, and the practical are conducted in a small groups of students for the better understanding of the course content. 50 per cent counselors reported that student asks the queries during the counseling sessions. The counselors get the cooperation from the study center staff and the students. They get their salaries in time.
5. The counselors have expressed the need of orientation programme at least once in a year because this is the innovative professional degree programme through the distance education.

6. Evaluation pattern of the programme is reported most appropriate by all counselors.

CONCLUSIONS

In the present communication, the need and importance of Distance Education as a vehicle for development and change has been discussed. The B. Sc. HTM is the programme as a representative of achievement to the challenges like implementing the professional programmes through the distance education mode. A pilot study of the programme evaluation for B. Sc. HTM programme in respect of study material appropriateness, counseling session's conduction, programme implementation etc has been discussed.

The B. Sc. HTM programme has been described by the counselors a landmark proagramme in the sense that in India, no other programme has been launched which is so much professional in nature; caters to the need of middle class and is offered through the Distance mode.

This programme has an enrolment of about 1500 students annually. About 90 per cent of the students attend the counseling and practical sessions regularly. The passing per cent is around 90 per cent and the dropout rate is around 10 per cent as per the examination records. The study conducted on a sample of 30 counselors revealed that the construction, the syllabus, the study material is good. The services from the university are satisfactory. The only problem is with the late receipt of the study material. For the more perfection the text books needs some improvement. The pilot study on the counselors has shown that the professional programmes can be implemented in a successful manner through the distance education.

REFERENCES

Atkare, P.S. (1998) An evaluation of Diploma programme in fruit production offered by YCMOU, Nashik, A thesis submitted for fulfillment of the degree of M.Sc. Distance Education.

Bawiskar, Madhuri (1999) An evaluation of Diploma programme in vegetable production offered by YCMOU, Nasik. A thesis submitted for fulfillment of the degree of M.Sc. Distance Education.

Datta, Rudra (1990), "Distance education policies and strategies: A case study of India" in *Distance Education Development and Access*, edited by Ian Mug ridge, Marian Croft and Others Universidad Nacional Abierta, Caracas, pp. 67-69.

Joao, Oliveira and Greville Rumble (1992), *Growth Vocational Education at a Distance*, Kogan, p. 165.

Karen, Evans (1999) "Barriers to Participation of Women in Technological Education and the Role of Distance Education", *The Commonwealth of Learning*, 1995.

Motilal, Sharma (1990), "Lifelong Education", *Distance Education*, Asian Development Bank pp. 53/54.

Gujar, Rucha (2004), An Evaluation of Certificate in Beauty Parlor Management Programme of YCMOU. A thesis submitted for the fulfillment of the degree of M A Distance Education.

Gujar, Rucha (2006), Towards a new paradigm of professional education through distance mode: A case study of diploma in Interior Design and Decoration Programme of YCMOU, *Indian Journal of Open Learning*, IGNOU, Delhi May 2006.

Neelam, Soni (1995) "Post Literacy and Continuing Education", Extension Education in Colleges and Universities in India, Student Aid Publications p. 35.

Panda, Santosh (1993) "Programme evaluation in distance education: A perspective and proposed agenda of action", All India Association for Educational Technology, New Delhi p. 63.

Passornsiri, Nittaya (1990) "STOU in its first decade" in *Distance Education Development and Access*, edited by Ian Mug ridge, Marian Croft and Others Universidad Nacional Alberta, Caracas, pp. 34-36.

Prasad, V.S. (1993) "Vocational programmes through distance mode: Dr. B.R. Ambedkar Open University Experience" in *Technical and Vocational Programmes through Distance Education* edited by R.V.R. Chandrashekhar Rao Dr. B R Ambedkar Open University, Hyderabad, p. 115.

Reddy, V.V. (1999) "Reaching out unreached: Experiences of IGNOU" Paper presented at the IDEA conference held at YCMOU, Nasik, 30-31 Jan 1999.

19

Female Literacy in India

A Long Road Ahead

Lokanath Mishra

Women constitute almost half of the population in the world. But the hegemonic masculine ideology made them suffer a lot as they were denied equal opp. ortunities in different parts of the world. The rise of feminist ideas has, however, led to the tremendous improvement of women's condition throughout the world in recent times. Access to education has been one of the most pressing demands of theses women's rights movements. Women's education in India has also been a major preoccupation of both the government and civil society as educated women can play a very important role in the development of the country.

History of Women's Education in India: Although in the Vedic period women had access to education in India, they had gradually lost this right. However, in the British period there was revival of interest in women's education in India. During this period, various socio religious movements led by eminent persons like Raja Ram Mohan Roy, Iswar Chandra Vidyasagar emphasized on women's education in India. Mahatma Jyotiba Phule, Periyar and Baba Saheb Ambedkar were leaders of the lower castes in India who took various initiatives to make education available to the women of India. However women's education got a fillip after the country got independence in 1947 and the government has taken various measures to provide education to all Indian women. As a result women's literacy rate has grown over the three decades and the growth of female literacy has in fact been higher than that of male literacy rate. While in 1971 only 22 per cent of Indian women were literate, by the end of 2001 54.16 per cent female were literate. The growth of female literacy rate is 14.87 per cent as compared to 11.72 per cent of that of male literacy rate.

Importance of Women's Education in India: Women's education in India plays a very important role in the overall development of the country. It not only helps in the development of half of the human resources, but in improving the quality of life at home and outside. Educated women not only tend to promote education of their girl children, but also can provide better guidance to all their children. Moreover educated women can also help in the reduction of infant mortality rate and growth of the population.

WOMEN'S EDUCATION IN INDIA

"An educated girl ensures the progress of the country". This one-liner, often found at the back of auto rickshaws in our country one of the Government's awareness initiatives for the education of the girl child. Some of these slogans and campaigns have been really good. But what does it mean to the average woman in India? Has it made a difference? Have the efforts paid off?

Immediately after India overthrew the British rule, the government of India appointed the University Education Commission in 1948-49. Headed by Dr. S. Radhakrishnan, scholar, philosopher, and a President of India, the Commission focused on higher education. The Commission report, prepared by Dr. Radhakrishnan, opens with an angry statement damning the British Government for their lax approach towards women's education.

A large portion of the report is dedicated to women's education, and it reiterates the importance and relevance of the same, along with a mention of the government's obligation to provide equal educational opportunities for married as well as unmarried women. Although it suggests that unmarried girls might want to be gainfully employed—and that was a big advance at the time—the report emphasizes with equal vigor that motherhood and home making are, and will forever remain, central to the lives of women. There is nothing wrong with the viewpoint. Educated mothers make a huge difference to the thinking of the entire family. In fact, decades after this report, it has been proven that in communities where the literacy rate of women is higher, instances of dowry deaths and female infanticide are far fewer.

Further, the Constitution of India, formed in 1951, asserted the equality of all citizens in the eyes of the law. In addition, it identified women (along with the country's various tribes and formerly untouchable castes) as one of the weaker sections of society—

sections that have been wronged and discriminated against for several generations. Through the subsequent years, the Government has emphasized education as one of the tools for the advancement of these sections. Interestingly, this happened long before governments of other nations had even thought of it. But where have these 55 years of proactive policy–making led us?

Even today, we need slogans like "Women Empowerment" and "Shikshit mulgi, surakshit parivar" to be written at the back of auto rickshaws to remind us that girls need to be educated. This makes it amply clear that government programmes and policies are empty rhetoric. Nothing will change unless society's approach to the issue changes and some real opportunities are made available to women.

Why would a lower middle class family, in globalised, liberalized, urbanized India, send their daughter to school when the immediate impact is one less hand to earn a living? For example, in Maharashtra, despite incentives such as free education for girls, including free books, uniforms, and even food, most bais choose to pull their daughters out of school. They would rather have them "learn the trade" and make themselves fit for a livelihood later in life than waste time in school. It doesn't matter that the child does not know to count or calculate the change that a shopkeeper ought to give her.

That's not the only thing. It's also interesting to note that in urban India, even among the educated sections of society, the remunerations for men and women are different. Women are paid less. This adds to the reluctance of lower middle class families to invest huge amounts in the higher education of their daughters.

What, then, is the solution? Why are almost 50 per cent of the women in India still uneducated? There are no straight answers to this one. It's a complex issue and needs sorting out at various levels. We might even have to sort out some more issues like female infanticide before we arrive at women's education.

While it may be near impossible for our society ensure an "education" for every daughter, it is definitely possible, I daresay, easy, to make her literate. If our efforts are consistent, we may see more women in rural India who can at least scrawl their name.

I know it's a mammoth effort and would take the next fifty years to get there. I think our best hope is the "Each one teaches one" policy. The way I see it, the educated urban youth need to find their way into every village and small town in India to ensure at least basic literacy. In our own homes, we can contribute by home–tutoring children.

The media has a huge role to play as well. The reach of radio and television is phenomenal. The depiction of women on the idiot box can make an impact that can only be imagined. Rural women have to be made aware of their potential beyond the house. In all this, the media should be careful not to project all urban, career–oriented women as selfish people who cannot care for their families. Street plays and other audio–visual media can also be leveraged effectively.

Similarly, in the depiction of rural women, there should be no attempt to preserve or glorify their rustic beauty. We need to treat them as people who need to be made aware of their rights and potential. After all, these same women are behind success stories like "the cooperative movement called Amul" and the hugely inspiring Lijjat Papad. To these women, the benefits of working in an industry should be emphasized. They should be made aware of incentives like maternity leave and housing loans. Awareness is the key.

Of course, there is no denying that many of the efforts over the last 55 years have paid off. But a lot remains to be done. It's about time that women made an effort to exercise the equality made legally available to them. I know there's a long way to go. But I also know that we have it in us to do it.

Obstacles: Gender discrimination still persists in India and lot more needs to be done in the field of women's education in India. The gap in the male–female literacy rate is just a simple indicator. While the male literary rate is more than 75 per cent according to the 2001 census, the female literacy rate is just 54.16 per cent.

Prevailing prejudices, low enrollment of girl child in the schools, engagements of girl children in domestic works and high dropout rate are major obstacles in the path of making all Indian women educated

According to la. St Census held in 2001, the percentage of female literacy in the country is 54.16 per cent.

The literacy rate in the country has increased from 18.33 per cent in 1951 to 65.38 per cent as per 2001 census. The female literacy rate has also increased from 8.86 per cent in 1951 to 54.16 per cent. It is noticed that the female literacy rate during the period 1991-2001 increased by 14.87 per cent whereas male literacy rate rose by

11.72 per cent. Hence the female literacy rate actually increased by 3.15 per cent more compared to male literacy rate.

LITERACY STATUS IN SOUTH ASIAN COUNTRIES

Country	*Total Non-Literate Population 15+age (in million)*	*Literacy Rate 15+ (%)(2000-2004)*		
		Total	*Male*	*Female*
Maldives	--	96	96	96
Sri Lanka	--	91	92	89
India	268.42	61	73	48
Bhutan	--	--	--	--
Pakistan	48.81	50	63	36
Nepal	7.66	49	63	35
Bangladesh	52.53	43	52	33

Source: Education for All–Global Monitoring Report-2007.

India: Population in 15-35 Age-group

Age-group	*Persons*	*Males*	*Females*
Total Population			
15-19	100,215,890	53,939,991	46,275,899
20-24	89,764,132	46,321,150	43,442,982
25-29	83,422,393	41,557,546	41,864,847
30-34	74,274,044	37,361,916	36,912,128
15-35	347,676,459	179,180,603	168,495,856
Literate Population			
15-19	79,462,115	45,837,429	33,624,686
20-24	65,731,454	38,574,667	27,156,787
25-29	55,931,949	32,863,958	23,067,991
30-34	45,813,001	27,948,542	17,864,459
15-35	246,938,519	145,224,596	101,713,923
Literacy Rate	71.03%	81.04%	60.36%
Non-literate Population			
15-19	20,753,775	8,102,562	12,651,213
20-24	24,032,678	7,746,483	16,286,195
25-29	27,490,444	8,693,588	18,796,856
30-34	28,461,043	9,413,374	19,047,669
15-35	100,737,940	33,956,007	66,781,933

FACTORS RESPONSIBLE FOR POOR FEMALE LITERACY RATE

Historically, a variety of factors have been found to be responsible for poor female literate rate, viz.

1. Gender based inequality
2. Social discrimination and economic exploitation
3. Occupation of girl child in domestic chores
4. Low enrolments of girls in schools
5. Low retention rate and high dropout rate.

Strategies Adopted by the Government for Increasing Female Literacy in the Country

The main strategies adopted by the Government for increasing female literacy in the country include: National Literacy Mission for imparting functional literacy

Universalization for Elementary Education Non–Formal Education

CONTRIBUTION OF LITERACY CAMPAIGNS TO FEMALE LITERACY

The provision of educational opportunities for women has been an important part of the national endeavor in the field of education since India's Independence. Though these endeavors did yield significant results, gender disparity persists with uncompromising tenacity, more so in the rural areas and among the disadvantaged communities. This is not only a matter of national anxiety and concern but also a matter of national conscience. It is with this concern that the Government of India launched the National Literacy Mission in 1988 for eradication of adult illiteracy. Since women account for an overwhelming percentage of the total number of illiterates, the National Literacy Mission is for all practical purposes a Mission of imparting functional literacy to women. Total literacy campaigns launched since 1988 under the aegis of the National emphasis on making efforts to:–

Create an environment where women demand knowledge and information, empowering themselves to change their lives.

Inculcate in women the confidence that change is possible, if women work collectively. Spread the message that education of women is a pre-condition for fighting against their oppression. Highlight the plight of the girl child and stress the need for Universalization of elementary education as a way of addressing the issue. Some of the significant ways in which the literacy campaigns have contributed to the promotion of female literacy and women's empowerment are as follows:–

HEIGHTENED SOCIAL AWARENESS

Literacy campaigns have heightened social awareness among women regarding the importance of education, both for themselves as well as for their children. Large numbers of women have been participating whole–heartedly in the literacy campaigns as learners and volunteers. Because of the campaign mode and creation of a positive environment for literacy, women receive a social sanction to participate in the literacy programmes. As women came out of their homes and take part in the campaigns with great enthusiasm, they acquire a heightened sense of self-awareness and desire to gain knowledge of host of women's issues.

INCREASED SCHOOL ENROLMENT

The literacy campaigns have also motivated and encouraged women learners to educate their children, particularly girls by enrolling them in formal schools. An evaluation study of the literacy campaign ion Birbhum District shows that the biggest achievement of the adult literacy programme in Birbhum has been its impact on girls' education. The confidence of the girls, as they perform drill or play football, is the result of the awareness among neo-literate parents that girls need to be educated and outgoing. The need to provide equal opportunity to both girls and boys has also had effect of generating greater demand for the quantity to both girls and boys has also had effect of generating greater demand for the quantity and quality of primary schooling.

INCREASE IN SELF–CONFIDENCE AND PERSONALITY DEVELOPMENT

The literacy classes conducted under literacy campaigns have given women as opportunity to break the isolation which is socially structured into their lives, giving them a chance to meet other women and learn collectively–rather than learn singly as individuals. The newly acquired literacy skills have enhanced their ability to solve family problems and learn new skills. Women are communicating how they have started feeling more confident, how their articulation has improved, how they have become more discerning and how they have learnt to function autonomously.

GENDER EQUITY AND WOMEN'S EMPOWERMENT

Total literacy campaigns have provided illiterate adult women, who have been denied access to formal schooling, with a great opportunity for reading, writing, increasing awareness levels and skills training. Literacy campaigns have thus actively promoted gender equity and have sought to empower them as to decision making about themselves, their families and their communities. The impact of literacy on women's life has often been dramatic. Experiences of Poddukuttai in Tamil Nadu (where women learnt how to bicycle and acquired ownership right in stone quarries) and Nellore in Andhra Pradesh (where a lesson in the literacy Primer inspired women to launch anti-arrack agitation that later engulfed the entire district and the state) have shown how women have been empowered at individual and collective levels as a result of their participation.

STATUS IN THE FAMILY

Literacy campaigns have played a significant role in improving the status of women within their own families. Whereas traditionally, women have little say in the family decision making, they, through participation in literacy programmes, have begun to express their newly found self-belief in having say both within and without the family.

EDUCATIONAL EQUALITY

Another area in which women's equality has shown a major improvement as a result of adult literacy programmes is the area of enrolment of boys and girls in schools. As a result of higher participation of women in literacy campaigns, the gender gap in literacy levels is gradually getting reduced. Even more significant is the fact that disparity in enrolment of boys and girls in neo-literate households is much lowered compared to the non-literate householders.

WOMEN AS ENTREPRENEURS

Participation of women is literacy campaigns have opened several opportunities for neo-literate women to step out of the households and involve themselves in some enterprise or a new vocation. The Dumka campaign in Bihar has demonstrated how literacy campaign has helped women has demonstrated how literacy campaign has helped women to take charge of their lives. They have formed a group called "Joga Behna" (Awake sister), which tries to sensitize the women to the need of collective action against social ills. These women have also set up "Didi Bank" (Sister Bank) which promotes the habits of thrifts and savings. Here women have also learnt to maintain hand pump thereby breaking their dependence for repair on mechanics from outside the village. SHG in orissa also improve the economic condition of women

HOUSEHOLD SAVINGS AND ACCESS TO CREDIT

In almost all the districts, the literacy campaigns have gone beyond the transaction of mere literacy skills and have served to enhance knowledge and skills for better management of expenditure and improving earning capacities. In several districts, the women participants in literacy campaigns have begun to set aside their earnings not only in regular banks but also in specially thrift societies. Such societies, as for example in Dumka are run by the women themselves.

HEALTH AND HYGIENE

Literacy campaigns in most districts have taken up health and hygiene issues as an integral component of adult education programmes. Literacy campaigns have helped to spread knowledge about health care and nutrition, thereby enabling mothers to keep their family in better health and to care better for their children. Literacy campaigns have also disseminated information for creating awareness about problems of early marriage, spacing and small family norms.

20

Role of Facilitators in a Total Literacy Programme for Women

An Analysis of Jyothirgamaya Programme

C. Naseema and *V.K. Jibin*

After the Declaration of total literacy in Kerala in 1990, no mentionable follow up work was conducted in the Literacy programme. It was assumed that the state of Kerala is still a leading state in India with almost total literacy.

But as evidence against this belief, Nilambur Gram Panchayat in Malappuram District of Kerala State conducted a detailed survey about the present status of literacy rate including other factors like health and socio-economic status of the Panchayat. 2700 volunteers selected for the purpose participated in the survey for collecting data from about 7000 houses situated in the Nilambur Gram Panchayat.

The survey revealed that more than 1500 people of the Gram Panchayat are either illiterate or educated below 4th standard. Among the identified group, 800 are illiterate and 700 are educated below 4th standard *i.e.,* the dropouts of primary education.

The above facts lead to the idea of a project towards the total Primary Education Programme which was aptly named as 'Jyothirgamaya'–which means "leading from darkness to light". This was an ambitious project which covered the illiterates and dropouts at lower primary level at the age group of 15 to 50 with a purpose to give them education at least up to the 4th standard.

This project was an innovative one and first of its kind in the country–A gram panchayat aiming at the achievement of total primary education programme. *Jyothirgamaya* and was organized with the support of Kerala State Literacy Mission.

Jyothirgamaya was an attempt to popularize total primary education without any financial assistance from any leading agency but with the support of the enthusiasm and integrity of the youth participating in the total primary education campaign. This was really encouraging and promising.

The term facilitator here refers to those who facilitate learning. Facilitation describes a range of pedagogical techniques whose shared goal is to guide and assist learning processes, while encouraging high levels of learner ownership and participation. Facilitation places learners at the center of educational activities, values knowledge that learners have acquired through lived experiences, and shifts the focus of processes and activities to the learners themselves. In short, facilitation makes learners much more responsible for their learning than more traditional pedagogical approaches.

The objectives of the study are: 1. To study the extent of the involvement of facilitators in the implementation of the Total Primary Education Programme; 2. To find out the difficulties faced by the facilitators in the implementation of the Total Primary Education Programme.

METHODOLOGY

Tool: Questionnaire on the Functioning of Total Primary Education Programme (for Facilitators)

Sample: 180 Facilitators randomly selected constitute the sample of the study.

Statistical Techniques: Percentage analysis was carried out as the statistical technique.

MAJOR FINDINGS

Data collected from 180 facilitators randomly selected from the population were analyzed and summarized as follows:

1. Involvement of Facilitators in the Implementation of the Total Primary Education

Programme.: The economical background of the facilitators voluntarily participated in the Jyothirgamaya project is presented below

(i) *Economic background of the Facilitator*: Table 20.1 shows the distribution of family monthly income of the facilitators.

Table 20.1: Details of Family Monthly Income of the Facilitators

Sl. No.	*Family Income (in Rupees)*	*Percentage*
1	Below 1000	62.5
2	1001 – 5000	32.5
3	5001 – 10,000	2.5
4	10,000 and above	2.5
	Total	100.00

Table 20.1 reveals that majority (62.5 %) of the facilitators' family earn an income below

Rs. 1000. 32.5 per cent of the respondents' family income was between 1001 to 5000, 2.5 per cent of respondents family income was in between 5001–10,000 and 2.5 per cent reported their family income as above 10,000 per month.

It is clear from the Table 20.1 that most of the facilitators belong to lowest economic status and they, with all the burden, supported the primary education project for its success with their voluntary services.

(ii) *Class time*: Class timings opted by the facilitators of the Primary education programme is shown Table 20.2

Table 20.2: Class time of the Learning Centres

Sl. No.	*Class time*	*Percentage*
1	2 pm – 4 pm	31.25
2	4 pm – 6 pm	31.25
3	6 pm – 8 pm	30.00
4	8 pm – 10 pm	7.50
	Total	100.00

It can be seen that 31.25 per cent of respondents opted the time between 2 pm to 4 pm or between 4 pm to 6 pm. Only 30 percent of them conducted their classes between 6 pm to 8 pm and 7.5 per cent of the respondents opted 8pm to 10 pm for teaching.

(iii) *Previous experience of the facilitators*: Table 20.3 indicates whether the facilitators had previous experience in any literacy programmes.

Table 20.3: Previous Experience of the Facilitators in Literacy Programme

Sl .No.	*Previous Experience-response of facilitators*	*Percentage*
1	Yes	16.25
2	No	81.25
3	No response	2.50
	Total	100.00

81.25 per cent of the respondents were having no previous experience in any literacy programmes while 16.25 per cent had previous experience.

(iv) *Factors inspired for voluntary participation in Jyothirgamaya Project:* Table 20.4 indicates the factors inspired the facilitators to participate in total primary education programme voluntarily, without any external motivation.

Table 4: Factors Inspired the Facilitators for Voluntary Participation

Sl. No.	*Inspiring Factors*	*Percentage*
1	Interest in social service	90.00
2	Interest in Teaching	82.50
3	Interest in Literacy Programme	70.00
4	Freedom from family atmosphere	2.50

Table 20.4 shows that for the 90 per cent of the respondents their interest in social service inspired them to co-operate with this programme and 82.5 per cent of facilitators told that they have interest in teaching. Interest in literacy programme (70 %) and freedom from family atmosphere (2.5 per cent) are the other factors compelled them to participate in the programme.

(v) Teaching Methods Used

Table 20.5 shows the response of the facilitators regarding the teaching methods they used in classroom.

Table 20.5: Teaching Methods Used by the Facilitators

Sl. No.	Method of teaching	Percentage
1	Learner friendly methods	76.25
2	Conventional method	16.25
3	No Response	7.50
	Total	100.00

Majority of Respondents *i.e.,* 76.25 per cent reported that they used Learner friendly methods for teaching their adult learners, while only 16.25 per cent responded that they used conventional method for teaching the learners.

It shows that majority of the facilitators were aware about the needs and problems of their learners and they used learner friendly methods like teaching "from words to letters" methods, activity oriented methods etc.

(vi) Awareness About the Ability of Learners

Table 20.6 shows the awareness of the facilitator about the personal capability of each learner.

Table 20.6: Awareness of Facilitator About the Abilities of the Learners

Sl. No.	*Awareness about the learners*	*Percentage*
1	Yes	97.50
2	No	2.50
	Total	100.00

Majority of the facilitators *i.e.,* 97.5 per cent reported that they were personally aware of the capabilities of each learner. Only 2.5 per cent responded that they don't know their abilities personally.

This shows that the most of the facilitators succeeded in understanding each of their learners' ability in learning which an important quality is required for an effective facilitator.

(vii) Improvement in Total Life of Learners

Table 20.7 shows the opinion of the Facilitators about the improvement in total life of learners.

Table 20.7: Facilitators' Opinion About the Improvement in Total Life of Learners

Sl .No.	*Improvement in life of the learners*	*Percentage*
1	Not at all	3.75
2	To some extent	31.25
3	To a great extent	58.75
4	No response	6.25
	Total	100.00

58.75 per cent of Facilitators responded that total life of learners have improved to a great extent, while 31.25 per cent said that total life of learners have improved only to some extent, while only 3.75 per cent responded that it has not at all improved. 6.25 per cent have not responded to this question.

Majority of the Facilitators have the opinion that the total life of the learners have improved as a result of Jyothirgamaya Project. Total improvement in life is assessed based on the learners' improvement of self confidence, knowledge in health related aspects, political awareness, legal literacy, knowledge about social responsibilities, care in the education of children, interest in conservation of nature, willingness to present views and opinions, awareness about external affairs and ability to react.

2. Difficulties Faced by Facilitators

The facilitators felt some difficulties to teach learners of the total primary education programme according to their different standards and different memory power. Most of them found that it is difficult to come down to the level of learners as they are very slow in learning. Poor hearing capacity, poor eyesight and old age of the learners were the major obstacles faced by the facilitators in interacting with them and teaching the learners.

Many facilitators are of the opinion that the time they got to spend for the learners was insufficient. 60 percentages expressed that the time was not enough to teach the learner each day as the learners are from different family and social background. In their opinion at least four hours of teaching and learning is essential for effective study.

Different linguistic styles of the learners, use of different colloquial styles, lack of punctuality in attending the class and difference in class timings are the other problems faced by the facilitators in their venture. Many Facilitators complained about the lack of primary essential facilities of the learning centres. They complained about the seating, roofing and furniture of the centres. Lack of electricity was also a major problem in some learning centres.

CONCLUSION AND EDUCATIONAL IMPLICATIONS

The analysis revealed that a total primary education project can be made successful with the sincere support of facilitators. The problems listed by them in the implementation of the programme and their remedial measures can be considered as the suggestions for the better functioning of any literacy programmes.

Most of the facilitators belong to lowest economic status and they, with the entire burden, supported the primary education project for its success with their voluntary services. For the 90 per cent of the respondents their interest in social service inspired them to co-operate with this programme and 82.5 per cent of facilitators told that they have interest in teaching.

76.25 per cent reported that they used Learner friendly methods for teaching the adult learners. Most of the facilitators succeeded in understanding each of their learners' ability in learning which an important quality is required for an effective facilitator.

One thing specially to be noticed is that if some of the facilitators are trained in teaching of Adult learners, the effectiveness of the literacy programmes or total primary education programmes could be increased. Majority of the Facilitators have the opinion that the total life of the learners have improved as a result of Jyothirgamaya Project.

REFERENCES

Naseema, C. (2008), *Evaluation of Jyothirgamaya Project—A Total Primary Education project in Nilambur*

Gram Panchayat of Malappuram District (2008), A Project report submitted to University Grants Commission, New Delhi.

www.Asian–University.org

www.nlm.nic.in/women.htm

www.globaled.org/curriculum/wlit.html

www.indiaedu.com/education–india/**women**-edu.html

21

Developing an Interdisciplinary Concept for Sustainable Global Milieu

Hemant Kumar Khandai and *Shabnam Khan*

Nowadays, the changes in the international environment are associated with the fast exchange of new ideas and technological innovation. The globalization of jobs is an inevitable result of the knowledge–driven economic development. The job market is expanding and becoming global. Indian industry finds a serious shortage of skills. Employers have complained that they are unable to find required talent in their drive to become world class, owing to the pressure of competition as a result of globalization this gap between institutional input and industrial requirements can be filled only by inculcating two capabilities in students. The first is task performance capability focused on acquiring skills required by employers. The second involves building conceptual performance which is not job related but behaviour related. These can be obtained by practicing Interdisciplinary Approach in higher education. Corporate today have realized the importance of Interdisciplinary Approach to solve these complex problems.

INTERDISCIPLINARY APPROACH

Interdisciplinary enables integration of concepts, theories, techniques and perspectives from two or more disciplines to advance fundamental understanding or to solve problems whose solutions are beyond the scope of a single discipline." All cutting edge developments in technologies occur at the interface of two or more disciplines. Interdisciplinary is a key to sustaining knowledge–based development (KBD), since any single discipline can be capable of dealing adequately with the complex realities of the knowledge

Societies Integrating Interdisciplinary Approach to academic programmes can become an efficient means to cope up with the complexities. This approach is intended to provide the intellectual synthesis. In such a programme, general subjects–social sciences, languages, etc.–are incorporated with specialized subjects (mathematics, physics, computing, management, etc.).

Its outcomes are

- Ability to use knowledge in practice.
- Ability to design and investigate.
- Ability to create and innovate.
- Ability to manage and compete.
- Ability to communicate proficiently in the international community.
- Understanding the significance for self-development and life-long learning.
- Understanding social, professional and ethical responsibility.

SIGNIFICANCE OF INTERDISCIPLINARY APPROACH IN GLOBALIZATION

Interdisciplinary education is growing in importance across the globe, with an increased focus on innovation through research and development in order to advance towards a more 'knowledge–based' economy. Also, today Interdisciplinarity is being recognized to be essential for innovation and Universities are unique environments where high academic standards and a vast range of disciplines meet and flourish. In recent years, the spectacular growth of knowledge in science and technology has been made possible by the integrated efforts of scientists, engineers and social scientists, in addressing complex problems from the perspectives of different disciplines. There was a time when a person would remain in one profession for a lifetime. Now a US survey has shown that on an average a person changes at least 10 professions in his lifetime. The Global job market demands Interdisciplinary skills including good team work skills Today, in business and in science, to use multi–functional and intercultural teams to cope with complex problems has become a widespread practice. Business experts state that this is the only way to assemble the knowledge and breadth required to pull off many complex tasks the business faces today. The main concern for education experts is to provide their graduates with a wide variety of skills required for the new knowledge–based economy, which needs professionals who can learn, explore, analyze, design and innovate.

Most of the innovations that you see today are interdisciplinary and we are in the nascent stage when it comes to sectors like telecommunications, pharma and alternative health sciences." the cell phone revolution and the making of the Nano car exemplary examples of the application of interdisciplinary science to modern day needs and feels that indigenous discoveries and inventions in pharmacy and technology were delayed and hampered due to our closed minds

GLOBAL (INTERNATIONAL) EDUCATIONAL CHALLENGES

- Rapid technological progress and innovation.
- Globalization of the manufacturing base.
- Emergence of the knowledge–based society.
- Enhanced international cooperation.
- Increased need to communicate efficiently in the worldwide community.
- Faster economic growth.
- Increased competition.
- Increased government regulation of business.
- Socio–cultural and demographic changes.
- Formation of multicultural communities.
- Increased workforce mobility and customized global job market.
- Emergence of the idea of sustainable social development.
- New career opportunities (globalization of jobs, new job growth overseas, new career prospects).
- New threats and uncertainties (unemployment, displacement of jobs, Polarized work opportunities).
- Increasing diversification and specialization of knowledge.
- Rapidly evolving educational environment.
- Enlarged competition in order to retain and attract talents.
- Increased demand for higher education in relation to lifelong learning.
- Integration of the concepts of sustainability into all levels of education.
- Reorganization of knowledge delivery.

- Providing new opportunities to students in the context of the job market customization and lifelong learning.
- Providing computer–based learning to enhance knowledge and to change the way students learn.
- Providing multidisciplinary education to satisfy the requirements of the knowledge–based Economy.
- Developing a learning environment based on information and communication technologies (ICTs).
- Developing and making use of a set of management and pedagogical tools to provide improved knowledge acquisition
- Creating resourceful organizational environment to provide a more explorative and creative
- Learning, and ensure students' intellectual and professional growth

FORMS OF INTERDISCIPLINARITY

Interdisciplinarity of Neighboring Disciplines

Under this heading one could include cases in which two areas of science are becoming so closely involved with each other that there is an overlap to which both disciplines can contribute both methods and concepts.

Interdisciplinarity of Problems

In this one could apply to certain problem groups which cannot be included in a specific discipline and contain so many aspects that they could not be taken care of by just one discipline.

Interdisciplinarity of Methods

This type of interdisciplinarity is most likely to occur when methods peculiar to one discipline can be used for research in other disciplines as well.

Interdisciplinarity of Concepts

This type of interdisciplinarity refers to a situation in which models and concepts have been developed in one discipline and are then used to supplement research in another discipline or even supplant existing models and concepts.

Interdisciplinarity Through Themes, Topics or Ideas

The use of a theme as an organizing or integrating element can be used to show how different disciplines interrelate in the elaboration and illumination of the theme. This both assumes a disciplinary base and strengthens the understanding of the disciplines themselves as they are used in sequence or in concert to pursue a given theme or topic.

Interdisciplinarity in Practical Thinking

There are, however, areas of the curriculum which do not fall into traditional subject areas. These are in the main practical areas whose importance is made clear by individual or social demands. Civic education is a case in point.

Interdisciplinarity Through the Learner's Own Interested Inquiry

A further variation of approach is to make the learner's own interested inquiry the basis of the curriculum. This, by its nature, cannot be a discipline–bounded approach, it commences with the interests of a student. It will be an interdisciplinary approach where a variety of relevant disciplines is used to illuminate and structure the inquiry

The Sectors of Education Concerned by Interdisciplinarity at the Primary Level

At the primary level the interdisciplinary is most widespread. It is at this level too that is less contested and easier to apply. The primary school–teacher is not a specialist in one subject, and he is more prepared to accept and apply an interdisciplinary approach.

At the Secondary Level

At the secondary level it is more difficult to persuade teachers to accept interdisciplinarity, because they are less prepared for the pedagogic aspects of teaching than for proficiency in their subject. They are also much less versatile in respect of their training and their ideas than primary–school teachers. Subjects at the secondary level are taught in greater depth and the structure of the discipline is the object, often the principal one, of its teaching

At the Upper Secondary Level

Interdisciplinary is rarely applied, for the reasons that ignorance of the problem and of the different forms and possibilities of interdisciplinarity on the part of teachers and education authorities.

Occupational Training

Occupational training should be a privileged area of interdisciplinarity, since it is aimed directly at preparing the pupil to deal with occupational situations. But quite often, when the teaching departs from the purely occupational aspect and covers a theoretical aspect or a general theme, the teacher tends to revert to disciplines

At the University Level

At the university level the problem of interdisciplinarity arises in a more complex manner, because on the one hand it must be designed at three levels: teaching, research and service to the community and on the other hand the university aims to inculcate professional abilities and abilities to solve complex problems, as well as research and abstraction abilities.

NEW CAREER AVENUES AND INTERDISCIPLINARITY

- *Biomedical Engineering:* It deals with the integration of medicine and instruments, *i.e.* material engineering sciences with life sciences catering to the endless needs in diagnostics and internal medicine sensors (bioinstrumentation).
- *Cognitive Science* is the study of mind or the study of thought. It embraces multiple research disciplines, including psychology, artificial intelligence, philosophy, neuroscience, linguistics, anthropology, sociology and biology. It is used extensively in the fields of artificial intelligence and robotics.
- *Nanotechnology* is very diverse, ranging from extensions of conventional device physics to completely new approaches based upon molecular self-assembly and developing new materials with dimensions on the nanoscale.
- *Applied linguistics* is an interdisciplinary field of study that identifies, investigates, and offers solutions to language–

related real-life problems and is used widely in the technology space.

- *Biophysics* is an interdisciplinary science that employs methods of the physical sciences for the investigation of biological systems.
- *Astrobiology* is the study of the origin, evolution, distribution, and future of life in the universe. It makes use of physics, chemistry, astronomy, biology, molecular biology, ecology, planetary science, geography and geology.
- *Cybernetics* is the interdisciplinary study of the structure of regulatory systems. It connects the fields of control systems, electrical network theory, mechanical engineering, logic modeling, evolutionary biology, neuroscience, anthropology and psychology.
- *Econophysics* is an interdisciplinary research field, applying theories and methods originally developed by physicists in order to solve problems in economics.
- *Computing Graphics* are graphics created by using computers. It has revolutionized the animation and video game industry, it blends fine arts, pixel art and vector graphics.
- *Materials Science* aims at revolutionizing the construction industry, and is essentially built around materials, nanotechnology, engineering, architecture, design and environmental sciences

ADVANTAGES

Interdisciplinarity has numerous and important advantages. It provides an overall grasp of reality which makes possible a better understanding of its complexity, its interrelationships and its interactions. Furthermore, it provides a unifying framework for concepts and methods which can be used in different situations and in different disciplines. It is a manner of tackling problems which is more operational and more relevant to the social and physical environment It shows how the complex and imbricate problems of the contemporary world, which involve numerous disciplines, should be studied. There are also many advantages from the point of view of educational psychology. Firstly, interdisciplinarity is better adapted to the overall and harmonious development of the pupil as an individual. Secondly, it is better able to ensure the transferability of what is learned, thereby making the pupil more capable of dealing with real situations and new problems. It is an appropriate method of taking advantage of the pupil's experience and helping him to build up his knowledge on the basis of meaningful situations It is oriented towards 'open' learning, the critical analysis of situations, and creativity; furthermore, its dynamic probably conforms more to the ways in which learners perceive, organize and transform knowledge And at the primary level it is better adapted to children's overall approach and sensibility. Generally speaking, it provides greater incentive because the subjects studied are seen by the children to be more relevant to their concerns and interests. Interdisciplinarity has the great advantage of establishing dialectic between the school and the environment; it enables better use to be made of the situations and resources of the environment to organize relevant educational activities. Lastly, interdisciplinarity is a practical necessity because disciplines embrace such an increasingly wide field of subject matter that it is no longer possible to teach everything separately.

PROBLEMS FOR INTERDISCIPLINARITY

- Teachers at higher levels, tend to see themselves as specialists in a subject rather than experts in the development of abilities and attitudes.
- Interdisciplinarity sometimes encounters resistance on the part of parents, who no longer recognize the type of school they themselves attended
- Another difficult problem to which much effort must be devoted is the production of interdisciplinary textbooks. The rigidity of timetables is also a major obstacle
- The lack of materials, the lack of financial resources necessary for the innovation, in particular for the training of teachers are the most important obstacle to the introduction of an interdisciplinary reform
- The teacher has no methodology of interdisciplinarity which could provide him with a clear frame of reference and a specific guide for his teaching.
- The problem of evaluation in interdisciplinarity was raised several times. It was considered to be an essential one, but difficult to solve. Traditional evaluation is not appropriate to interdisciplinarity.

SUGGESTIONS AND PROPOSED LINES OF ACTION

- To attain the necessary level education managers have to create the environment distinguished by integrity, manageability, diversity of all subsystems within the entire system, flexibility, ergonomics, and the focus on the learner's requirements.
- Interdisciplinary Education can only be accomplished in the highly integrated educational environment (HIEE), which must be responsive to changes in technology, new developments in pedagogy and management, and the importance of lifelong learning.
- The integrated Educational Environment, where students can have an opportunity to create and to enhance their creative thinking and their creative potential, is an efficient means of preparing students for productive and satisfying careers in the knowledge–based economy
- We need the Educational Environment with clear connections to the social and global contexts of the profession, which provides a broad education.
- Teachers must be convinced, persuaded and trained.
- Evaluation must involve the affective as well as the cognitive aspects; it must cover overall abilities to grasp a problem, make a decision, and design, organize and implement an activity or a project.

THE OPINIONS AND EXPERIENCES

- We have currently is a steel box of a system within which there are smaller boxes with no interaction with the outside or with each other. There is a need for Interdisciplinary Experiences and this should help students sustain themselves when the demands of a particular job market change.

  The Yash Pal Committee Report on Renovation and Rejuvenation of Higher Education laments that what.
- "We need to go beyond multidisciplinary options to towards an interdisciplinary approach. All cutting edge developments in technologies occur at the interface of two or more disciplines."

  M. Anandakrishnan, Chairman, Board of Governors, (IIT)–Kanpur,

- DR. C V Raman has worked on the structure and function of the ribosome successfully combines the traditional domains of physics and chemistry. "Even modern biology has become very mathematical, based on genetics, quantum mechanics and other stream *Dr. Ra Mashelkar, President of INSA*
- "At present, there is a palpable demand for interdisciplinary professionals in the fields of environmental science, health sciences and computing specializations".

P. Banerjee, Director NISTADS, Delhi

CONCLUSION

Educational institutions are knowledge–based organizations, since knowledge is their major resource, knowledge delivery and knowledge creation being their main goal and their basic activity. They should provide their students with the opportunity to get professional knowledge and obtain professional skills. They should operate in a complicated educational environment, which includes pedagogical, organizational, managerial, and technological aspects. Pedagogical aspect includes pedagogical strategies that focus on the learning goals, learning process and learning outcomes. Technological aspect plays a key role in the educational environment based on information and communication technologies. An educational organization should develop an efficient educational environment capable of providing sustainable learning process. Management support ensures the coordination and cooperation of the available resources. On the one hand, education managers should distribute and use the organizational resources in order to ensure knowledge delivery/acquisition, knowledge sharing and new knowledge construction within the educational environment. On the other hand, they should gather the necessary information about the environment (how effectively the resources are engaged, what resources are needed, etc.), process this information and transform it into Knowledge. Using the obtained knowledge, education managers work out their strategy for the educational environment evolution. The aspects mentioned above are interconnected and mutually dependent. They provide the framework for creating the educational management strategy, which will involve a variety of management tools, as well as a combination of traditional and innovative pedagogical tools.

REFERENCES

American Educational Research Journal, Vol. 29.

Cheema, D.S., Degrees of Deception, *The Tribune*: Saturday, May 24, 2003

Lan, Zou, Striving for Change: Introducing an Interdisciplinary Approach into the urban primary school of China; International Education Studies; www.ccsenet.org/journal.htm.

Martin, Davies and Marcia Devlin, Interdisciplinary Higher Education: Implications for Teaching and Learning;

Repko, Allen F., *Assessing interdisciplinary learning outcomes*, University of Texas Arlington.

Van, R. Wood, Globalization and Higher Education: Eight Common Perceptions from University Leaders.

22

Lifelong Learning in Indian Higher Education: Challenges in Current Global Scenario

Hemant Kumar Khandai and *Anshu Mathur*

Education is not merely imparting knowledge in a particular faculty or subject. Education should be training in pragmatic and logical thinking and should help the coming generations adjust to the available environment. Education is not run now a days for its traditional basic goals: reading, writing, arithmetic, But to work for knowledge and skill development. In short, everything required to live and to communicate with the environment, everything that a person needs to participate in the life of his/her society is in education. Higher education as an integral part of Indian education system contain the terms, Lifelong learning and extension. *Lifelong learning* includes formal education as well as non-formal (organized educational activities that are not a part of the formal education progression system) and informal (individualized or group activities which are not provided through an educational institution. "The acquisition of knowledge, abilities and skills by using all systems of education (formal, non-formal and informal) in the lifespan of an individual for socio-economic, cultural and political emancipation leading to the holistic development of the community is called Lifelong learning." Three constituents of lifelong learning are—learning for life, learning for livelihood and learning throughout life. Lifelong learning in higher education attracts adults in changing global scenario for a higher education qualification to fulfill career-related reasons and/or for personal fulfillment; add to additional qualification for career change and to accomplish these needs of development.

The term '*globalization*' means integration of economies and societies through cross country flows of information, ideas, technologies, goods, services, capital, finance and people. There is no question that lifelong learning has become an essential part of life in the time of globalization, which has been called by some the new "Learning Age." Learning is needed throughout life, whether in formal settings or in informal ways will become integrated as a normal part of life. 11th plan guidelines on lifelong learning and extension emphasize upon the importance of lifelong learning/ education in India what is increased in recent times. In the era of globalization Lifelong Learning and extension in Indian higher education is viewed as medium to attain the equalization of opportunities, Promotion of human resources social competencies and economic empowerment. It requires a strong team of people with an aptitude to serve the community.

Players of Indian Higher Education to meet with the challenges of globalization

- University Grants Commission (UGC) set up under UGC Act 1956 is responsible for coordination, determination, and maintenance of standards and release of grants to universities and research organizations.
- Professional councils responsible for recognition of courses, promotion of professional institutions and provision of grants to undergraduate programmes.
- UNESCO (founded in 1945) with the goal "Education for all" by 2015 that includes Basic literacy, Post literacy and Continuing education programmes.
- Universities have also pooled and outreached its resources to the community. It has paved a way for equalizing educational opportunities for unreached population through various forms.
- Various private institutes who are running programmes of education through part time and distance mode and pre-service and in-service training programmes for the employees.
- India has an Open University system to encourage distance learning. Indira Gandhi National Open University (IGNOU) was the pioneer and now there are seven open universities in India offering over 500 courses. IGNOU has about 11,87,100 students on its rolls.

- National Literacy Mission and various flagship programmes associated with it are being organized at the formal institutional levels and through adopting non-formal approaches.
- Jan Shikshan Sansthans launched the Total Literacy Campaign, Post Literacy Programmes and Continuing Education Programmes
- Quality assurance at higher education by establishing
  - Quality Assurance Cells
  - Academic Staff Colleges
  - State Resource Center
- In higher education domain, the University Grants Commission has accepted the extension as the third dimension Strengthened and established the Departments of Adult, Continuing Education and Extension and Outreach in about 100 Universities.
- Establishment of the Departments of Adult Education (Lifelong Learning).
- Training the manpower, Documentation and dissemination, Preparation of Directories, Allocation of financial resources, Special assistance for research Seminars and Symposium, Promotion of professional bodies.

BARRIERS IN IMPLEMENTATION OF VARIOUS PROGRAMMES

Educating adults differ from educating children in several ways. Adults have accumulated knowledge and experience that can add to or hinder the learning experience. They frequently apply their knowledge in a practical fashion to learn effectively, so there is a need to improve education system with more real life experiences and to make it more meaningful with the concept of earning while learning. There is also need to attract rural population towards new industries or new methods of latest technologies, but the condition of majority of government schools/colleges (on which majority of Indians depend in villages) is pathetic. Major population of India in villages is educationally and facilities vise almost deprived. That is why no less than a revolution is needed in the extention education system in India. But there are some bariors in this field to achive the targets. Technical barriers include lack of infrastructure, multiple controls, outdated programmes with inflexible structures, lack of qualified teachers/trainers, shortage of basic facilities like training centers, libraries, latest technological gadgets or equipments including computer and Internet facilities, not having communication channels to approach. On the other hand there are some Behavioural barriers are also hitting the aim of extension education–Some adults feels that "higher education is for others–not for me." some adults feel that they are "too old" to return to education.

Secondly, Time, money and energy are the three biggest barriers facing by adults. Because they are dealing with family, work, and other commitments, time for education is very limited. Money for education is often limited as well, and takes a lower priority than family needs. Lastly an adult has difficulties understanding complex course selection, admissions procedures, classes' time, rules of attendances, course duration, lack of flexibility in course structures, transportation problems, etc. In many cases, universities do not provide sufficient information and guidance to receivers.

CURATIVE IDEAS TO EDUCATION SYSTEM, COPING WITH GLOBALIZATION

The impact of globalization on education and the manner in which the system should respond to the needs of globalization would require to be developing under following headings.

DEVELOPMENT OF PERSONAL LEARNING ENVIRONMENT

Personal Learning Environments are systems that help learners take control of and manage their own learning by providing support for learners to set their own learning goals, manage their learning; managing both content and process communicate with others in the process of learning by providing them environment full of study materials, libraries, laboratories, technological facilities, internet etc. We should find avenues of higher learning like science and technology in our regional languages too.

SMART COURSES

Education should fulfill the aspiration of the learner and leads to economic benefits. Global competition has to keep in mind so that the courses and curriculum are structured accordingly. Regular updating for the field functionaries, monitoring the adult literacy programmes, organizing both short term and long term courses on full time and part time basis for catering to the needs of the field Strategies, Establishment of the Departments of Adult Education everywhere, Training the manpower to develop human resources, Documentation and dissemination of latest technologies, Preparation of short term effective training programmes for rural population, Allocation of financial resources, Special assistance for research Seminars and Symposium, Promotion of professional bodies are the platforms to work on can be the weapons to fight the battle of globalize complexity.

EMPOWER DISTANCE EDUCATION

Distance education is the main player in the game of lifelong learning. This can fulfill Indian mindset of collecting Degrees as well as can give opportunity to rural population for their higher education. Re-structure the system of education leading to the equalization of educational opportunities through distance mode. We need a coherent education system for primary to higher level for everyone to acquire knowledge, skills and basic training in a particular vocational/trade.

FLEXIBLE EDUCATION

Education should be accessible to Anybody, Anytimeand Anywhere. Flexibility in courses, duration, admission, attendance, examination and fees structure can attract everybody towards higher education. Human resource development should be the main objective of education. Working adults need immediate and convenient access to learning opportunities throughout their lives. And these learning opportunities must be available and should be fit into the new life patterns of adults. The Lifelong Learning model should recognises that each person has individual learning goals and needs, and offers ways for the learner to design a course or programme to suit these needs.

GLOBALIZATION OF INDIAN EDUCATION

Expansion of activities across boundaries, which includes establishment of campuses abroad, attracts foreign students and creates virtual universities for extension. Indian education system should go for development of theoretical models based on the research, practices and involving the academic staff with different backgrounds and aptitudes. There is inadequate support for research, fellowships, training in research methodology, dissemination of research findings etc. Inter–disciplinary research in lifelong learning is with some opportunities for post graduation and research leading to M. Phil and Ph. D. in lifelong learning, is what required in the system.

EXPANSION OF QUANTITY AND QUALITY

Enhance productivity and make the education system factory of quality students and qualified youth, who can compete with the world market. It's a multi–dimensional concept, which includes all functions and activities that is teaching, research, cadmic environment, staffing, students, infrastructure and courses. Quality of Education can be checked thru independent body that timely evaluate the current position and needs as public service. International dimension of higher education should be an inherent part of quality.

EXPLORE DIFFERENT LEARNING PARADIGMS

Learning is relatively permanent is to emphasize that behaviour is flexible and not genetically pre-programmemed in form or function. Learned behaviours may exist for a lifetime, but they may also not appear throughout an individual's life. Most learning that takes place outside of a classroom can be characterized in groups and community only. Sharing, communication, and collaboration are the keys of learning. Learning requires individuals to engage in dialogue and discussion with understanding such kind of paradigms should be explored for Indian education system.

BRIDGING THE GAPS FROM EDUCATION

Lifelong learning and extension education with formal or non-formal ways can bridge the gap of rural and urban population, what seems to be very difficult. Learning can and does take place in different forms for example, formal settings such as schools, colleges and universities and all of them can be used to hit the target. Lifelong Learning Model should be "anytime–anywhere," based on multiple locations and multiple modes of learning which conveniently meet the needs and learning preferences of potential students. Online learning, face-to face learning, individual tutorial sessions, work-based learning, self-paced learning, computer–

based learning, and combinations of these are used to provide a variety of modes, which enhance learning. Globalization of Education is an important asset for any country to justified use of communication and tries to bridging gaps of education.

INDIAN SCIENCES TO BE EXPLORED

Govt. should give ample opportunities to grow Indian sciences like Ayurveda, Homeopathy, Yoga or any other kind by research and development at international level to expand the knowledge of India abroad. Universities can make a tie-up with foreign campuses to run these courses there.

EDUCATION WITH INDIAN VALUES AND CULTURE

Indian culture and values should be treated as advantage. Promoting the dominant cultures and values of some advanced areas and accelerate cultural transplant from advanced areas to less developed areas can help society grow and can face the challenges of losing local identity in overwhelming globalization. Curriculum should be effective and relevant to meet people's needs and developing a sense of value among them.

EDUCATION WHICH ENCOURAGES ENTREPRENEURSHIP

It is the task of the education system to change the mindset of rural people. It also has to inspire the youth for the necessary courage for entrepreneurship. Rural people should recognise their talent and use it for not only themselves but for country also. They should get encouragement and financial help accordingly, which will help them to change their vision. Their should be policies to attract youth towards agriculture, as agriculture is the backbone of Indian economy. We have to Identify "Basic" Skills of students and groom them as professionals. Former president Dr. Kalam said that our education system should highlight the importance of entrepreneurship and develop such skills right from the college to provide them with opportunities for creativity and freedom and ability to generate wealth through setting up ventures producing, marketable products.

E-APPROACH TO EVERYONE

The whole population should have a direct access to modern technological if every village is connected with Internet facilities.

They can have a direct contact to modern technological advancements through such facility and can share their knowledge with the other countries. Distance and online learning provide greater flexibility in time and place. Self-paced computer programmes and the Internet are being used increasingly for individualized just-in-time learning.

TECHNOLOGICAL EXPANSION

Access to technology is constrained by electricity, number of PC's, telephone mainlines and Internet hosts. Their working is far from satisfactory. If we have to make an improvement in computer access for our students these problems have to be addressed on priority. Increasing technological gaps and digital divides between advanced countries and developing countries are hindering equal opportunities for fair global sharing. The possible strategic solutions are like granting autonomy to leading institutes with quality, establishment of powerful industries and organizations to build the nation.

EXPANSION OF AGRICULTURAL CAMPUSES

Strengthen agriculture as nation's backbone of economy, our policies must therefore, create an environment. There should be more effective policies for agriculture courses and researches to be implemented by certified agricultural people so that it reaches to common former. Which encourage the outcome for globalization. We should Support new Interdisciplinary, Cross–Cultural Collaborations in agricultural education.

MORE PARTICIPATION OF WOMEN

National policies and all other development plans are promoting the overall development and empowerment of girls but we have not been able to achieve the targets. Organizing different type of educational programme in rural and urban areas, short term courses to enhance their own potential, linking of literacy programme with all around development and providing help line services with placement and change of jobs as per their need. Meaningful partnership between men and women is important to move forward together in these global requirements.

CONCLUSION

Education plays a significant role to put nation in the list of developed countries. After analyzing the weakness in the present education system it is noticed that the revamping of this system needs to carry out an immediate basic to be fit to survive in this competitive world. UNESCO describes–"A key to the twenty first century, learning throughout life will be essential for adapting to the evolving requirements of the labour market and for better mastery of the changing time frames and rhythms of individual existence".

Our "Think Tank" has to plan accordingly. Need of nation and its people must be the aim. We have recognized that Globalization is a reality, which cannot be denied and should not be avoided. However, it needs to be managed. To do this, it is necessary to continue the process of opening up of the economy to international competition, which was initiated in the 11th plan period, while making parallel efforts to strengthen the potential of Indian industry to compete effectively in world market.

Globalization should lead to expand our economy, culture and social values, education and knowledge across political boundaries of nations. As a global citizen one can have knowledge based learning society with multiple opportunities to work and grow in a healthy competitive and democratic environment to survive with own beliefs and values, and control over conditions to stay strong in ever changing surroundings. We should live like a global joint family rather than living with disintegration and an environment of cutthroat competition for survival. Literacy for all, adult literacy in particular could be thought of as the engine to spread head a revolution, which will shapeup coming generation in real sense.

REFERENCES

Knowles, M. (1984) *The Adult Learner: A Neglected Species*, Third Edition. London: Gulf Publishing Company.

Naik, S.P. (2004) *Education for Twenty First Century*, New Delhi, Amole Publications Pvt Ltd.

Rao, D.B. (2004) *General Secondary Education 21st Century*, New Delhi Discovery Publishing House.

Tilak, B.G. and Jandhyala (2003) *Education, Society and Development, National and International Perspectives*, APH Publishing Corporation.

Schultz, T.W., (ed.) (1982)"The value of higher education in low income countries, in B.C. Sanyal" *Higher Education and the new international order*, IIEP, UNESCO, Paris, p. 52.

Sharma, K. Hitesh (2008), The impact of globalization on higher education. *Vivek* Journal of Education and Research Vol. 1 no. 1, April.

Uberoi, N.K., Some Current Developments in India's Higher Education. *Newsletter*.

www.league.org/publication/abstracts/learning/lelabs0699.htm

http://www.ericfacility.net/ericdigests/ed414961.html

www.cdtl.nus.cdu.sg/Idcas/iot12.htm

Tagg, J. (1998). "The Decline of the Knowledge Factory: Why Our Colleges Must Change." *The World and I*, June 1998. www.worldandi.com/archive/mtjun98.htm

23

Corrective Approaches for Sustainable Extension Education Services in Rural India

Hemant Kumar Khandai and *Anshu Mathur*

India aspires to be powerful, it wants to play a role in the international community, for that to happen, its economy has to grow multifold and for that to happen, it requires a huge force of entrepreneurs who could transform it into a nation which produces, from the one which only consumes. India needs a huge force of innovators who could make it self reliant in all kinds of sciences and technologies. India needs artists who could make its culture the most popular in the world. A culture which is not only saleable itself but also helps in selling India's products across the world. In a nutshell, India needs more changes in existing education system and we need more effective extension education system to reach villages and to find more talents and use it as our human resources. After the independence there are recommendations of various Commissions and the UGC guidelines issued from time to time for Adult, Continuing Education and Extension, it is evident that one of the goals of the UGC is to transform the university system into an active instrument for social change through the institutionalization of Extension as the Third Dimension and by ensuring that the university system is adult learner friendly and pro life long learning Its objective was to extend knowledge and other institutional resources to the community and vice-versa and to gain insights from a contact between knowledge resources and socio-cultural realities with a view to reflecting these in the entire curricular system of higher education including teaching and research. It was to be a two-way process between the experts and the people, an intellectual intervention in the community's living problems, which need to be overcome through an educational process.

It was to be that education which helped students to face life and its challenges and which created an ambience for a learning society. But the condition of majority of government schools (on which majority of Indians depend in villages) is pathetic. Major population of India in villages is educationally and facilities vise almost deprived. That is why no less than a revolution is needed in the extention education system in India.

Some of the suggestions are:

1. Appointment of Graduate Teachers in Each Village

On an average, one extension personal covers one thousand clients in India. To a certain extent the extension worker should have the knowledge to resolve the problems and to help rural people by taking decisions. There is a severe shortage of quality teachers. Morality and character of majority young teachers and teen students are almost non-existent. Accountability of teachers and school administrators is at its lowest, mainly because of political interference at every level. Cheating and corruption is the rule of the day. There should be quality teachers in every area of extension to spread knowledge.

2. Best Talents of the Country Working in the Rural Education Sector

Education is one of the highest profit making 'industries' in the service sector, but its workers are the least paid compared to those working in somewhat glamorous sectors like the IT industry. This has to change. Specially in rural areas govt should pay more attractive sailleries and perks to magnetise youth.

3. Education which Encourages Innovation and Creativity

Rural people have so much talent in working fields, small scale industries, house holds etc. Extention worker should encourage them and should provide them facilities to improve their talent. Govt. Should provide required training, workshops and finencial help to village persons.

4. Education which Encourages Entrepreneurship

It is the task of the education system to change the mindset of rural people. It also has to inspire the youth for the necessary courage for entrepreneurship. village people should recognise their talent and use it for not only themselves but for country also. They should get encouragement and financial help accordingly. Which will help them to change their vision.

5. Need to Bring Improvement in Agriculture Related Programmes of Mass Media

Television channels like Doordarshan (DD) and Etv. are telecasting agriculture related programmes everyday but due to unavailability of TV sets with farmers, non-suitability of timings and unavailability of location specific or region specific programmes, farming community is not getting real advantage out of these programmes. To bring the desirable result the following changes are obligatory in the present system.

- Government, cooperative societies or NGOs working in the villages should take initiative to provide TV sets and VCRs in each village to watch and record the programmes related to the crop of the area.
- Agriculture related programmes should be telecast at the most convenient time of farmers and the frequency of the programme should be at least twice in a day.
- Development of video library regarding the area specific crops and practices would be very helpful to the farmers.
- At least once in a week, one-way video and two-way audio live agricultural programmes should be organized on television to establish direct contact between farmers and scientists. Such type of two-way programmes could be organized even in radio.
- More programmes on successful farmers should be made for TV, radio and print media to encourage the others.
- Villagers are also viewing different channel in their TV through cable. If information regarding agricultural practices is given on a strip through cables, people can get interesting information on agriculture while watching entertaining programmes.
- Regional FM radio station especially for agriculture can be established through which agricultural information can be given with a variety of entertainment programmes for twenty-four hours. Such type of special TV channel on agriculture can also be started.

6. Adaptation of Simplicity

Usually the language and simplicity is what effects on rural population. For example agricultural chemicals like pesticides; fungicides and herbicides are bearing very complex and lengthy names. These names are very difficult to understand and remember for farmers. It would be better to give simple and common name to these chemicals, so that the farmers can easily remember them. So the communication should be in their language or extension worker should simplify the programme, lesson or any information.

7. Improve People's Participation and Practicability of New Technology to Adopt in Various Extension Programmes

From finding out specific problems, its solution, planning, implementation to evaluation of the programme, people participation must be encouraged to carry out research and extension programmes successfully. The programme must be implemented from bottom to top level. The recommendations for any thing are made in terms of availability of that in particular area. Any new technology can be adopted by its practicability only. Extension worker should improve both.

8. Combination of Traditional and Electronic Method

Nowadays many modern types of equipments like computer and interactive television programmes are being utilized for dissemination of agricultural technologies. But most of the old aged people like traditional methods like puppet show, street plays, folksongs etc., while younger generations like modern devices such as Television, Computers etc. The combination of these traditional and electronic methods helps to attract a wide range of younger to old aged audience. For example telecasting of drama, puppet show and folksongs etc, related to technology dissemination attracts both elder and younger rural population.

9. Availability of Rural Libraries

Many magazines and journals are available in urban areas, but agricultural publications what they really want are rarely available in rural areas. So, the establishment of rural libraries for agricultural publications is obligatory for the literate framers in rural area. In addition to this audiovisual materials like Audio/videocassettes and CDs should be made available on new technology to the young entrepreneurs.

10. Internet Facilities at Village Level

The villagers from villages can have a direct access to modern technological if every village is connected with Internet facilities.

They can have a direct contact to modern technological advancements through such facility and can share their knowledge with the other villages and countries. This will have positive impact on faster dissemination of agricultural technologies. The young educated farmers can be trained and their services can be utilized for this purpose. In Orissa, the KVK has started Information Center where Internet and other required facilities have been installed.

11. Use of Local Resources Available

Old villagers are rich sources of indigenous technologies. But in modern age, no one have awareness regarding the importance of this technology. Extension worker should accumulate such knowledge from the aged farmers and after proper scientific test it should be transferred to the younger farmers, entrepreneurs and motivate them to use locally available indigenous. Extension functionaries for the younger should also arrange field visits.

12. Encouragement to Private Extension Service

Private extension service provides job opportunities to the unemployed agricultural graduates. For them it is one of the best fields to start self-employment ventures. To encourage such service, Government should provide some financial help to the agricultural graduates at the initial stage so that the unemployed agricultural graduates can be motivated towards such kind of activities.

The acceptance of Extension as the Third Dimension equal in importance to teaching and research was in the context of a growing realization that the universities and colleges having institutional resources–knowledge, manpower and physical–have an obligation to develop sensitivities to involve the development of the community with particular reference to the overall and diverse learning needs of all the segments of the people of the community. Today India claims to be the biggest human resources supplier for the world, We supply bureaucrats to the government, software engineers to the IT companies around the world, highly paid managers to the multinationals, we supply engineers and science graduates as researchers to the foreign universities. Then why we are ignoring our rural men power? Though they are the real assets. they are providing us our basic needs to grow. We should take steps for their sustainable developement and through extension education it is quite possible to fulfill the dream of emerging India.

From my point of view as a developing country we should improve our Extension education system for:

- Making education relevant to real life situations in all over India.
- For preventing the alienation of the educand from society
- For developing a sense of responsibility towards society in rural populations.
- To empower the village youth for a developed country.
- To improve education system with more real life experiences and to make it more meaningful with the concept of earning while learning.
- To attract rural population towards new industries or new methods of latest technologies.

However, success of all programmes in past has been limited by the lack of efficient administrative mechanisms, the limitation of resources, the magnitude of the task, and the lack of willingness to change the status. Many of the programme results appear better on paper than the actual results in the field because of lack of implementation and poor monitoring. We should revise and rethink about it.

CONCLUSION

For widespread and sustainable development of India, present system of rural education needs to be changed. For this, policy makers should involve research and extension activities of different fields and appoint Graduate teachers in each village, bring improvement in agriculture related programmes of mass media, adopt simplicity in naming the agricultural technology, develop practically adoptable new technology, improve peoples' participation in various extension programmes, use combinations of traditional and electronic extension methods, make available rural libraries and facility of Internet at village level, use experiences of successful farmers for the extension of technology, establish farm clinics and service centers in villages, motivate NGOs to change their role for marketing oriented work and encourage private extension services. These implementations will play an important role to increase agriculture, handicrafts, small-scale industries and other productions. The only requirement is for Govt. who should allocate more resources and introduce strict accountability for different government run programmes.

Contributors

Anjum Ahmed, Department of Education, Aligarh Muslim University, Aligarh.

Anshu Mathur (Ms.), Assistant Professor (Education), Bhopal School of Social Sciences, Bhopal.

B.K. Passi, Former Vice-Chairman, NCTE, New Delhi

Baiju. K. Nath (Dr.), Lecturer (Education), Calicut University, Kerala.

C. Naseema (Dr.), Professor of Education, University of Calicut, Kerala.

D. R. Kapoor (Dr.), Associate Professor and HOD—Educational Research, MIER College of Education, B.C. Road, Jammu.

D.D. Pandey (Dr.), Faculty Member, National Institute of Public Cooperation and Child Development, 5, Siri Institutional Area, Hauz Khas, New Delhi.

Gaurav Singh (Dr.), Sr. Lecturer, Rakshpal Bahadur Teachers Training Institute, Bareilly (U.P.).

Geetika Agarwal, Lecturer, CRSCE, Noida.

Hemant Kumar Khandai (Dr.), Head B.Ed. Department, Barkatullah University, Bhopal.

Jibin V. K., Research Scholar, Department of Education, University of Calicut, Kerala.

Kajal Manhas (Dr.), Assistant Professor, P.G. Department of Education, Jammu University, Bahu Road, Jammu.

Kalika Yadav (Prof.), Director, Department of Continuing Education and Extension, Barkatullah University, Bhopal.

Loknath Mishra (Dr.), Principal, Vivek College of Education.

Nityananda Pradhan (Dr.), Head, P.G. Department of Education, D.A.V. College, Koraput.

Noushad Husain (Dr.), Associate Professor, Maulana Azad National Urdu University, College of Teacher Education, MHK-ITC Campus, , Bhopal (M.P).

Poonam S. Kharvar (Dr.), Lecturer (Education), Ramabai Govt. Girls P.G. College, Akbarpur, Ambedkar Nagar, U.P.

Rucha Gujar (Mrs.), Senior Assistant Professor, School of Continuing Education, YCMOU, Nasik.

S.S. Chaugule (Dr.), Reader and Head Special Project, Research Centre YCM Open University, Nasik, Maharashtra.

Shabnam Khan, Research Scholar, Barkatullah University, Bhopal.

Smriti Bhosle (Dr.), Associate Professor, Department of Sociology, L.J.N.J. College, Vile Parle (E), Mumbai.

U.C. Vashistha (Prof.), Department of Education, Lucknow University, Lucknow, U.P.

Vandnere (Dr.), Professor, School of Continuing Education, YCMOU, Nasik.

Vani N. Laturkar (Dr. Mrs.), Faculty, SCMS, SRTM University, Nanded, Maharashtra.